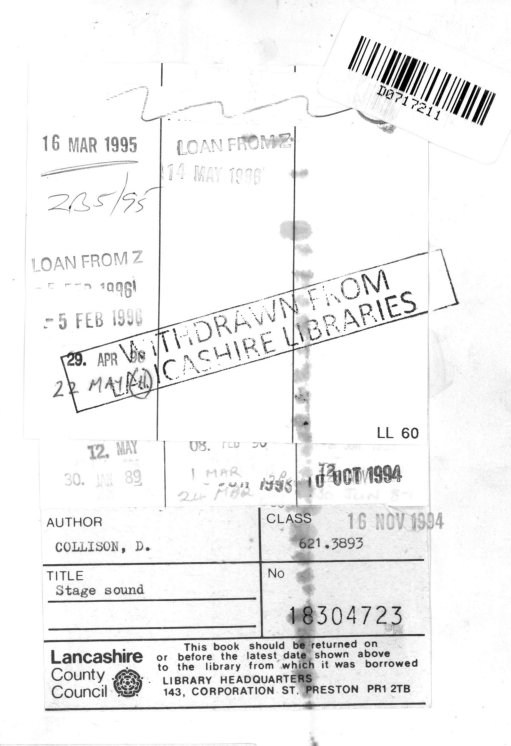

STAGE SOUND

DAVID COLLISON

**Foreword by
Sir Peter Hall**

Cassell London

First edition:	*To Annie*
Second edition:	*To Annie, Mark, Dominic and Robin; a lot can happen in eight years.*

Cassell Ltd
Greycoat House, 10 Greycoat Place, London SW1P 1SB

Copyright © David Collison 1976, 1982

First published 1976
Reprinted 1976
Second edition, first impression 1982

ISBN 0 304 30987 7

Set in Univers Light by Georgia Origination, Liverpool

Printed in the United States of America by The Book Press

Contents

Acknowledgements

There are many people who have been kind enough to lend their assistance in the preparation of this book. I should particularly like to thank John Pilcher not only for his interest but also for the many hours spent on the technical drawings. It is difficult to know how to express my gratitude to Robert ('you-can't-say-that') Higham who with tremendous patience, verging on enthusiasm, vetted the technical sections of the book. I am also extremely grateful to Bill Kelsey for his contribution to the chapter on outdoor systems.

I am indebted to BASF United Kingdom Limited for permission to draw liberally from their booklet on tape recording. And I am similarly obliged to AKG Equipment Limited for allowing me to include sections from their booklet on microphones. I am grateful to Blandford Press for allowing me to use items from *Hi-fi in the Home* in the glossary, and to the Altec Corporation for allowing me to quote from their technical publications.

I have to thank Peter Hall as the director who first inspired and encouraged me in my chosen profession and, later, Michael Elliott who has the foresight to allow his creative technical team the freedom of experimentation. I was very lucky to meet and team up with lighting designer and founder of Theatre Projects Ltd Richard Pilbrow during one of Michael Elliott's productions. And in 1962 on the Lionel Bart musical *Blitz* I was fortunate enough to meet Antony Horder who has been my close friend and colleague ever since.

Finally, I feel I must mention three great innovators. Men who started the first three firms specializing in electronically reproduced sound for the British theatre. I am proud to be able to say that I knew, and learned a great deal from all three: Jack Bishop, R. G. Jones and Bill Walton – the theatre is in their debt.

Foreword

As a young director, I filled my plays with sounds. They not only gave atmosphere; at dramatic moments, their sudden absence made silence even more telling.

So I went to enormous pains to create a world of sound for each play. I think that the actors, once they were over the first moments of the dress rehearsal where it appeared that they had to share their lines with rampant bull-frogs and incessant crickets, were supported and helped by the sounds around them.

All the same, I hadn't yet learned that all effects in the theatre which are nice but are not absolutely necessary should be cut. I think I quickly understood one thing: atmospheric sound in the theatre must be so faint as to be almost indiscernible. Noticeable sounds can only be supported by noticeable (and essential) actions. The amount of sound, evident or subliminal, depends of course on the play. Shakespeare does not need perpetual soundtracks; but the poetic realism of Tennessee Williams does.

I was fortunate twenty-one years ago, in those early experiments in sound, to encounter a technician of genius: David Collison. He could cue a sound to a tenth of a second – by hand on a pickup. We didn't use tape then. Surrounded by three or four turntables and a mass of records, he built up a soundtrack which was at one with the dialogue. He would have made one of the great Dubbing Mixers (the man who balances all the various sounds in the final stages of a film) of all time.

Fortunately, he stayed in the theatre. His work with Theatre Projects has provided excellent sound facilities for every kind of theatre. And although he has for many years been able to do the impossible with sound, he has the humility of every great theatre technician. He knows the sounds, lights, and elaborate stage effects are nothing if the words are not just, and the actor expressing them true.

This book is like the man: modest, precise, and unexpectedly humorous. I believe it will prove invaluable.

Peter Hall
11 June 1975

Introduction

The aim of this book is to assist (and, I hope, inspire) the non-technical user of sound equipment whether for a play or musical, a fashion show or an after dinner speech.

The first section is devoted to an explanation of basic electronic and acoustic facts which can directly affect the handling of sound equipment. Although this information will be elementary to some readers it can still serve as a useful reference. Others will find it a great help in fully appreciating the later chapters.

The second half of the book discusses aspects of the practical handling of sound equipment, the creation of sound effects (both live and recorded) and the application of different types of loud-speakers and microphones under various conditions. Techniques and problems are high-lighted by many examples taken from my own experience.

I was very pleased, though somewhat daunted, to be asked to write this book not only because of the honour it afforded but because I was becoming increasingly aware of the lack of any publication covering this particular field. This, however, is not altogether surprising. Electron-ically reproduced sound has only in the 1970s reached a sufficiently high standard in the theatre to be generally accepted as a technical art. Before then it suffered from a lack of interest caused largely by an ignorance of its potential, and a resultant lack of money. For these reasons the equipment was often not of the best quality and the person handling it not the most experienced.

As far back as the thirties, lighting designers began to use remote control switchboards and in the sixties miniaturization and duplicate 'preset' switchboards came in with the development of the thyristor dimmer. It was all becoming very sophisticated. Even scenery began to be more motorized and mechanized, while sound remained very much the poor relation. Audio engineers in other spheres such as radio, films and recording studios would scoff at the efforts of the few enthusiasts who were striving for better standards in the theatre. It was not until 1973 that I actually met a television sound engineer who, at a recording of a theatre show, asked if he could take a direct feed from the theatre system. Acceptance at last.

In the days before microphones, gramophone records and tape recorders, sound in the theatre depended on mechanical and live effects. The creation of these was a great art and was usually the domain of the property department. Thunder storms, avalanches, railway trains and collapsing buildings, all could be created by a team of well rehearsed stage hands. I believe that as late as the 1940s the great Sir Donald Wolfit, for his storm scene in *King Lear,* had a carefully worked out sequence using the constant backing of a mechanical wind machine varying in speed and pitch as required plus, on cue, one person rattling a metal thunder sheet, another performing rumblings and crashes on a large bass thunder drum, while a fourth person was actually inside an enormous galvanized tank savagely be-labouring the sides with two padded drumsticks. (It is said that Sir Donald could make himself heard above the lot and while doing so was able to detect if any one of the 'elements' was not performing strictly as rehearsed.)

When I began stage managing in the mid-fifties, although gramophone records had very much taken over, stage management still often preferred to do certain effects live. And managements, rather than hire expensive sound equipment and records, would insist, say, that a mechanical wind or wave machine be used. Extremely effective they could be too.

If recorded effects were required the stage manager would go with his shopping list to one of the theatre sound companies and purchase discs of the fairly limited range of stock items. He would then arrange the hire of some equipment which would duly be delivered and installed in the theatre. After that it was up to the stage management and the director to get on with it. It was simply unfortunate if the loudspeakers were the wrong type, if there was insufficient power to achieve the required effect, or if nobody knew about loudspeaker placing or the sound absorbent properties of various scenic materials, etc.

I was fortunate enough at that time to be working with some directors who liked using sound. And as I very much enjoyed operating sound equipment I found myself becoming a specialist. This was at the beginning of the tape revolution which took place in the British theatre during the late fifties and early sixties. The 'quality' revolution really got under way in the seventies and is still continuing.

Microphones for speech reinforcement were used in the forties and fifties. But the systems remained pretty crude until the late sixties when certain composers, used to having complete control over a sound balance inside a recording studio, began to write material for the stage which necessitated similar techniques. Producers were forced to pay for it and a new range of theatre sound equipment emerged. The rock movement, from the Beatles onwards, also helped, because people began to accept electronic sound. Prior to this period of change the poor stage manager had once again to assess the microphone requirements and organize the rental of what he deemed to be suitable equipment. This usually consisted of microphones on raised stands along the front of the stage, a set of two or four column loudspeakers driven by one or two amplifiers and a simple mixer with an overall master and tone controls. Once installed the usual procedure was: turn the master knob up for songs and down for dialogue. This is a far cry from the sophisticated mixing desks that are now installed in theatres where the balance engineer individually controls sometimes thirty or more microphones.

However, it is early days. For although the sound man is now an accepted member of the theatrical creative team there is still much to do to improve the equipment and the techniques. Hopefully, this book may help somebody along that road.

Eight years on

When I began work on the first edition of this book in 1974 we were at the start of an electronics revolution which has affected all our lives in one way or another. The easily reproduced printed circuit board and, more latterly, the encapsulated micro-circuit (or chip) have caused the market to be flooded with electronic aids and gadgets most of which would have been unimaginable a decade ago. And if one were asked to single out an area where the new technology has particularly affected theatre sound it must be in the emergence of the relatively cheap high performance mixing desk. We can now walk down the high street and purchase a mixer with more facilities than were available to most studio engineers during the great pop recording boom of the 'swinging sixties'.

I remember describing only eight years ago with what trepidation we specified a 'studio quality' mixing desk for the new National Theatre of Great Britain, and how it was deemed by many to be completely over the top. Yet what is happening now? Mixers two and three times that size are by no means unusual as part of a temporary installation for a run-of-the-mill musical. The reduction in costs coupled with the increase in technical possibilities has created a veritable explosion of knobs – too many and varied for most mortals to contemplate. But fear not; a number of interested parties around the world are hell-bent on harnessing the computer to the theatre sound console. *Memory sound* is upon us. The first production model memory lighting control emerged in the United Kingdom around 1965 at a time when the manually operated electronic consoles sprouted too many channels for one person (or even two) to handle. The same situation now prevails with the larger sound installations.

All this is very exciting stuff because what the major professional theatres have today the school halls will have tomorrow. But there is a spin-off from these technical advances which, in my estimation, gives cause for concern: this is the growing reliance by performers upon the microphone and the apparent acceptance by audiences of 'electric'-sounding voices.

In June 1981 a young American lighting designer on her first visit to England was enthusing about the plays she had seen in

London when she casually remarked that it was 'fascinating to listen to natural voices in a theatre'. She might have taken the stunned silence of the assembled British theatre technicians as a feeling of shame and deprivation that we could not afford the sound systems they have on Broadway, for she went hastily on to assure us, her voice tinged with surprise, that there was no problem of audibility at all. This, she explained, was probably due to the fact that English actors were better trained than their American counterparts. I wonder if she would have said that if an American actor had been present?

I have always been taught that all the scenic and technical elements of a production must be designed and executed so as to be integral and related parts of the whole. In other words, the *only* justification for the technician's existence is to serve the performer; and the performer, it must be remembered, is a human being. Unfortunately a great deal of the amplification one is forced to endure in musicals these days is out of scale with the human being.

It reminds me very much of the period in lighting when a filament light source was found powerful enough to project scenery on a large scale and we all gasped at the vast colourful backgrounds which the lighting designers could change at the flick of a slide; and those great skeletal sets with static or moving platforms designed to give the actors interesting spaces on which to perform without, of course, detracting from the impressive cycloramic projections. The trouble was that when the poor little actors were placed in the middle of all this technical splendour they were entirely lost. Those intimate scenes which worked so well in the rehearsal room and even the big company dance routines no longer had the impact. The scale was wrong.

I suggest that the current artistic numbness in the audio world has arisen because technical advances, including the introduction of the graphic equalizer and, particularly, digital time delay, have provided the means by which it is the turn of the sound designer to have his ego-trip. And surprisingly he is aided and abetted by producers, directors, authors and composers.

I am often asked – and it always irks – why theatre sound is 'always so bad'. My answer is to point out that bad sound is obvious whereas good sound, unless, of course, it is some great dramatic sequence of sound effects, will go unnoticed. How many shows have you seen, I ask, where you have not given the sound system a thought? That is what it is all about.

I am hopeful, though not over-confident, that producers and directors will sooner or later come to realize that the actor/audience relationship is not necessarily best served by having gigantically over-sized stage sets, blindingly bright lights or sizzlingly loud sound.

David Collison
February 1982

Part 1

I
What is sound?

Pressure waves

Sound is essentially the movement of air in the form of pressure waves radiating from the source at a speed of about 1,130 feet (350 metres) per second. These waves consist of alternate regions of high and low pressure travelling *in all directions* like a continually expanding sphere. Sound cannot travel in a vacuum because a medium is required on which the pressure waves can act and all solids, liquids and gases will transmit sound to a greater or lesser degree.

In order to understand the behaviour of sound waves a useful analogy may be drawn from a study of the ripples that are set up when a small stone is dropped into a pond (remembering that water ripples move in one plane only and sound waves expand in all directions). Small waves travel outwards, gradually diminishing in height; in sound terms, diminishing in intensity or loudness. However, although the ripples get smaller the distance between adjacent peaks, the wavelength, is constant. One cycle of vibration occurs when the water surface at a given point changes from peak to trough and back to peak again, i.e. a complete cycle of events.

Frequency

If the stone were attached to a piece of string, it would be possible to vibrate it up and down at the surface of the water. If this could be done one hundred times each second, one hundred waves would be created each second and there would be one hundred cycles of vibration each second at a point on the water surface, (see point A in figure 1). Thus the frequency of the vibration would be 100 cycles per second, and the unit used for measuring cycles per second is Hertz (Hz). The rate of vibration is the frequency or pitch of the sound and so the higher the rate at which waves pass a given point, the higher is the pitch of the sound. An oscilloscope is a device for displaying visually an electronic signal. It is used for accurately studying the characteristics of a signal. Figures 2, 3, 4 and 5 show oscilloscopes displaying different frequencies.

Intensity

To obtain a greater intensity of sound at the same pitch we require the same number of cycles per second, but the movement between peak and

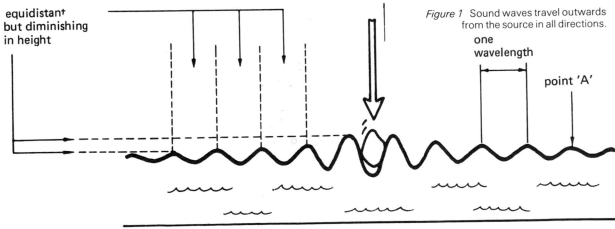

equidistant but diminishing in height

Figure 1 Sound waves travel outwards from the source in all directions.

one wavelength

point 'A'

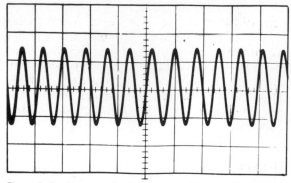

Figure 2 Oscilloscope displaying a pure high frequency tone.

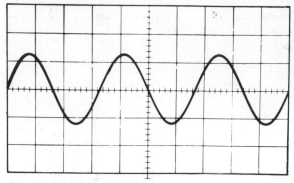

Figure 3 Oscilloscope displaying a pure low frequency tone (fewer waves – or cycles – per second).

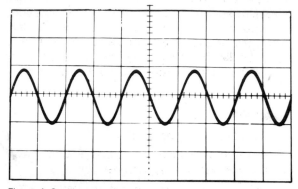

Figure 4 Oscilloscope displaying a pure tone at a given intensity.

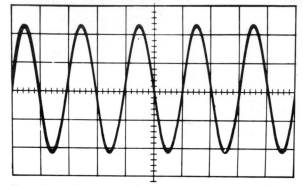

Figure 5 Oscilloscope displaying the same tone at increased intensity.

trough must be greater. Returning to the water analogy, if a larger stone had been vibrated 100 times every second, 100 larger waves would have been produced. The greater the size or amplitude of the pressure waves, the greater the intensity or loudness of the sound.

The human ear is capable of hearing sounds with a very wide range of intensities. In terms of air pressure changes, the loudest sound which does not quite cause physical pain is about one million times greater than the quietest sound which the ear can just detect. Because such large numbers are inconvenient to handle, sound intensities are often referred to in terms of decibels (dB). Strictly, the decibel refers to the ratio of two intensities or amplitudes, and it is calculated logarithmically. By this means we achieve a convenient unit in which one decibel represents about the smallest change in sound intensity which the human ear can detect.

The difference in intensity between the sound of leaves rustling gently and a symphony orchestra at its loudest is about 100 dB. If we set our standard level of 0 dB intensity at the sound of rustling leaves, the orchestra will be + 100 dB of

sound. Alternatively, if we set our 0 dB for the orchestra, the sound of rustling leaves will then be −100 dB. Figure 6 shows the intensities for various sounds.

Sound levels are subjective, however, and the ear quickly adjusts to growing intensities. Not until the sound equipment is being overloaded are some people convinced of the loudness.

Doppler effect

It is interesting to note that an approaching sound, say of a police siren, appears to be higher pitched than a receding sound. This is because as the source approaches you are receiving more cycles each second than when it is going away from you. This phenomenon is called the Doppler effect after an Austrian, Christian Johann Doppler (1803–53), who first explained it.

Harmonics

Pure sounds (i.e. single undistorted frequencies) occur very rarely in nature and are produced mainly by electronic apparatus especially

Threshold of pain	140	Jet aircraft at 15 feet
		Artillery fire
Threshold of feeling	120	Underground train
	100	Noisy industrial plant Large symphony orchestra (forte)
Envelope of hearing	80	Listening level of a Hi-Fi addict! Inside a family car Noisy office Conversation
	60	
		Suburban street
	40	Quiet home
	20	Bedroom Quiet whisper Empty theatre Rustling leaves
Threshold of audibility	0	Inside a heavily treated room (e.g. recording studio)

Figure 6 Chart showing typical sound pressure levels measured in dB where 0 dB is defined as the threshold of audibility (commonly known as the dBA Scale).

designed for the purpose. A variable frequency oscillator is one such piece of equipment used by engineers to test other electronic equipment. It produces the pure waves as depicted above on the oscilloscope. Electronic organs and synthesizers are based on the oscillator with distortion deliberately introduced to vary the quality of the sound.

Most sounds consist of a complex mixture of frequencies at differing intensities.

Sounds produced by musical instruments usually consist of the basic note or fundamental and small amounts of integral multiples of this frequency or harmonics (in musical terms, overtones). Thus a piano note of fundamental frequency 200 Hz will contain proportions of 400 Hz, of 600 Hz, of 800 Hz, etc. No two instruments will produce exactly the same proportion of harmonics and it is this varying characteristic which determines the *timbre* of each instrument.

In most musical instruments, sound is produced by causing part of them to vibrate. When the bow is drawn across a violin string, this vibration imparts energy through the bridge to the body of the violin which tries to follow the vibration. In so striving the wood produces pressure waves which, though not the same, are nevertheless related to the fundamental vibra-

tions of the string, i.e. harmonics. We therefore have a combination of frequencies which are characteristic of the violin. Similar examples are the vibrations of reeds in woodwind instruments and the shock waves of drum skins or cymbals when struck. Trumpet and horn players cause their own lips to vibrate in the mouthpiece of their instrument.

The ear

We shall see in later chapters how the tiny movements of the diaphragm of a microphone when struck by sound waves set up electrical vibrations or impulses. These impulses in turn may be electronically amplified and made to cause a loudspeaker to vibrate similarly, setting up pressure waves and thereby reproducing the sound.

Functions

Pinna: collects sound waves

Tympanum (ear drum): vibrates sound waves (like a microphone diaphragm)

Ear ossicles (malleus – hammer, incus – anvil, stapes – stirrup): tiny bones which pick up and intensify vibrations

Cochlea: contains sensitive nerve endings which convert vibrations into nervous impulses to pass along the auditory nerve to the brain

Eustachian tube: carries air, keeping pressure in middle ear constant with outer atmosphere

Semi-circular canals: three tubes at right angles contain sensitive nerve endings affected by the fluid in the canals as the body moves. Important in balancing the body

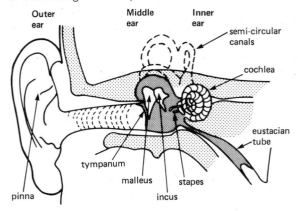

Figure 7 The human ear.

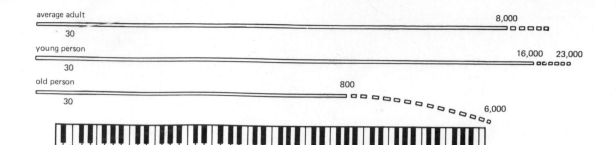

Figure 8 Frequency range of human hearing

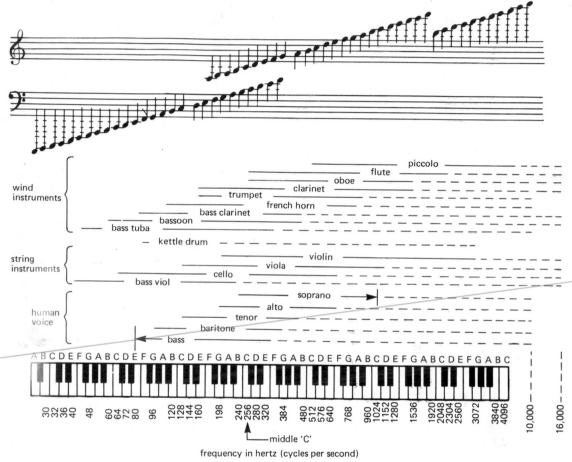

middle 'C'

frequency in hertz (cycles per second)

Figure 9 Useful frequency comparisons.

Sound waves cause the ear drum to vibrate just like the diaphragm of a microphone. These tiny movements are transmitted to the base of the cochlea which contains an incompressible fluid. The fluid transmits the vibrations equally to all surfaces of the cochlea where numerous nerve endings react and transmit auditory sensations to the brain.

The average human ear can hear sounds from 16 Hz to 16,000 Hz, although some people can hear as high as 23,000 Hz. Frequencies below the lowest which can normally be heard are called infrasonic and those above the highest are called ultrasonic. Sensitivity to higher frequencies deteriorates with age so that, typically, someone in their sixties does not hear any-

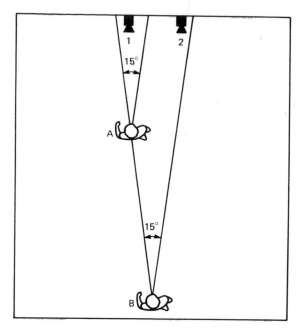

Figure 10 Listener A can easily pinpoint the locations of loudspeakers 1 and 2, but listener B cannot tell the difference.

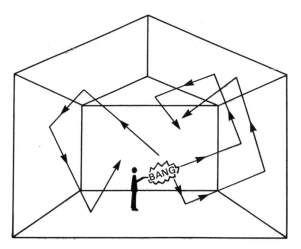

Figure 11 Sound reflects off all surfaces and will carry on reflecting until it is eventually absorbed.

thing above 6,000 Hz. The human voice ranges from 40–1,200 Hz, and a piano ranges from 30–4,000 Hz. See figure 8 for further comparisons.

Although the ear transmits to the brain all the sounds it manages to collect we are able, to an amazing degree, to select what we want to hear. (Just pause for a moment and listen to the sounds that are going on around you. Many of them will have been subconsciously blocked out.) We can be selective in another way when listening to complex sounds; it is possible, for example, to identify the different instruments playing in a full orchestra and even to 'tune in' to one in particular.

The human ear collects sounds forwards and sideways and can determine the source of sounds within approximately 15 degrees horizontally. Because the ears are positioned on the sides of the head we find it more difficult to determine the source of sounds vertically. This deficiency should be borne in mind when placing loudspeakers on a stage.

Reverberation (*Multiple echoes*)

Sound which is reflected several times between the surfaces of an enclosed space before reaching the ear is known as reverberation, and the

greater than about $1\frac{1}{2}$ seconds, then direct speech tends to overlap and intelligibility is impaired.

Sounds emanating from above or behind a listener arrive after being reflected at various surfaces like walls, floor, ceiling, etc. Depending upon their acoustic properties, these surfaces will alter the sound by absorbing certain frequencies and accentuating others. Basically, soft surfaces (drapes, clothes) absorb sound and hard surfaces reflect it. Since the reverberation may be greater in square or rectangular halls, theatres are usually designed to avoid parallel walls.

There is less reverberation at the higher frequencies (which give intelligibility to speech and 'brilliance' to music) because they are generally more easily absorbed. Therefore in practical terms high frequencies can be looked upon as directional.

It is generally known that as the intensity of a sound is increased the resulting audible reverberation will be proportionately longer. This fact can be used to advantage for sound effects. For example, if a recording of a gunshot is played in an auditorium and then, without changing the intensity, it is repeated with some artificial reverberation added (see Chapter 6) the effect will be of a louder sound.

2

Basic equipment?

Having discussed some of the properties of sound, we shall now consider how to capture, amplify and reproduce it. For this certain basic items of equipment are required, which, leaving aside the process of recording which will be dealt with in a later chapter, fall roughly into five categories.

1 *Units which transmit a signal* such as microphones, tape and disc reproducers. We can also include radio tuners, electric guitars, synthesizers and a host of electronic devices which have one thing in common: they require amplification.

2 *Preamplifiers*. These are usually built in to the mixer, amplifier, tape recorder, etc, in order to amplify incoming signals to a standard level (commonly known as line level). If this is done it is much more convenient to handle the signal through such devices as filters, bass, treble, presence and volume controls which we shall meet later.

3 *Mixers*. These are used for combining a number of signals. Each input on the mixer has a volume control which varies the amount of the input signal to be mixed into the final output.

4 *Amplifiers*. The final blended signal from the mixer is fed to an amplifier which magnifies that signal to a level at which a loudspeaker will respond.

5 *Loudspeakers*. These translate the electrical 'vibrations' (variations in the electrical signal) from the amplifier into physical vibrations (movements of the loudspeaker diaphragm) thereby creating pressure waves. Pressure waves produce sound and so the cycle is complete. Strictly speaking *headphones* should come into this category, but most headsets are sensitive enough to operate from a preamplifier stage at line level.

So the principle of electronic sound reproduction is that sound pressure waves are transformed into an electrical signal with an equivalent pattern. This signal when amplified causes a loudspeaker diaphragm to vibrate similarly, thereby reproducing the original pattern of sound waves.

The five basic elements can be assembled in various formats; for example, figure 13 shows a small sound system with two loudspeakers being driven by a power amplifier which is receiving a

Figure 12 The basic system falls into five categories: 1 units which transmit a signal 2 preamplifiers 3 mixers 4 amplifiers 5 loudspeakers.

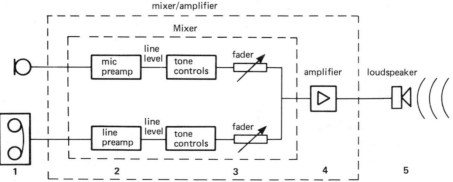

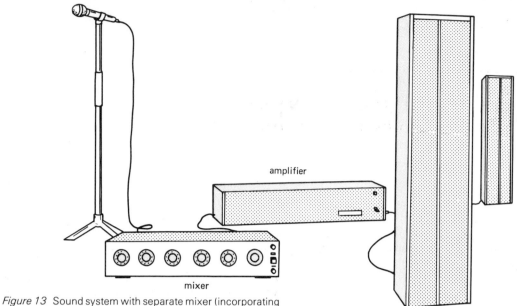

amplifier

mixer

Figure 13 Sound system with separate mixer (incorporating preamplifiers), power amplifier and two loudspeakers.

standard or line level signal from a mixer. This mixer has four microphone inputs, a tape input, and a master volume control. The necessary pre-amplifiers for the different types of input signal are built into the mixer. In figure 14 the mixer and

Figure 14 Sound system with combined mixer/amplifier.

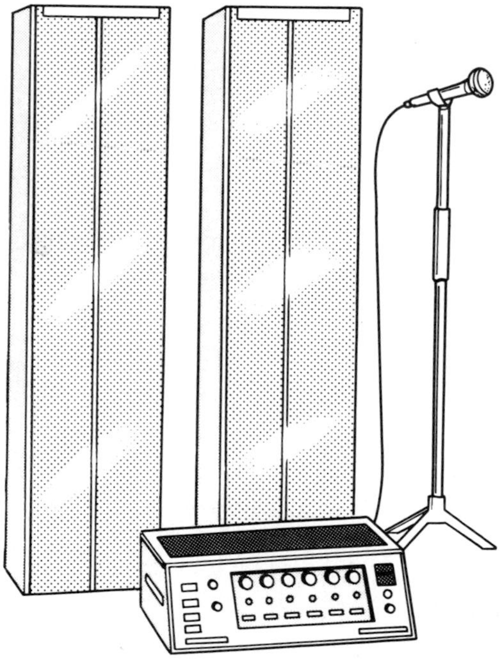

mixer/amplifier

the power amplifier are in the same package. This combination is known as a mixer/amplifier.

The portable sound system in figure 15 incorporates the mixer and the amplifier into the loudspeaker cabinet. This arrangement is commonly used for the amplification of electric guitars and organs.

So, all sound systems are broadly based upon the format:
SOURCES — PREAMPLIFIERS — MIXER — AMPLIFIER(S) — LOUDSPEAKER(S).

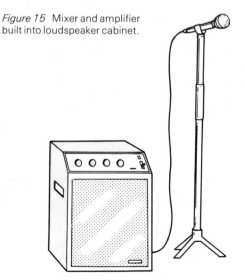

Figure 15 Mixer and amplifier built into loudspeaker cabinet.

mixer/amplifier/loudspeaker

19

Inputs and outputs

Because of the varying standards of connections in sound equipment, one has to use units which are designed to be connected together.

We must ascertain the following information about the inputs and outputs of the equipment: whether it is microphone level or line level, high impedance or low impedance, balanced or unbalanced. There is a further complication with the connection of amplifiers to loudspeakers, since loudspeakers can either be fed at low voltage or at high voltage.

To understand what is meant when we talk about inputs and outputs, it is necessary to know a little about voltages and impedance. Let us look for a moment at another water analogy, this time with reference to electricity. Imagine water flowing through a pipe:

1 The pressure of water = voltage – volts
2 Restriction of water flow in the pipe, i.e. smallness of bore = resistance – ohms or impedance
3 The rate of flow = current – amps

Impedance

Impedance is similar to resistance but the term impedance is reserved for use with alternating current (AC). For limiting the amount of current passing a given point, we can use resistors, inductors and capacitors (condensers). The unit of resistance used when measuring the resistance of resistors and the impedance of inductors and capacitors is called an ohm.

Inductors and capacitors have another very important property in electronic circuits in that they have different effects on low and high frequencies. A simple tone control could consist

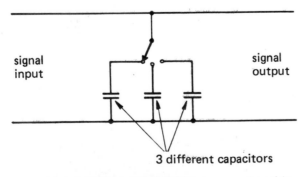

3 different capacitors

Figure 16 A simple tone control. Selecting one or other of the different capacitors will short out more or less of, say, the high frequencies relative to the low.

of a selection of capacitors connected across the signal wires. Depending upon which capacitor is chosen more or less of the high frequencies would be shorted out relative to the low frequencies.

Signal levels

The input and output levels of equipment are given by the manufacturer either in volts or millivolts (mV) (a millivolt is one thousandth of a volt) or in decibels (dB). We met the decibel earlier as a ratio of sound intensities; it appears again as a ratio of voltages.

So that everybody knows what they are talking about, a standard reference level has been set in which 0 dB is equivalent to 0·755 volts.

The British Post Office, who regulate such standards in the UK, chose this voltage many years ago because it gave the required power into their 600 ohms cables. Although 0·775 volts is rather an odd value it does not really matter because it it seldom necessary to convert backwards and forwards.

Conversion table

Decibels	Voltages
+20 dB	7·75 V
+ 2·2 dB	1 V
0 dB	0·775 V
−17·8 dB	100 mV
−20 dB	77·5 mV
−37·8 dB	10 mV
−40 dB	7·75 mV
−57·8 dB	1 mV
−60 dB	0·775 mV
−80 dB	0·0775 mV

i.e. each time the decibels drop by 20 the voltage is divided by 10.

The voltages usually found between microphones, preamplifiers, mixers and amplifiers range between −80 dB and +10 dB, i.e. between about 1 millivolt and 3 volts. These are quite small voltages when compared with mains of 250 volts. Even the signal from an amplifier to its loudspeaker only reaches 40 volts for a 16 ohm loudspeaker delivering 100 watts.

It is here that we have one of the main compromises in handling sound. If the signal voltage is too small it is very susceptible to interference or noise (hum, clicks, hiss, etc.), and special precautions have to be taken against this by using expensive screened cables and boxes to house the equipment. Conversely, if a large signal voltage is chosen it is difficult to achieve this level without distortion and the amplifiers become inconveniently large and heavy. So a compromise is made where the signal levels between preamplifiers, mixers and amplifiers is about 1 volt or 0 dB (zero level).

Signal levels of sound systems are divided broadly into two categories: microphone levels and line levels.

Microphone levels

Microphones generate small voltages from about −80 dB up to about −20 dB, depending on the loudness of the sound and the method used in the microphone to convert from sound to electricity. There are two main categories, however.

1 *Low impedance microphones*. These are in the range 30 and 600 ohms. Professional ribbon microphones are usually 30–50 ohms. Professional dynamic and condenser microphones are usually 200 or 300 ohms.

2 *High impedance microphones*. These are mainly the cheaper domestic variety. Many are

dynamic microphones of 50,000 ohms (50K ohms). The really high impedance units, e.g. very cheap crystal microphones, are of two million ohms (two megohms).

Microphone inputs to amplifiers are stated by the manufacturer and will be as follows: (a) 'Low' – 30 to 50 ohms or 200 to 600 ohms (b) 'High' – or greater than 50,000 ohms and often as high as 2 megohms.

It is worth noting that satisfactory results may be obtained if a microphone is used with an input of higher impedance, for example a 30 ohm microphone with a 300 ohm input, but the amplification will be less than it would be with the correct input. The reverse, however, is not true. If a high impedance microphone is used with a 'low' input, serious distortion and loss of bass frequency will result. This is summarized in figure 17.

Line levels

Usually the voltages of line level outputs (i.e. the pre-amp stages of tape recorders, mixers, etc.) are greater than those of microphones, and range from about −20 dB up to 0 dB (*zero level*).

Figure 17 A guide to suitable inputs for various microphone impedances.

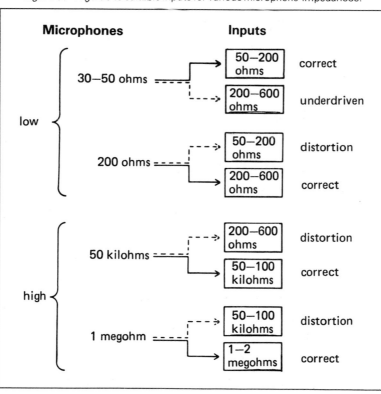

The impedances usually found at line inputs and line outputs vary widely even in professional equipment. The original standard was that a line output was 600 ohms and this could be connected to the 600 ohm line input of the next piece of equipment in the chain. In this way the two items of equipment were said to be matched. However, this arrangement is operationally inflexible because, although one microphone should never be connected to more than one microphone input of an amplifier, it is often necessary to connect the line output of a mixer to the line inputs of several loudspeaker amplifiers. The technique used today is to keep the line output (usually) well below 600 ohms, typically 50 to 100 ohms, and the line input never less than 2,000 ohms and usually about 10,000 ohms.

Returning to our water analogy, we see that a high resistance can be likened to small-bore pipe and a low resistance to a large diameter pipe. It is obvious that a large pipe can supply water to many other pipes of small-bore without difficulty and that adding a further small-bore pipe will not appreciably affect the flow in all the others. This is the principle of 'low into high' where one low impedance output can be connected to several high impedance inputs. Futher high impedance inputs can be added without affecting the exist-

Figure 18 Low impedance at line level can feed into high impedance just as a large bore water pipe can feed many small bore pipes. The addition or subtraction of a single small bore pipe will not noticeably affect the main flow (or signal).

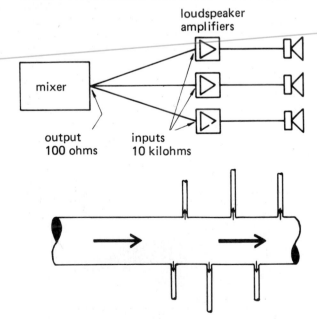

loudspeaker amplifiers

mixer

output 100 ohms

inputs 10 kilohms

ing signal levels. There is obviously some limitation to the total number of inputs which can be connected to one output and with typical values of 100 ohms for the line output and 10,000 ohms for the line input it would usually be quite satisfactory to connect up to ten. High impedance inputs such as these are also known as bridging inputs.

The 'low into high' arrangement is highly recommended for professional and semi-professional installations where flexibility is important.

Caution: This technique only applies at line level because a microphone produces such a very small voltage it has to be connected to the correct impedance. Occasionally, and particulary with some domestic equipment, other standards of voltage and impedance are found and equipment using these will not always work satisfactorily with a professional installation. However, it may be possible to achieve an acceptable result after some experimentation.

Balanced or unbalanced

In addition to the voltage and impedance at inputs and outputs of equipment we also need to know whether the connections are 'balanced' or 'unbalanced'. An unbalanced system uses interconnecting cables with one conductor and an overall braided screen (co-axial cable), whereas a balanced system has two conductors plus a screen (twin-screened cable). It follows that plugs and sockets for unbalanced systems need two pins or connections while for a balanced system three are required.

Unbalanced

Let us look first at the disadvantages of the simpler and cheaper unbalanced system. As stated earlier, the signal voltages used are quite low, just under a volt for line level and about a millivolt for microphone level. All cables will pick up hum and other forms of electrical interference to some extent and there is particular danger at microphone level because the unwanted signal (the interference) may be almost as loud as the wanted signal from the microphone. Even at line level the interfering signals can be much too loud to ignore.

Hum is the most common defect of the unbalanced system and is caused by the electromagnetic radiation or magnetic fields from nearby electrical cables and equipment. Such

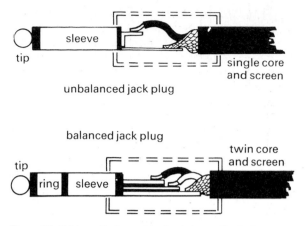

Figure 19 Wiring of balanced and unbalanced jack plugs.

radiation can have an influence over quite a considerable distance depending upon the type of mains cable, whether it is encased in metal or not, the type of current flowing, etc. The screen of the cable does nothing to eliminate this type of interference – it is there to guard against another kind of interference: electrostatic. The magnetic field induces different voltages in the centre conductor and the surrounding screen and while those induced in the screen have an easy path to earth (ground), those induced in the centre conductor add to the wanted signal.

A further difficulty arises with the interconnection of unbalanced equipment because the screen of the cable which is carrying the signal links the cases of the mixer and amplifier. Both cases should also be connected to earth for safety and there is thus a continuous, circular

Figure 20 Earth (ground) loops causing hum in a balanced system should be broken by disconnecting the screen in one or more of the plugs. In an unbalanced system all but one of the mains earths (usually at the mixer) should be disconnected. *Note:* this should only be done where equipment will not be unplugged from the mixer, thereby breaking the earth connection and making the equipment dangerous.

path from the earth at one mains plug, through the mains cable to the mixer, through the mixer chassis to the screen of the link cable to the amplifier chassis, and thus back to earth via the amplifier mains cable. Although very small, the earth current flowing from the mixer can now divide between its own mains cable route and the route through the screen of the co-axial cable to the earth via the amplifier cable. This earth current combines with the signal in the co-axial cable giving hum in the background of the signal.

We can break the earth loop by disconnecting the earth wire in all but one of the mains plugs. This can be very dangerous but may be justifiable in a fixed installation where the equipment remains *permanently* connected and earthed by the screened cables.

Balanced

With a balanced system this kind of hum loop will not occur because there are two signal wires which are completely independent of the earth (ground) connection. However, a slight hum can still appear via the earth loop formed by the screens of the interconnecting leads and the mains earths. This loop can easily be broken by disconnecting the screen at one end of the cable. Normally this is done at the mixer, which is the central piece of equipment.

Hum from magnetic fields will not occur because the two conductors are alike (rather than the single conductor and screen forming the circuit in an unbalanced system) and they are also 'balanced'. Balancing is achieved by fitting a transformer at each input and output, as shown in figure 21, which has the effect of isolating the interconnecting signal wires from the rest of the system. Because the two wires are alike local magnetic fields will induce a similar voltage in each. The wanted signal is flowing round the loop, forwards in one wire and back in the other,

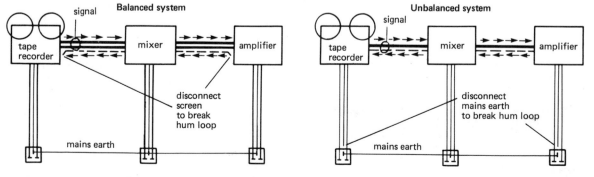

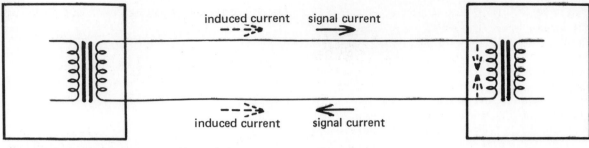

Figure 21 Balancing transformers at either end of an interconnecting cable will make both cores in that cable alike. Similar negative and positive voltages will cancel out *induced* voltages.

but the induced voltage causes currents in the same direction in both wires, say forwards. Thus it adds to one wire and subtracts from the other, giving a net effect of no interference.

So, in order to prevent hum caused by earth loops and magnetic induction a balanced system is preferred, especially for long cable runs. It is sometimes acceptable on the grounds of cost and convenience to use an unbalanced system for linking closely associated pieces of equipment.

Recommendations

Impedances: It is now standard practice in broadcasting and other professional organizations for interconnecting circuits to be fed from low impedance outputs to high impedance inputs.

All inputs should be balanced and high impedance, at least 2,000 ohms and preferably 10,000 ohms.

All outputs should be balanced and low impedance, less than 100 ohms.

All inputs and outputs associated with the mixing desk should be at a standard level (zero level) to permit flexibility in their interconnection.

Earthing: It is essential that each item of equipment remains earthed either to the mains or via interconnecting screened leads.

Loudspeaker connection

Low voltage systems

Loudspeakers have an impedance, which can be somewhere between 2 ohms and 30 ohms, and amplifiers are designed to feed to a specified load, usually of 4, 8 or 16 ohms, so problems may arise in connecting them. Some amplifiers

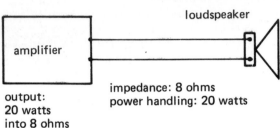

Figure 22 Correct amplifier loading.

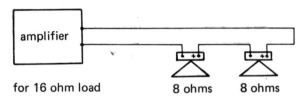

Figure 23 Loudspeakers wired in series to match amplifier output.

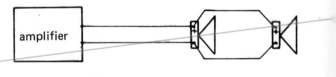

Figure 24 Loudspeakers wired in parallel to match amplifier output.

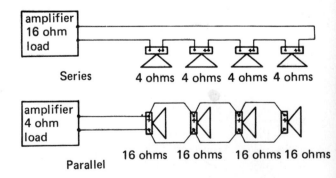

Figure 25 For N number of loudspeakers of the same impedance, Y, in series the combined impedance is N times Y, and in parallel the combined impedance is Y divided by N.

have several outputs to cater for different loads and others have one output with facilities to adjust the correct working load, but usually the manufacturer states, for example, 'Output 20 watts into 8 ohms'. This means that the amplifier will give its optimum performance with a load of 8 ohms, when it will deliver 20 watts.

From an amplifier designed for a loudspeaker of 16 ohms it is possible to run two 8 ohm loudspeakers by wiring them in series to make the total load 16 ohms. Some slight loss of quality will result but for most purposes this is acceptable. Alternatively it is possible to run two 16 ohm loudspeakers from an amplifier designed for a load of 8 ohms by wiring them in parallel. This is a better method of feeding two loudspeakers from one amplifier. The same principles can be applied to a larger number of loudspeakers.

If an amplifier designed for, say, 16 ohms is connected to one of, say, 4 ohms the result will be a louder and perhaps distorted sound, and the amplifier may suffer damage. Conversely, if an amplifier designed for a 4 ohm load is fed to a 16 ohm loudspeaker the result will be a loss of output level.

Although amplifiers can usually accept a load from half to double the one specified, the only sure way of getting reliable results is to follow the manufacturer's instructions. Ideally, where cost is not the determining factor, each loudspeaker should have its own amplifier.

When applied to the requirements of a theatre installation these restrictions produce three problem areas:

1 Where different combinations of loudspeakers are required to be switched on and off, thereby varying the impedance of the load on the amplifier.

2 Where a large number of loudspeakers are required to operate in a series or series-parallel arrangement, generally producing a high impedance load (for example in a dressing-room paging system).

3 Where long cable runs are required which may result in power being lost in the cable and a worsening of the damping factor (see below).

1 and 2 are usually solved by employing a high voltage system to feed the loudspeakers; the third restriction can also be handled in this way, but the use of cable of sufficient size (i.e. low enough resistance) is usually a satisfactory solution.

Damping factor of loudspeaker and amplifier

Manufacturers of loudspeaker amplifiers usually state a damping factor in addition to the normal load impedance, for example: 'Normal load 8 ohms, damping factor 20'. This is a measure of the output impedance of the amplifier itself. Thus,

$$\text{Damping Factor} = \frac{\text{Normal Load Impedance}}{\text{Amplifier Output Impedance}}$$

and in this example

$$20 = \frac{8}{\text{Amplifier Output Impedance}}$$

giving an Output Impedance of 0·4 ohms.

It is important that the impedance 'seen' by the loudspeaker 'looking back' into the amplifier should be as low as possible because the loudspeaker cone is springy in its mounting. If a signal corresponding to a single push of the cone is fed to the amplifier, the cone, of course, moves forward, but when returning to its rest position it can overshoot and oscillate backwards and forwards for a few cycles. This extends the duration of the sound and is a kind of distortion. It must be kept to a minimum by damping the oscillations with as large a damping factor as possible, i.e. as small as possible an impedance seen by the loudspeaker. We saw above that two 8 ohm loudspeakers could be connected in series and connected to an amplifier designed for 16 ohms. If this amplifier has a damping factor of 20, the amplifier output impedance is $\frac{16}{20}$ or 0·8 ohms. If the diagram is now slightly rearranged (see figure 26), we find that the impedance seen by the right-hand loudspeaker is now a combination of the amplifier and the left-hand loudspeaker, i.e. 0·8 ohms and 8 ohms. The total impedance seen is 8·8 ohms and the damping

Figure 26 Loudspeaker damping.

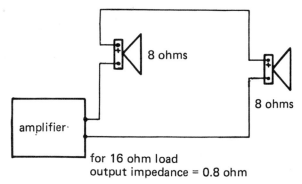

for 16 ohm load
output impedance = 0.8 ohm

factor for the right-hand speaker is $\frac{8}{8\cdot8}$ or $0\cdot9$, which degrades the performance rather too much for true high fidelity.

These problems also occur, although to a lesser extent, if the cable used to connect the amplifier to the loudspeaker has too much resistance. In figure 27 we have a loudspeaker driven over a long run of cable of $1\cdot2$ ohm resistance.

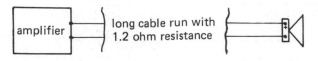

output impedance = 0.8 ohm   impedance = 16 ohms

Figure 27 A cable with too much resistance (i.e. not large enough) can also affect the damping.

The loudspeaker now sees a combined impedance of the amplifier output and the cable, i.e. $0\cdot8+1\cdot2$ or 2 ohms and the damping is reduced from 20 to $\frac{16}{2}$ or 8. Such a reduction would normally be regarded as an acceptable degradation but it is important that the cable is of sufficient size for the intended use.

Cable sizes in low voltage systems

There is a useful rule of thumb which can be followed to avoid losing too much signal in the cable and making the damping factor too low: this is that the cable resistance should not exceed one tenth of the loudspeaker resistance. If this is kept to, the damping factor will not be less than 10 and the signal lost in the cable will not exceed 1 dB.

Thus for an 8 ohm loudspeaker the cable resistance should not exceed $0\cdot8$ ohms. On a short run of only a few feet a lightweight cable will be adequate but on longer runs the cable resistance must be considered.

High voltage system

The high voltage system was devised to overcome the many problems which arose with feeding an amplifier directly to several loudspeakers over long cable runs. This method is especially useful in a system utilizing a number of loudspeakers of various types dispersed around a theatre, and when different combinations of loudspeakers are required for each sound effect, etc. The high voltage system is much more flexible, but in a very high quality system the slight limitation of the frequency response at the

loudspeakers, caused by the introduction of extra transformers, may not be acceptable. In this case the only solution is to install an amplifier at each loudspeaker and feed at line level to the input of each amplifier. The high voltage system is quite simple and we will first consider feeding from an amplifier to one loudspeaker. Remembering that

watts = volts × amps   and   volts = amps × ohms,

an amplifier designed to feed a 4 ohm loudspeaker with 25 watts is producing 10 volts. As part of the amplifier, a transformer is introduced to step up this voltage to 100 volts, see figure 28. (In the USA and Canada, also, for safety reasons, in hospitals in the UK, it is more common to use 70 volts.) At the end of the cable run, inside the loudspeaker enclosure, a similar transformer is fitted to step down the 100 volts to 10 volts to feed the loudspeaker itself. The reader may well wonder what has been achieved apart from the purchase of two large and moderately heavy transformers. The advantage is that here we have used a transformer of step-up ratio 10 volts to 100 volts, i.e. 10 times, and a transformer, in stepping up the voltage 10 times, steps up the impedance 100 times, i.e. the square of the voltage ratio. So the output impedance of the amplifier with transformer becomes 100 times greater and the cable resistance is now of much less significance.

Further advantages appear in a system where one amplifier is to feed several loudspeakers, see figure 29. Here the same amplifier and transformer is used to feed four 6 watt loudspeakers, so that the total load is 24 watts, just inside the capability of the amplifier. The transformers at the loudspeakers are not the same as in the previous example; in this case we have a 6 watt, 4 ohm (say) loudspeaker which requires almost 5 volts to drive it fully and the transformers here have to step down from 100 volts to 5 volts. This is the only way in which four such loudspeakers can be fed from such an amplifier while paying attention to quality, and all the cable can be 'lighting flex' instead of 15 amp cable for a typical length of run in the theatre.

Despite these complications the system is simple to operate. There will be a 100 volt output at the amplifier and there will be a similar input at the loudspeaker. It is usual also to provide at the loudspeaker a means of varying the power taken from the 100 volt line up to the maximum permitted by that particular loudspeaker. Thus a 10 watt-maximum loudspeaker may have set-

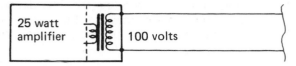
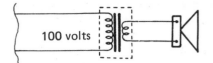

25 watt loudspeaker

Figure 28 Feeding a loudspeaker at a high voltage to ensure that there is no loss of impedance on a long cable run.

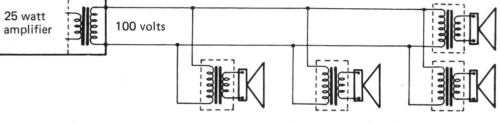

4 loudspeakers; each 6 watts power handling

Figure 29 Feeding a number of loudspeakers at a high voltage with no loss of impedance.

Figure 30 One 40 watt amplifier feeding two 10 watt capacity loudspeakers at 10 watts each for maximum efficiency, and four 10 watt capacity loudspeakers at 5 watts each to obtain less output.

transformers set at 10 watts

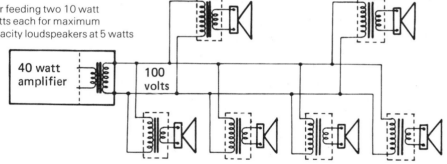

transformers set at 5 watts

Figure 31 Overloading of amplifier output (example A).

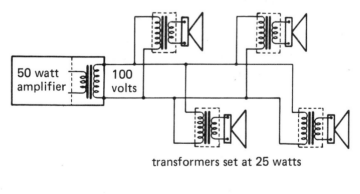

transformers set at 25 watts

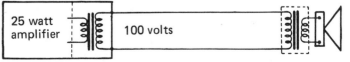

transformers set at 50 watts

Figure 32 Overloading of amplifier output (example B).

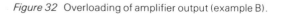

tings for 3, 6 and 10 watts. This permits such combinations as shown in figure 30 which uses six 10 watt units fed from a 40 watt amplifier to cover an auditorium with sound while keeping the source of sound apparently at the front of the hall.

It is important that the amplifier is not overloaded with loudspeakers: a 50 watt amplifier, for example, will not fully drive four loudspeakers set at 25 watts, indeed the amplifier may be damaged by doing so.

This high voltage system has the tremendous advantage of allowing loudspeakers to be switched on and off almost at random without affecting either the amplifier or the remaining loudspeakers. It also permits the development of systems in which several amplifiers can be fed to any of a number of loudspeakers. It is, of course, essential that the switching does not allow the outputs of two amplifiers to be connected together.

3
Loudspeakers

A loudspeaker is in many ways the reverse of a microphone. Its purpose is to create movements of air by the controlled oscillation of a cone or diaphragm, thereby manufacturing sound pressure waves.

But how does it work? In figure 34 you can see a section through a normal cone loudspeaker. Within the rigid metal frame is suspended a paper or plastic cone. This is known as the diaphragm and it can be caused to oscillate to produce sound waves in the air. To allow the necessary movement the cone is attached to the frame at the front and rear by a flexible surround. A coil of wire known as the 'voice coil' is rigidly fixed to the diaphragm and held within the magnetic field of a specially designed magnet. The ends of this coil are connected to an amplifier from which they receive alternating positive/negative voltages corresponding to the audio signal. The electrical current flowing in the coil in one direction (say positive) causes the coil to move within the magnetic field. When the current flow is reversed (negative) the movement of the coil is reversed and the resultant oscillation of the voice coil causes the movement of the attached diaphragm (figure 35).

Loudspeakers come in many different sizes. There are two main factors which determine the size of the cone. Firstly there is the question of the required loudness, or sound pressure level.

Figure 33 Loudspeakers come in many different sizes.

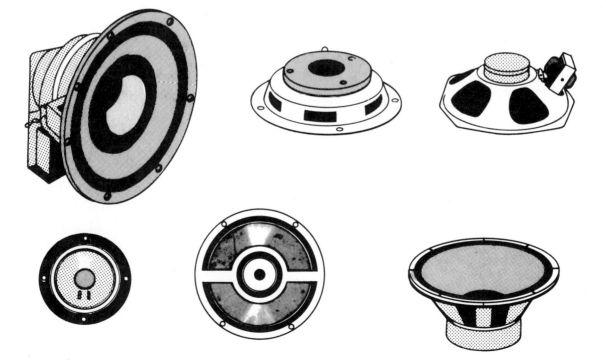

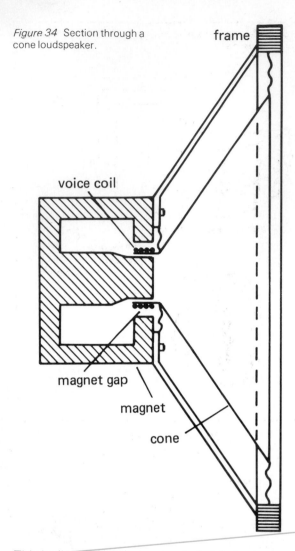

Figure 34 Section through a cone loudspeaker.

frame

voice coil

magnet gap

magnet

cone

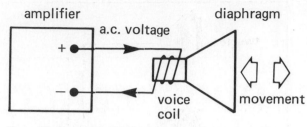

amplifier

a.c. voltage

diaphragm

+

−

voice coil

movement

Figure 35 Alternating positive/negative voltages cause the voice coil held within a magnetic field to move.

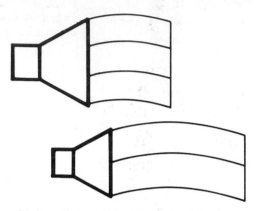

Figure 36 A small cone has to move *farther* than a large cone to produce the same amount of energy.

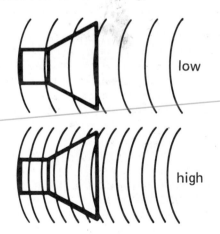

low

high

Figure 37 The higher the frequency the greater the number of cone movements per second.

This is dictated by the amount of air being moved by the cone. Therefore at a given frequency (or rate of oscillation of the diaphragm) a small cone has to move *further* than a larger cone in order to translate the same amount of energy (figure 36). Some loudspeaker systems actually employ a number of small loudspeakers to move the same amount of air as one large one.

Secondly, the rapidity of cone movement must be considered. For the higher the frequency the greater are the number of cone movements necessary per second.

It is as difficult to make a large cone move rapidly with any accuracy as it is to get a small cone to move a large amount of air slowly (which is necessary to produce a deep bass sound). Hence the need for large cone loudspeakers ('woofers') of up to 15 in. or 18 in. (380 or 457

mm) in diameter and small 'tweeters' down to $1\frac{1}{2}$ in. or 2 in. (37 or 50 mm). Sometimes a loudspeaker cabinet also contains an intermediate size of loudspeaker suited to handling the mid-frequency range.

A cross-over (or dividing) network is necessary to segregate the range of frequencies and to allow the most efficient operation of the loudspeakers. This network also protects the units as

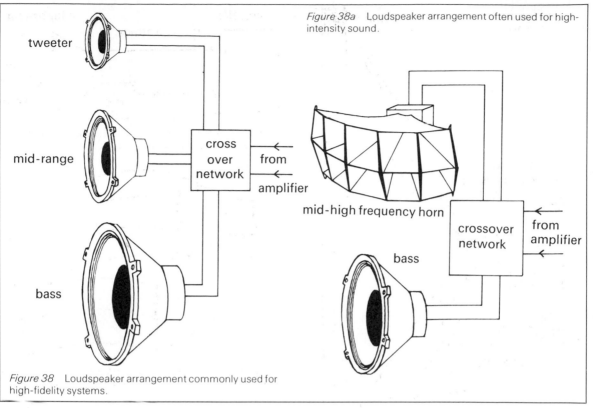

Figure 38a Loudspeaker arrangement often used for high-intensity sound.

tweeter

mid-range

bass

cross over network

from amplifier

mid-high frequency horn

bass

crossover network

from amplifier

Figure 38 Loudspeaker arrangement commonly used for high-fidelity systems.

a tweeter could be damaged when trying to cope with powerful bass sounds. A complete loud-speaker system operates rather like a choir where the soprano never gets the bass or baritone parts and vice versa, but she will overlap slightly with the contralto, who will overlap slightly with the tenor, and so on.

For certain applications requiring a great intensity of high frequency sound the paper or plastic cone is considered too flimsy and a Pressure Unit is employed (figure 39). The drive mechanism operates in exactly the same way as the cone loudspeaker with the voice coil moving in the magnetic field, only this time the diaphragm is in the centre of the coil and it is made of aluminium. Although the diaphragm is very small it is only required to reproduce the higher frequencies, and being robust it can cope with excessive movement in order to produce loudness.

Pressure units are usually attached to some form of horn, or flare, the size and shape of which will determine the distribution pattern of the sound. Many of these horn loudspeakers are designed for announcement systems where

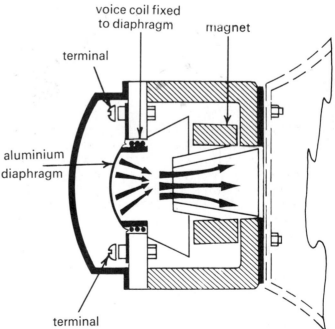

voice coil fixed to diaphragm

magnet

terminal

aluminium diaphragm

terminal

Figure 39 Horn pressure unit. The aluminium diaphragm is capable of a much greater intensity of mid/high frequencies than a paper cone. A horn is fixed on the front to direct the sound.

31

Photograph 1 Cutaway section of a dual concentric. *Photo courtesy Tannoy*

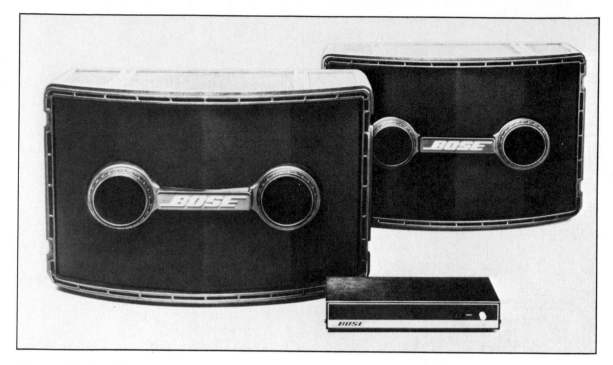

Photograph 2 'Bose' Model 802 loudspeakers measuring 520 mm × 326 mm × 334 mm high. These small, high-power loudspeakers of unique design incorporate 8 cone drivers mounted on four separate facets for smooth dispersion. The two circular vents at the front are reactive air columns which increase the bass output while lowering distortion on bass-heavy material by reducing cone movement. The loudspeakers are supplied with an active *equalizer for* optimum performance and can each handle 160 watts into 8 ohms. Horizontal dispersion: 120 degrees; vertical dispersion: 100 degrees (60 degrees if stacked in pairs). *Photo courtesy Bose UK Ltd*

Figure 40 Examples of pressure units driving into different types of horn: a) multi-cellular horn b) radial horn c) exponential or trumpet horn d) exponential horn (folded back upon itself to conserve space) e) horn with acoustic lens designed to provide a wide dispersion with a soft edge for short-throw sound (10–20 metres).

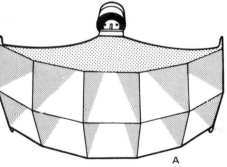

A

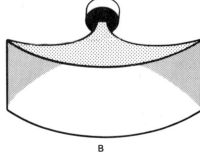

B

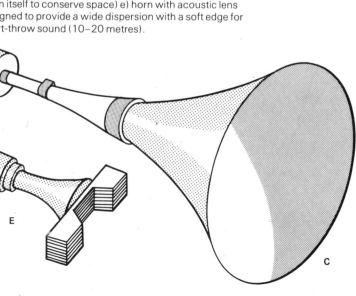

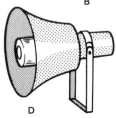

C

D

E

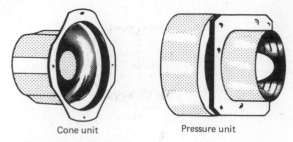

Cone unit   Pressure unit

Figure 41 Examples of tweeters.

power and intelligibility are more important than quality, i.e., they reproduce the higher frequencies in the voice range at a great intensity. High frequency tweeters may be either cone or pressure units. Their performance can be equally good. But in a powerful system where high sound pressure levels are required the more robust pressure units are usually employed (figure 41).

Cabinets or *enclosures*

All cone loudspeakers have to be mounted in an *enclosure* (or box) of some sort and the design of these will significantly affect the performance of the speaker.

It could be said that a loudspeaker mounted behind a hole in an infinite wall with equal air pressure either side would be operating under ideal conditions: this is because the primary function of an enclosure is to separate sound waves emanating from the front of a loudspeaker from sound waves emanating from the rear of the loudspeaker so that they do not cancel each other out. This cancellation occurs because the two sets of pressure waves are 'out of phase'.

Let me explain: imagine the movement of a diaphragm; when it moves forwards it compresses the air at the front and rarefies the air at the rear; conversely, when it moves backwards it compresses the air at the rear and rarefies the air at the front. Therefore the patterns of the pressure waves produced at the front and rear of a loudspeaker diaphragm are always out of phase; and the interaction when they meet will cause a cancelling effect at certain frequencies.

Now the Infinite Wall idea is not a very practical arrangement, but a compromise can be made by wrapping the hypothetical wall around the back of the loudspeaker to form an enclosed box, and the result is called an Infinite Baffle (figure 42). A drawback of the Infinite Baffle is that the volume of air trapped inside the box constitutes a 'stiff-

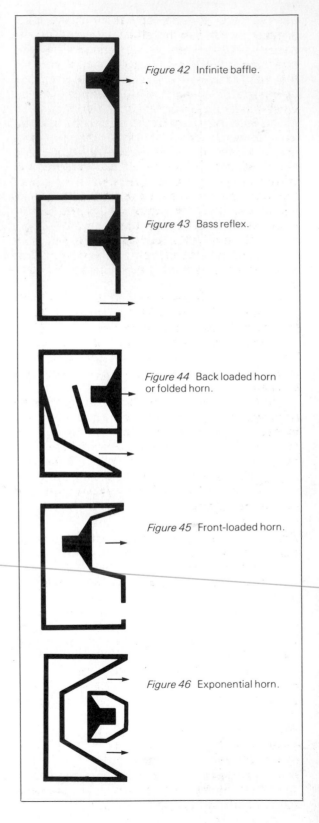

Figure 42 Infinite baffle.

Figure 43 Bass reflex.

Figure 44 Back loaded horn or folded horn.

Figure 45 Front-loaded horn.

Figure 46 Exponential horn.

ness' to the physical operation of the loud-speaker which has the effect of restricting the bass response. Therefore many enclosures have openings or *ports* carefully calculated to improve the bass response and also to minimize any unwanted resonances which may be set up when the loudspeaker is in operation.

The Bass Reflex enclosure (figure 43) is similar to an Infinite Baffle, but with a port or opening carefully designed to make use of some of the back radiations which would otherwise be absorbed in the box. In order to do this the size of the port is calculated so that low frequency sound waves coming out of the port are broadly out of phase with the rear of the cone. They are thus *in* phase with the bass sounds from the front of the cone and will add to them. In this way, the bass response, restricted in the Infinite Baffle, is enhanced.

As the bass frequencies we are dealing with have wavelengths of six feet and more the Back-Loaded or Folded Horn enclosure (figure 44) is designed to increase the length of the sound path from the back of the cone to the port as another way of obtaining the correct phasing between cone and port.

Other enclosures are designed to increase the bass response and also to improve the *directivity* of sound. The Front-Loaded Horn (figure 45) has the driver set back in a horn flare. The Exponential Horn enclosure (figure 46) has the driver enclosed and reverse mounted so that the reflected sound waves emanate from a flare the size of the cabinet.

Cost and size. In the theatre we are usually concerned with maximum sound pressure levels (loudness) coupled with a broad and uniform frequency response (quality). Unfortunately, this means large cost and sizeable units.

A fair comparison would be to take the hi-fi loudspeakers you have at home; try dividing the volume of the theatre by the volume of your room, then multiplying the size of your loud-speakers by the result. Use the same factor to multiply the cost and you will get a fair idea of what should be spent on theatre loudspeakers.

Power handling capacity. The power handling capacity of a loudspeaker, that is, how many watts received from the amplifier it will cope with successfully, is a guide to the achievable 'loudness' of the unit. However, some loud-speakers are so designed that they are not very

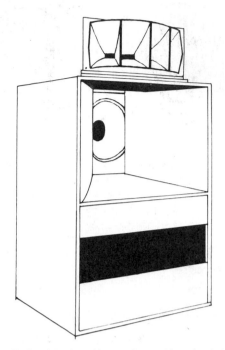

Figure 47 Combination of bass reflex and front loaded horn cabinet together with a mid/high frequency horn unit as seen in the famous Altec 'Voice of the Theatre' loudspeaker.

efficient. Therefore it is important to investigate for comparison with other units the published figures given for sound pressure levels.

It is generally advisable to allow for a larger power in the loudspeaker than that normally supplied by the power amplifier. The reason for this is that while overload of the amplifier results in distortion, overload of the loudspeaker may result in burnout or other physical damage. It is wise therefore to match a 35 watt amplifier with a loudspeaker capable of withstanding a constant electrical power of 35 watts and intermittent peaks of 50 watts. This would be stated as 35 watts RMS (Root Mean Square, a standard means of measuring the *effective* current) and 50 watts peak.

Remember that in 100 volt (or 70 volt) systems a stepdown transformer will be required with the loudspeaker. And this must be of the correct rating. (See Chapter 2.)

Conformity. All enclosures have their own particular characteristics so it is desirable that, as far as possible, similar types of loudspeaker and enclosure are used throughout the entire sound system. In this way the 'voice' of the sound will be uniform through the auditorium.

Phasing

When connecting up loudspeakers it is of prime importance to observe the correct phasing. In simple terms, all the 'positive' connections on the amplifier and loudspeakers should be wired to, say, the red wire and all the 'negative' connections wired to the black one.

If this is not scrupulously checked loudspeakers may be working out of phase, i.e. when one cone is moving forwards in its oscillating cycle the other is moving backwards. The result is a cancelling effect which reduces the bass response and also the apparent level when the listener is standing between the two loudspeakers.

Directivity

When dealing with speech reinforcement and public address systems directivity becomes a key factor. To achieve a uniform coverage of an auditorium with maximum potential gain before feedback or howl round from the microphones, directional microphones are used to point at the stage and directional loudspeakers are used to point at the audience.

The first rule to remember is that only high frequencies are directional. The bass tends to spread around in an uncontrollable fashion. Fortunately the 'speech intelligibility' frequencies or the 'presence' frequencies are in the higher range, and this factor can be used to advantage.

There are two methods of obtaining directivity in a loudspeaker. The first is by using a high frequency pressure unit driving into a horn, the size and shape of the horn determining the distribution pattern. The second is by placing loudspeakers, one above the other, in a column or line.

Line source loudspeakers. It is a physical fact that each time you place a like loudspeaker on top of another you decrease the vertical distribution, concentrating more power in the horizontal plane.

A line source loudspeaker is a column of cone units (usually) mounted in an infinite baffle enclosure. The resulting HF distribution pattern is fan-shaped in the horizontal plane with striking and definite perimeters (figure 48). With some hiss through the system you can test this for yourself by finding where the sound sharply

drops away. With a good line source unit it will be noticeable within a matter of inches.

The other great advantage of this type of loudspeaker is that, when correctly positioned, the maximum power output can be directed at the rear of an auditorium while the front rows are only receiving the benefit of the lower one or two cone units in the cabinet. The farther back you go the more benefit you receive from the loudspeaker.

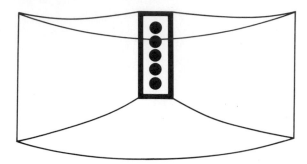

Figure 48   Coverage of columnar loudspeaker; typically the effective coverage of a good line source loudspeaker might be 60 degrees in the horizontal plane and 30 degrees in the vertical.

Figure 49   The Bozak range of columnar loudspeakers provides a wide horizontal and narrow vertical coverage by virtue of the number of cone units in each column. The two-way column incorporates separate low and high frequency units for increased frequency response.

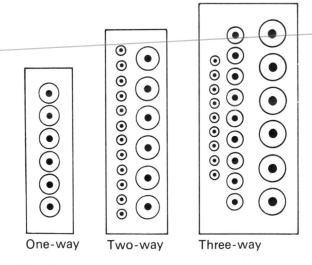

One-way   Two-way   Three-way

High frequency dispersal horns. The main advantages of using combinations of directional horn loudspeakers in conjunction with separate bass units are frequency response and power. There is no substitute for a properly designed bass enclosure for power and performance, and a pressure unit is capable of handling more HF signal than an ordinary cone.

The disadvantages of this arrangement are size and quality. It is not always physically possible to mount large bass enclosures in an auditorium, and even if it is possible it is aesthetically not as pleasing as slim column loudspeakers.

As far as quality goes, it is possible to use the very best cone units in a column (although many manufacturers do not do so in the interests of economy), whereas it is difficult to produce a 'sweet' sounding HF horn. The nature of the beast is to be on the hard side, but where power and definition are required this is a distinct advantage.

4
Power amplifiers

A power amplifier takes a line level signal and amplifies it to a degree where it is powerful enough to make a loudspeaker respond. Without going into technicalities there is not a great deal one can add to what has been said in previous chapters about amplifiers. They come in many shapes and sizes with varying inputs and power ratings. Each year smaller and more powerful amplifiers come on to the market with the advances in circuitry and transistor design (photograph 3).

Photograph 3 Twin channel professional power amplifier providing 220 watts per channel RMS into an 8-ohm load, or 350 watts RMS per channel into a 4-ohm load. Operating as a mono power amplifier it will provide 440 watts RMS into 16 ohms, 700 watts RMS into 8 ohms or 1200 watts RMS into 4 ohms. Manufactured as *Crown* in the USA. *Photo courtesy HHB Hire and Sales*

Input

Straight amplifiers will have a line level input which in most cases will be unbalanced as they are usually closely associated to the mixer and long leads are not necessary.

Outputs

The output impedance will be stated and/or there may be a 100 volt output. In some cases there will be a choice of impedances, for example, 4, 8 and 16 ohms (photograph 4).

Power rating

The unit will have a power rating which is stated in two ways: the continuous maximum power

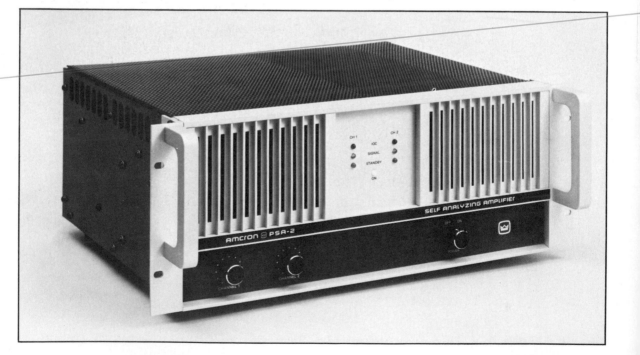

it will happily generate over a reasonable frequency range given an unvarying 0 dB signal (RMS), and the maximum burst of power it will handle above that figure when fed with a normal varying programme (this is known as a music or peak figure). The RMS figure is the more important one.

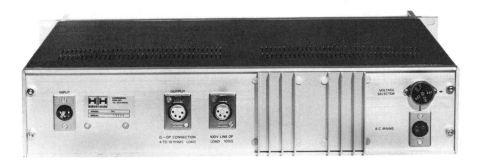

Mixer/amplifiers

Some amplifiers have inputs with gain and tone controls for microphones or other equipment. In other words, there is a mixer incorporated. These mixer/amplifiers are mainly used for small permanent or portable P.A. systems and can be very useful for rehearsal purposes (photograph 5).

Photograph 4 Rear of a mono power amplifier. H/H Electronics Ltd

Photograph 5 Mono power amplifier designed to accept a range of input and input combining plug-in modules. A flexible mixer/amplifier particularly useful for permanent announcement and background music application. *Photo courtesy Millbank Electronics Group Ltd*

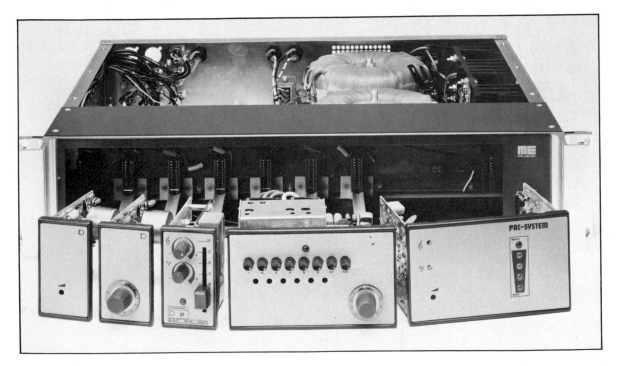

5
Mixers

At its most basic a mixer accepts a number of signals from varying sources, provides each with a volume control for 'balancing' purposes and sends out the blended result as one line level signal. In addition tone controls may be added either to each individual input channel or, more simply, to the overall blended signal at the output.

The mixer is the heart of any sound system and should be of the highest technical standard of performance.

The mixing *desk* is commonly used in stage sound systems and it is therefore important to become acquainted with its basic facilities and the terminology.

Figure 50 is a very simplified diagram of the signal paths of a stereo mixer where there can be any number of inputs on the left, mixing down to two outputs on the right. The input channels in this example are identical so let us look at channel 1. You will notice that there are two inputs to the channel, one for a line level signal and the other for a microphone level signal. Plug sockets will be available on the mixer for connecting a microphone or a tape recorder, gram deck, etc. On the control panel there will be

a switch to select either the microphone or the line level signal into the system. The selected signal then flows along until it meets the Input Fader. This fader, or volume control, adjusts the amount of signal on each input channel to reach the final output.

The signal then has to be routed to either or both of the output channels. In a stereo mixer this is achieved with a Pan Control. The pan control operates rather like two volume controls back to back working in opposite directions. Turn the knob to the left and the signal is routed full strength to output A. Turn it to the right and the signal is routed full strength to output B. In the centre position it goes equally to both outputs and in the intermediate positions it will be pro rata to each side. The pan control is a device which moves or 'pans' the sound from left to right within the stereo image. The pan controls on all the input channels are connected to a common conductor known as a 'rail' or 'bus bar' via which the mixed or blended signals arrive at the final outputs. En route will be the Output Faders which master the overall signals.

At the outputs, which are at line level, one can connect amplifiers which in turn will be

Figure 50 Diagram of the signal paths of a stereo mixer.

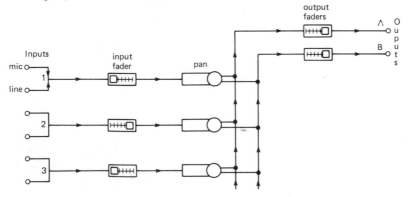

Figure 51 Four groups with input gain and tone controls.

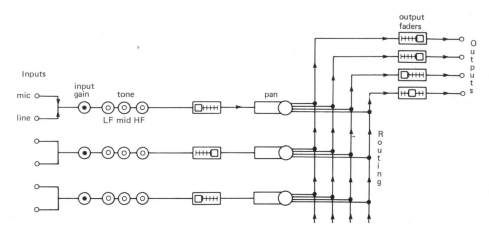

connected to loudspeakers. Alternatively, if the mixer is being used for recording purposes the outputs will be connected to the inputs of a tape recorder.

Additional outputs are necessary if one wishes to do multi-track recording. They also give us scope in the theatre for the convenient control of a number of amplifiers and loudspeakers. In figure 51 we have four output channels. It is now necessary to add additional switching for routing any of the input channels to the choice of outputs. These switches in the routing section may or may not be associated with the pan control; it will vary from mixer to mixer. As the output faders are mastering groups of channels they are sometimes called 'group output' faders and it follows, therefore, that the routing switches are sometimes called 'group select' switches.

Many of the larger mixers incorporate *subgrouping* whereby a number of input channels (say six microphones on a violin section) may be mastered as a pre-mixed group before being blended into the final output.

The mixer has to cope with varying signal strengths derived from different types of microphone, and indeed different types of performer, so it is conveneint to have an Input Gain control which can be preset as required. This allows the rest of the mixer to work within its designed parameters.

Unless the mixer is extremely basic it will incorporate Tone adjustment within each input channel. In this example we have a boost or cut of low frequencies (the bass), mid frequencies, and high frequencies (the treble). Mid frequency enhancement is sometimes called 'presence' for the simple reason that boosting the appropriate

mid frequencies can make a voice or an instrument stand out, be sharper or more present. The tone control section can be more or less complicated depending upon the mixer.

Monitoring what is happening within the mixer is very important. Meters (figure 52) are usually provided on each output to indicate visually the strength of each output signal. Should the meters be seen to be peaking too high or too low then appropriate action can be taken with the relevant fader or faders.

Facilities for Aural Monitoring will necessitate a gain control on each output channel allowing the required blend of signals to be mixed or switched to the monitor amplifiers and loudspeakers.

Facilities for Headphones are normally incorporated as it is not always convenient to monitor with loudspeakers, especially when one is working within an auditorium.

PFL or 'pre-fade listen' is another monitoring function. Each input channel has a switch inserted before the channel fader (pre-fade) to route the signal full strength to the monitoring system. Thus PFL allows the sound operator to monitor the signal on any channel no matter whether the input fader is open or closed. Somewhere in the monitoring control section of the mixer there will be a master gain control for pre-fade listen. As an example of its function, PFL is very useful for checking that a microphone is operating or that a tape cue is lined up while the channel fader remains closed.

Most mixing desks also have auxiliary facilities on the input channels for sending signals to separate outputs for 'foldback' and 'echo'.

Foldback (figure 53) is also a form of monitoring, but it is monitoring for the performer rather

Figure 52 Monitoring.

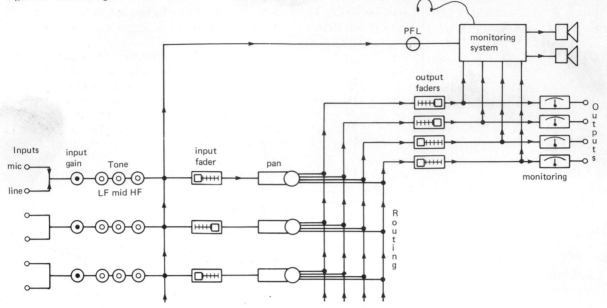

Figure 53 Auxiliary sends and returns.

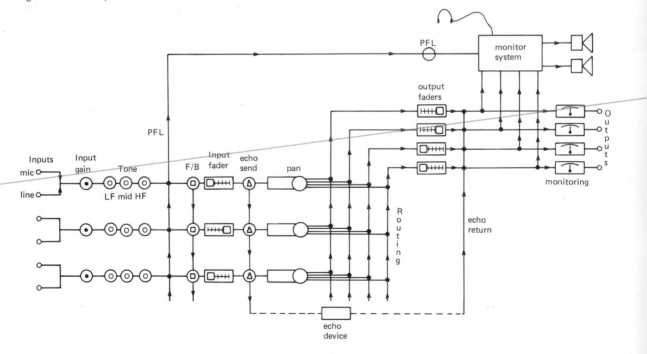

than the technician. Sometimes a singer on stage has difficulty hearing the important instruments in an orchestra. The singer will probably ask for foldback of certain key instruments, perhaps piano and drums. So, the foldback fader is turned up on the relevant input channel or channels and the signal is sent to the foldback output. Often a singer on stage using a microphone will complain that he cannot hear himself. This is because all the loudspeakers are directed away from him. A little judicious foldback will make him feel more secure. The foldback output which is at line level can be connected to a power amplifier driving loudspeakers which are placed on stage.

Foldback is so called because the signal arriving at the mixer from the microphone is literally folded back again to the performer. Some mixers have several foldback sends on each channel providing a variety of signal mixes to different performers. There is a growing tendency in big musicals and revues to use a combination of live sound and microphones, with tape recordings to which the artistes mime. This not only provides a more pleasing sound but allows the people on stage more freedom of movement. Tape foldback is an essential part of this operation.

The Echo Send is an identical facility in that each input channel has an echo send level control which sends the required amount of signal to the line level echo send output. However, instead of being connected to a power amplifier the echo send is connected to some form of echo or reverberation device. But having sent various signals into our echo unit we need to take the echoed signal and mix it back into our system so that we can hear the result. To this end the output of the echo unit is plugged into the Echo Return inputs and the processed signal is introduced into the mixer. Adjustment of the relevant echo return faders, or gain controls, will mix the echoed signal into the final outputs as required.

On the input channels the foldback and echo send facilities may be wired before or after the channel fader: Pre or Post fade. Sometimes they are switchable. In figure 53 the echo send is Post fade so that the channel fader effectively masters the echo send. But notice that the foldback send is *before* the fader – Pre fade – so that the foldback signal will remain constant no matter what happens to the channel fader.

Mixing consoles

Large permanent installations often have the mixer built into a console which includes all the ancillary facilities like loudspeaker switching, microphone and loudspeaker plug patch panels, tape remote controls, cuelights and intercommunication (photograph 6).

Sometimes even the tape machines and gram decks are also built into purpose-designed furniture. This idea was particularly prevalent in the UK during the 1960s when a new wave of theatre building coincided with the emergence of the Theatre Consultant. But although this is a very neat arrangement it is also extremely inflexible. The trend is now for smaller pluggable units

Figure 54 Example of the functions of a typical mixing desk.

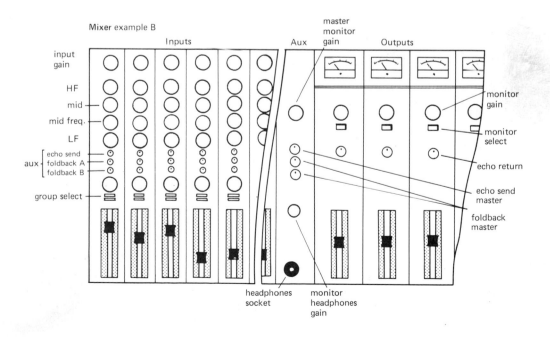

Photograph 6 Sound control room at the Lyric Theatre, Hammersmith, installed 1980. Mixer Cambridge Electronic Workshop. *Photo courtesy Theatre Projects Consultants Ltd*

which can be rearranged to suit individual operational requirements and can from time to time be replaced with more up-to-date pieces of equipment.

Output routing

In a theatre system which is used for the replay of sound effects some form of loudspeaker switching is necessary. This may be achieved at loudspeaker level *after* the amplifier or at line level *before* the amplifier (in which instance it is, strictly speaking, an amplifier switching system).

Switching to change location in a sound effects system is technically best handled when there is a correctly matched power amplifier associated with each loudspeaker (or group of loudspeakers). In this case the switching can be done between the mixer and the amplifier at line level (figure 55). As much routing as possible should be carried out at low level where it is easy to avoid impedance mismatching and electrical 'splats' which often occur at loudspeaker levels.

However, for reasons of economy it is sometimes necessary to switch at loudspeaker level (figure 56) in order to reduce the number of power amplifiers in a system. This is best carried out at a high voltage (100 volts or 70 volts) as discussed in Chapter 2. The major drawback is the possibility that all the loudspeakers may be switched to the output of a simple amplifier. This will inevitably overload the amplifier beyond its wattage capability.

Switching after the amplifier must be so arranged that it is impossible to connect more than one amplifier to any speaker or group of speakers. It is also inadvisable for any amplifier to be left without some form of load on the output. This need not necessarily be a loudspeaker, it can be what is known as a 'dummy load' in the form of correct value resistors. Hence, when a loudspeaker is rerouted the switching arrangement should cater for a dummy load to take its place.

With more ambitious output routing where there is a requirement for a number of signals to be routed to a variety of amplifier/loudspeaker combinations it will often take the form of a matrix of push buttons or switches. However, this arrangement is limiting in that it does not allow for *proportional* routing; i.e., a number of

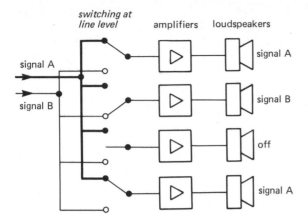

Figure 55 Switching at line level where each loudspeaker remains connected to its own power amplifier.

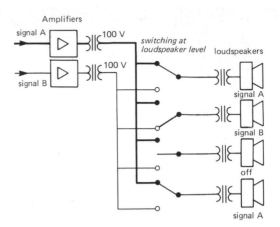

Figure 56 Switching at loudspeaker level (100 volts) with possible over-loading of amplifiers if too many loudspeakers are connected to one amplifier.

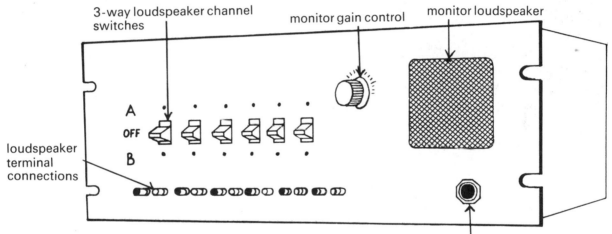

Figure 57 Loudspeaker switching unit suitable for two amplifiers feeding any combination of up to six loudspeakers via 100 volts line.

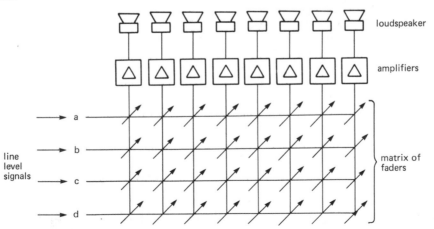

Figure 58 Diagram of output routing with variable cross-points.

loudspeakers receiving different mixes of signals. To achieve this end the matrix of routing push buttons is replaced with a matrix of faders (figure 58). This provides complete flexibility for the operator in that any signal from the mixer (or direct from a tape machine) can be routed in any proportion to any or all of the outputs. The possibilities for movement of sound and changes of texture and perspective are limited only by the number of inputs and output with their variable crosspoints and by the dexterity of the operator.

During the 1970s several attempts were made to design theatre mixers with all the sophisticated facilities previously described at the beginning of this chapter combined with some very complex output routing for the control of sound effects. The result in most instances has been a bewildering and uncontrollable array of knobs, switches and faders; and at excessive cost.

Photograph 7 Example of a theatre sound control room of the late 1960s with a six input, four output mixing desk with loudspeaker routing on the right. Extra microphone inputs come via small sub-mixer. Note the large opening window, the recessed and lit plug panel, the two remotely controlled tape machines and the sunken turntable unit with flush perspex lid. Mixer: Electrosonic Ltd. *Photo courtesy Theatre Projects Consultants Ltd*

Having been down that road myself I am now firmly convinced that mixers primarily designed for use with microphones should be kept separate from mixers whose purpose is to control and route sound effects. In the former the requirement is for a quantity of microphone input channels with full equalization and auxiliary functions to be mixed down to a limited number of outputs. The routing and control take place at the input stage. But in a sound effects system only a few tape/disc input channels with basic tone controls are normally required which need to be sent to a greater quantity of outputs. So here the routing and control to a large extent takes place at the output stage. In my opinion it is therefore preferable to have a standard mixer for microphones and general use (including the recording and preparation of tapes), and to have a separate mixer for the replay of sound effects.

Of course the development of mixers incorporating digital technology and microprocessor memory facilities might make me change my mind before too long. But it is better to have a simple system which can be operated well rather than confront the sound operator with a monster which remains a constant challenge to his mental and physical capabilities.

6

Echo and reverberation

Echo can be obtained by means of the record and playback heads on a tape machine. Take a straight signal, feed it also to a tape machine which is recording, take the signal from the playback head and mix it with the original and the result is tape delay echo.

For reverberation a different system is employed. A portion of the straight signal is sent to what is virtually the driving mechanism of a loudspeaker. This is attched to either one end of a long coiled spring (photograph 8) or, more expensively, to a large sheet of thin steel called a plate (photograph 9). The coil or plate is caused to vibrate and each vibration takes a certain amount of time to ripple along the length. At the other end a magnetic pick-up (as used in a gramophone pick-up) reacts to these delayed vibrations and sends them back to be mixed in with the original signal. Some degree of equalization (tone correction) is usually incorporated to obtain optimum quality from what is basically a crude device.

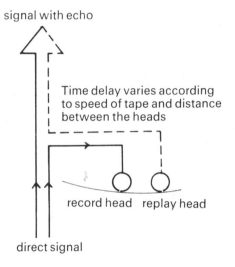

Figure 59 Tape delay echo.

Photograph 8 Echo Spring. *Photo courtesy Scenic Sounds Equipment, London*

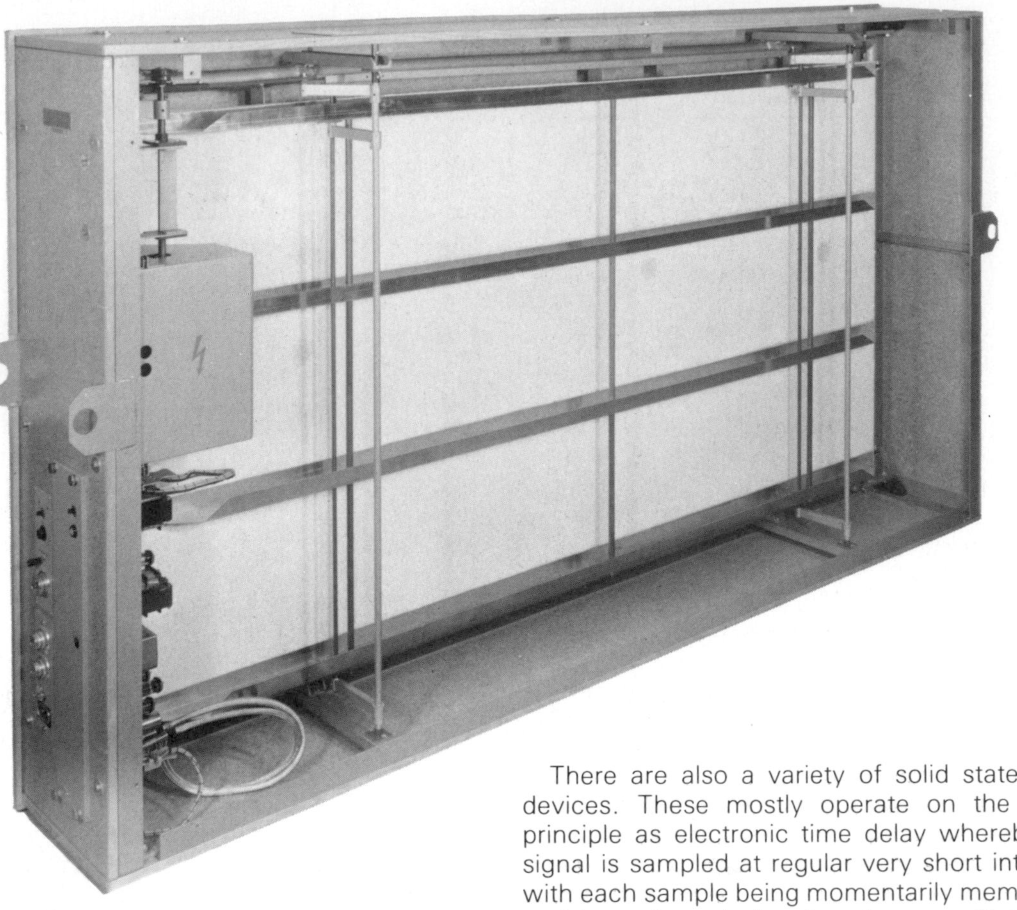

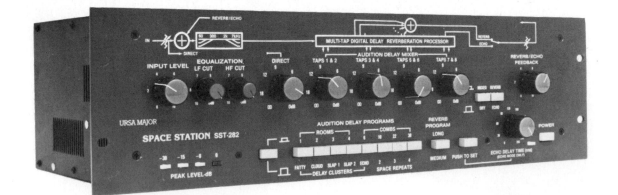

Photograph 9 Echo plate. *Photo courtesy F. W. O. Bauch Ltd*

Photograph 10 Solid state processing centre for reverberation, multi-tap digital delay, repeat echo plus many other effects. *Photo courtesy Feldon Audio Ltd*

There are also a variety of solid state echo devices. These mostly operate on the same principle as electronic time delay whereby the signal is sampled at regular very short intervals with each sample being momentarily memorized and then released a fraction of a second later. For repeat echo the signal is fed back into the system as many times as repeats are required. Apart from altering the time setting for short or long delays many units incorporate circuitry for changing equalization and processing the signal in different ways to create reverberation and other effects (photograph 10).

7
Disc replay

A disc replay (or playback) unit operates on the (by now familiar) principle of vibrations being turned into electrical impulses. The stylus sits in the groove of a revolving disc. The groove has a varying lateral pattern which the stylus is forced to follow and which causes it to vibrate; these vibrations are turned into tiny electrical currents by one of several methods depending upon the type of pick-up.

I shall not go very deeply into the technicalities of disc reproduction here. Suffice it to say that a gramophone pick-up is very similar in operation to a microphone, which is discussed in the next chapter.

The turntable

The essence of a good turntable is that it should run accurately at the set speed with no fluctuations and that the motor should not cause vibrations which can affect the pick-up, thereby causing an unacceptable low frequency rumble.

The unit should also be mounted so that any vibrations in the room such as footsteps, doors shutting, etc., will not be transmitted to the pick-up. Even a heavy tread on a wooden floor can make a modern lightweight pick-up arm jump a groove. The remedy is either very solid mounting or, at the other extreme, a sprung mounting, in which the springs upon which the unit sits will absorb any shocks.

Speeds of $33\frac{1}{2}$ and 45 r.p.m. are essential and 78 r.p.m. is useful for old recordings. A constantly variable speed facility is invaluable, especially for making up sound effects; a bell can be slowed down to lower the pitch, a wind effect can be speeded up to make it sound stronger, etc.

The pick-up arm. Some turntables come with their own arms and also incorporate a lowering device, a sensible addition which saves many a cracked groove.

If a separate arm is required choose one that is reasonably robust and has a counterweighted balance which can be adjusted to the correct weight for the cartridge. With old 78s (which require a different cartridge) or worn discs the reproduction is sometimes improved by slightly increasing the weight.

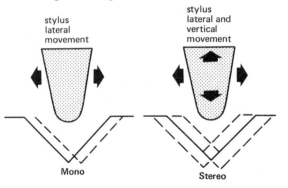

Figure 60 Mono and stereo grooves on a recorded disc.

Pick-ups. Crystal, ceramic, moving coil and semi-conductor pick-ups are all devices for turning vibrations into voltages. It is generally accepted that a crystal pick-up while being both cheap and robust does not provide the frequency range desirable in a first-class system. I would tend to go for a high quality moving coil with a diamond stylus – as this will last longer and be less damaging than a sapphire.

Preamplifier

It is good practice to incorporate a preamplifier into the disc unit, bringing the output of the pick-up head up to line level. It then becomes another standard item which can be used anywhere in the system.

Certain tone controls are particularly relevant to discs so it is convenient both operationally and electronically to incorporate them here. The basics are a 'scratch' filter (which just removes certain of the higher frequencies) and boost and cut of bass and treble. A more sophisticated unit would include:

1 Rumble filter. A switch which rolls away the bass below a certain frequency (usually about 60 Hz).
2 High frequency filters. Normally a choice of three frequencies (e.g. 5 KHz, 7 KHz 10 KHz).
3 Slope control. This determines how sharply the HF rolls away at the selected frequency.
4 Treble boost and cut.
5 Bass boost and cut.

It is also useful to have a Master Gain control, and headset socket which remains unaffected by the Master Gain (for cueing up discs), and a Mono/Stereo selector switch.

8
Microphones

A microphone is a device for converting acoustic power (sound pressure waves) into electrical power which has essentially similar wave characteristics. It is very similar to the human ear in many ways, the 'diaphragm' performing the same function as the ear drum.

There are five kinds of microphone:

1 *Carbon microphone*. The sound pressure waves acting upon the diaphragm compress the carbon granules, thereby producing an alternating electric resistance which modulates the current supplied by the battery (or by a low voltage mains supply). This system is still used today in the microphone part of a telephone. Carbon microphones are very robust but do not have directional properties and the frequency range is very limited. They are certainly not suitable for any form of 'quality' transmission.

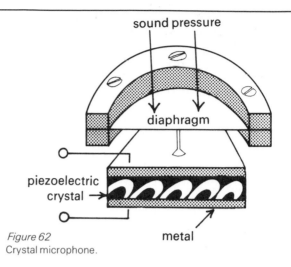

Figure 62
Crystal microphone.

2 *Crystal microphone*. The diaphragm presses against 'piezoelectric' crystals, deforming them so that they generate an alternating voltage. This is again a non-directional limited frequency range device. Since crystal microphones are robust, a convenient size and cheap to produce they are sold a great deal with the smaller domestic tape recorders.

3 *Ribbon microphone*. A 'ribbon' made of a corrugated strip of metal foil is fixed at each end to be between the poles of a magnet. The sound

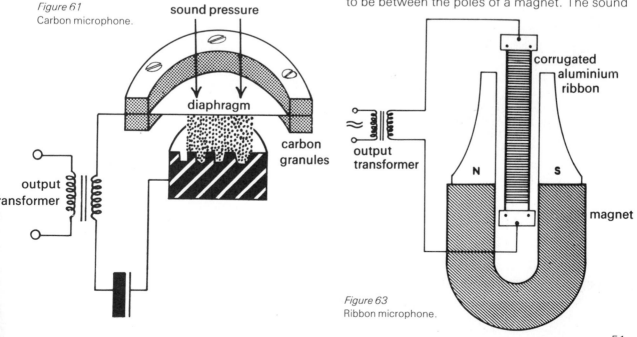

Figure 61
Carbon microphone.

Figure 63
Ribbon microphone.

pressure waves move the ribbon in the magnetic field between the poles of the magnet, generating a small alternating voltage between the ends of the ribbon. Ribbon microphones are usually sensitive front and back and relatively 'dead' on the sides. Good ribbon microphones are used in broadcasting and recording studios. The nature of their construction makes them fairly delicate and simply blowing on one can, and probably will, cause damage. They are medium priced.

4 *Dynamic moving coil microphone.* A metal coil rigidly fixed to the diaphragm moves in a magnetic field inducing a small current in the coil. Dynamic microphones, depending upon their design, can have any form of directivity of pick-up although they are most commonly found either with an all round pick-up (omnidirectional) or with one very definite live side (directional). The quality of the best of these microphones is excellent and they are reasonably robust.

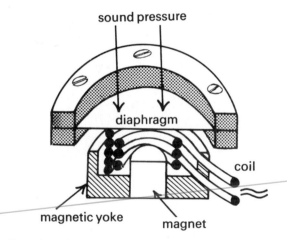

Figure 64 Dynamic moving coil microphone.

5 *Condenser microphone.* A thin diaphragm which forms one electrode of a condenser vibrates close to a fixed counter-electrode, thus producing variations in the capacitance (or impedance) of the condenser. The condenser is given a constant charge via a very high resistance and this produces a voltage between the plates of the condenser. This voltage varies with the changes in capacitance caused by the sound waves. It follows that a condenser microphone requires a power source to make it operate. A good condenser microphone is of the highest quality attainable. They are more expensive than most other microphones and require gentle handling.

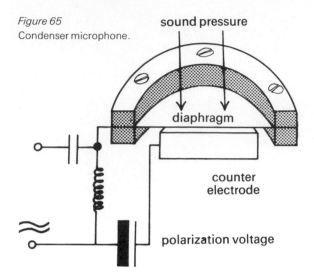

Figure 65
Condenser microphone.

Directivity

One of the big drawbacks of a microphone is that it 'hears' everything (within the boundaries of its design and construction). That is why so much care is taken to ensure that recording studios are absolutely silent and sound-proof against outside noise, and that the acoustics are favourable to recording techniques. Largely because of this lack of discrimination, microphones have been developed with differing directional characteristics to compensate for various conditions. They may be categorized as follows:

1 *Omnidirectional.* Also known as nondirectional. The microphone is equally sensitive in all directions. This is useful for, say, picking up a group of voices. Omnidirectional microphones are also used as 'chest' or 'lavalier' microphones attached to a halter hung round the neck of the speaker. Often to obviate the need for a trailing lead they are fed into miniature portable radio

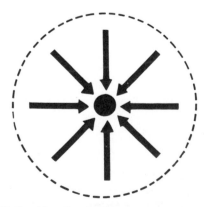

Figure 66 Omnidirectional pattern.

transmitters concealed on the person. An 'Omni' is preferred in this instance because of the proximity to, and the constant movement of the head. An omnidirectional microphone is not to be recommended for use in close proximity to loudspeakers where feedback is a problem; neither should it be used in reverberant conditions as it will pick up all the unwanted sounds.

2 *Bidirectional.* Also known as 'figure of eight', for obvious reasons. The pick-up pattern takes the form of a 'live ball' at the front and rear of the microphone with relative deadness at the sides, top and bottom. The pattern can vary with different makes of microphone; some are more sensitive at the front than the rear and most are remarkably dead at the sides.

Figure 68 Cardioid pattern (directional).

Figure 67 Bidirectional pattern.

Bidirectional microphones are useful for picking up speakers each side of the microphone or for recording instruments, e.g. strings, where you require the direct sound from the instrument plus some room acoustic to liven it up a little.

They are also extremely effective for broadcast drama work where an actor can seem to be walking into the distance merely by moving a few inches on to the dead side of the microphone.

3 *Directional.* Also known as unidirectional or cardioid. The word 'cardioid' derives from the heart-shaped pick-up pattern. The shape of the pattern varies with the make of microphone but a good cardioid is extremely sensitive at the front compared to the rear. One of the variations is the hypercardioid or the supercardioid which has a narrower front lobe with a slight rear pick-up but it is extremely dead to sound from lateral sources.

This type of microphone is, perhaps, the most useful in a live performance situation because of its exclusion of unwanted sounds and the possi-

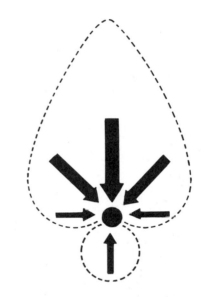

Figure 69 Hypercardioid pattern (very directional but with increased sensitivity at rear).

bility of keeping the dead side to the loudspeakers to minimize feedback. Directional microphones are also used extensively in recording studios to obtain maximum 'separation' between instruments.

A word about rifle or gun microphones: I would like to explode the myth that it is possible for a spy to set up an ultra-sensitive rifle microphone outside a window half a mile away and pick up a conversation inside the building. Theatre directors are constantly asking me to obtain one of these devices in order to amplify a singer thirty foot up stage on a twelve foot high rostrum – the sad truth is that this is still pure science fiction. However, gun microphones do exist. They are basically good directional microphones with perforated extension tubes on the front which are so designed that the higher frequencies are rejected from the sides, giving the effect of more directivity.

The unit can only be effectively used about three times farther away from the sound source than an ordinary cardioid microphone.

How directivity is accomplished

A If only one side of a diaphragm is exposed to the sound source while the other side is sealed against the environment, sound pressure waves from all directions will move the diaphragm with equal intensity making it an omnidirectional microphone.

B If both the front and rear of the diaphragm are exposed to the sound field, the force moving the diaphragm is due to the difference in the sound pressures in front and behind the diaphragm. This difference produces a directional effect.

C If both the front and rear are exposed to the sound field but the construction of the microphone is such that the pressure waves reaching the rear are delayed by a scientifically calculated amount of time (i.e. inverting the phase) then the result is a cardioid response.

D If both sides of the diaphragm are equally exposed to the sound field the result will be a figure-of-eight pattern (bidirectional effect).

Cables and connectors

Microphone cables must be twin core for the go and return and they must have lap-wound or braided screening with an overall PVC insulating sheath. Twin 14/0·0076 (metric euqivalent: 13/0·2) colour coded and screened PVC (or rubber) covered cable is recommended for most applications.

Since microphone cables are particularly susceptible to all forms of electrical interference, great care must be taken to keep them well clear of all mains cables and control gear and even from other audio wiring, especially high voltage speaker cables.

Connectors should be very robust, incorporating a 'solid' connection. Flimsy contacts can cause problems.

Tip, ring and sleeve (3 pole) jack plugs are often used as they are conveniently sized and priced. However, dirt can be a hazard with this form of connector; a small spot of grease or a little dust can produce a faulty connection.

Cannon XLR 3-pin plugs and sockets are recommended where possible.

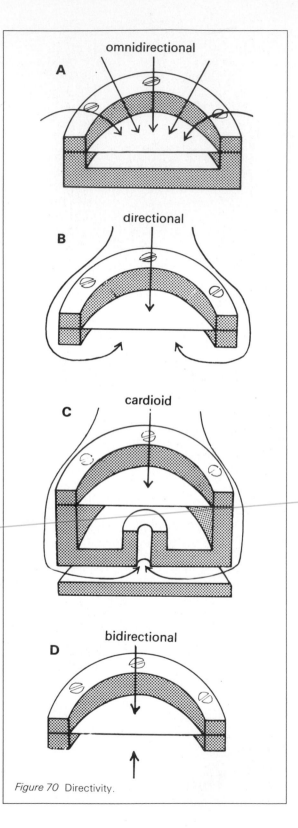

Figure 70 Directivity.

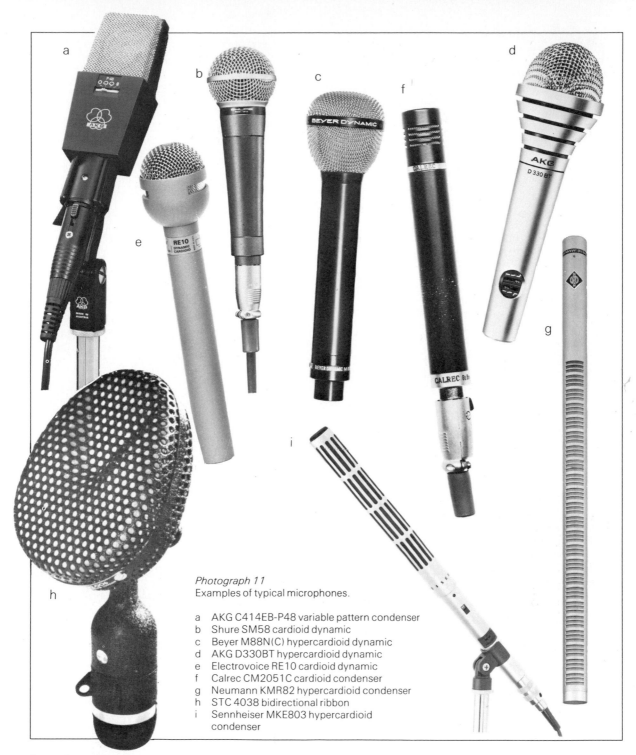

Photograph 11
Examples of typical microphones.

a   AKG C414EB-P48 variable pattern condenser
b   Shure SM58 cardioid dynamic
c   Beyer M88N(C) hypercardioid dynamic
d   AKG D330BT hypercardioid dynamic
e   Electrovoice RE10 cardioid dynamic
f   Calrec CM2051C cardioid condenser
g   Neumann KMR82 hypercardioid condenser
h   STC 4038 bidirectional ribbon
i   Sennheiser MKE803 hypercardioid
    condenser

Impedance

High impedance microphones should not be used in a properly engineered system. Apart from their greater susceptibility to interference, the capacitance in a long cable run at high impedance seriously reduces the microphone's high frequency response.

9
The tape recorder

The machine

A tape recorder is a device for recording, storing and subsequently reproducing sound. The storage medium is a continuous strip of material capable of being magnetized (tape) which is drawn at a constant speed across a recording head. Also known as a magnetic head, this is an electro-magnet consisting of a coil of wire on an iron core with an extremely narrow gap. Sound waves translated into electrical impulses or voltages via a microphone are first amplified by the record amplifier and then fed to the recording head. A magnetic field, the intensity of which varies synchronously with the original sound waves, develops across the gap in the head. The tape travelling past the head becomes magnetized to a greater or lesser extent depending upon the variation in this intensity. Therefore the intensity variation of the magnetization on the tape becomes a representation of the original sound waves.

Bias

In order to obtain a recording that is distortion-free, the tape must also be magnetized by a high frequency bias signal. Magnetic tape does not respond in an even and predictable way unless there is a certain minimum magnetic force from the recording head. The bias signal provides this minimum force at an ultrasonic frequency of between 40,000 Hz and 80,000 Hz. It only becomes audible if the tape recorder is faulty and in need of adjustment.

Playback

The playback process is pretty well the reverse of the recording process. The tape is drawn past the

Figure 71 Layout of heads on a normal three head recorder.

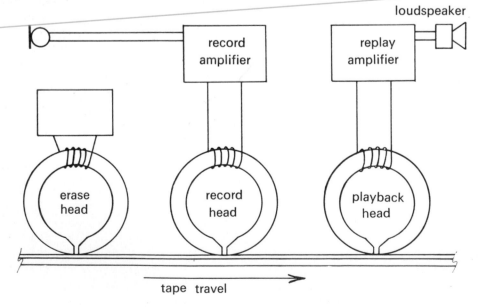

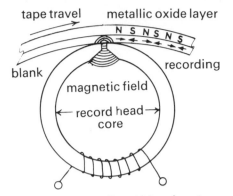

tape travel   metallic oxide layer

N S N S N S

blank

recording

magnetic field

record head core

record head   coil and bias signal

Figure 72 Record head.

playback head at exactly the same speed as when it was recorded and the varying intensities of magnetism on the tape induce corresponding voltages in the coil via the magnetic flux in the head. This pattern of voltages is then amplified by the playback amplifier and fed to a loudspeaker. The loudspeaker converts the electrical impulses into sound waves and the cycle is complete. On the cheaper domestic machines the same head and amplifier double for both the record and replay processes. In this case a suitable switching system is incorporated.

Erase

Once recorded, a tape can be used many times with no significant deterioration provided it is stored in a reasonable temperature and not exposed to other magnetic fields.

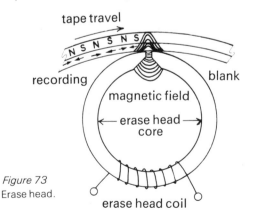

tape travel

N S N S N S

recording

blank

magnetic field

erase head core

erase head coil

Figure 73
Erase head.

But one of the attractions of tape is that it is simple to remove the original information and replace it with a new recording. For this purpose an erase head is incorporated into the system to clear the tape of any programme material before it reaches the recording head. The erase head produces a magnetic field induced by an ultrasonic alternating current that flows through the windings of the coil. This action demagnetizes the tape and the original recording disappears. Naturally, the erase head only comes into operation when one is recording. On playback the erase head is automatically switched off.

The basic system

The basic system consists of two main sections – one mechanical and one electronic.

The mechanical section, or tape-drive mechanism, transports the tape past the magnetic heads at a precisely controlled speed. The minutest variation of speed is noticeable in the form of an irregularity in the sound, often called 'wow' or 'flutter'. This same mechanism also accomplishes the high-speed rewinding of the tape. The capstan maintains a constant tape speed. The tape is kept in pressure contact with the capstan, which is a revolving shaft, by means of a pinch wheel. The diameter and the number of revolutions per minute of the capstan control the tape speed. The tape is drawn from the left-hand spool across the heads by the capstan and pinch wheel roller. The right-hand spool then takes up the slack tape as it leaves the capstan. This spool is driven either by a separate motor or by a belt drive from the capstan motor. For rewind purposes the supply spool is either driven by a third motor or again belt driven from the capstan. A three-motor transport is a better system. A set of tape guides is usually placed on either side of the head so that the height of the tape is kept at the same level to ensure the correct positioning of the tracks during recording and playback. Close contact between the tape and the magnetic head is achieved either by the tape tension alone or by a system of pressure pads. Most recorders are equipped with tape indicators or tape counters with which particular points in a recording may be located. These counters are coupled to the shaft of one of the reels and therefore do not indicate the footage of the tape itself or the playing time. However, they are accurate enough to find any desired spot on the tape, provided that the same type and thickness of tape with the same inside diameter of reel are employed both in recording and playback. Professional machines are often provided with fairly accurate counters which clock up the minutes and seconds.

The electronic section consists of an amplifier for the recording and reproducing process, recording level controls and an oscillator circuit which produces the high frequency current for the ultrasonic bias and the erasure.

Because of physical factors involved in the magnetic recording process, the low and high frequencies are attenuated by comparison with the medium frequencies. The amplifier is provided with an equalizing circuit which compensates for these losses both in recording and playback, so that all frequencies are reproduced as close to the original distribution as possible. Engineers call this a 'flat overall frequency response', and international standards prescribe the degree of equalization in order to ensure that tapes may be recorded on one machine and played back on another.

The amplifier of the electronic section is also operated by means of switches or press buttons. All recorders are equipped with one or more inputs for microphones and most have an additional radio input and a separate input for a pickup. The radio socket, which is at line level, is often combined for input and output (DIN socket). In this case the input serves for recording the radio programme and the output for the playback of the recorded tapes through the radio set or an external amplifier, or for copying to a second tape recorder. This input allows the copying of records (provided there are no copyright problems) or tape recordings. Some recorders are equipped with separate recording level controls for the different inputs, i.e. with an incorporated mixer.

Tape speeds

Most tape recorders offer a choice of speeds selected from 15, $7\frac{1}{2}$, $3\frac{3}{4}$, $1\frac{7}{8}$ and $\frac{15}{16}$ inches per second (38, 19, 9·5 and 2·375 cm/s). Generally, two speeds are provided, for example, $7\frac{1}{2}$ and $3\frac{3}{4}$ i.p.s. though three or even four speeds are sometimes available.

Obviously, the slower the tape speed the longer will be the running time. But as a general principle the higher the tape speed the better the quality of the recording. With a slow speed any imperfections in the tape itself become apparent. It is also mechanically more difficult to obtain a perfect speed constancy at a slow rate.

Recording studios normally use 15 i.p.s. In the theatre we have tended to standardize at $7\frac{1}{2}$ i.p.s. The frequency response and dynamic range at this speed are excellent and the amount of tape required held within reasonable limits. It is also a convenient speed for editing. At $3\frac{3}{4}$ i.p.s.

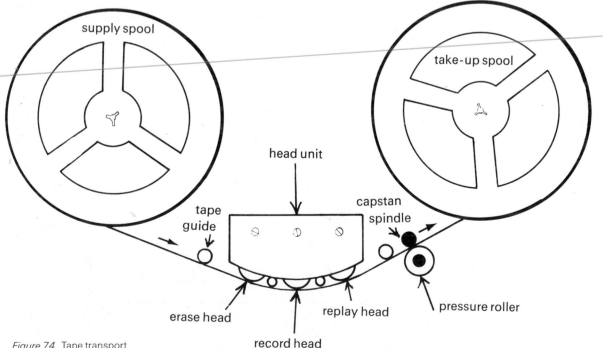

Figure 74 Tape transport.

cutting in on a bar of music or trying to edit out a 'click' starts to become difficult.

$3\frac{3}{4}$ i.p.s. is useful for long background effects or 'wallpaper' music, and some modern machines produce remarkable results at this speed. At $1\frac{7}{8}$ i.p.s. the loss of high frequencies must be taken into account. Speeds as low as $\frac{15}{16}$ are only really suitable for lengthy dictation or for recording conferences, etc., where the main consideration is a very long uninterrupted recording time.

Tape speed governs frequency range and although there are constant technical developments in both tape and electronics the highest frequencies reproduced by most non-studio quality recorders are approximately as follows:

$$15 \quad \text{i.p.s. up to } 25{,}000 \text{ Hz}$$
$$7\tfrac{1}{2} \text{ i.p.s. up to } 20{,}000 \text{ Hz}$$
$$3\tfrac{3}{4} \text{ i.p.s. up to } 12{,}000 \text{ Hz}$$
$$7\tfrac{7}{8} \text{ i.p.s. up to } 8{,}000 \text{ Hz}$$
$$\tfrac{15}{16} \text{ i.p.s. up to } 4{,}000 \text{ Hz}$$

Number of tracks

The idea of a number of tracks on a tape often causes confusion. First it must be understood that only one side of the tape is coated with an iron oxide solution which is capable of being magnetized. This working side is coated across the whole width and entire length of the tape. The tracks are created by the track configuration of a particular recording head. Thus a full track head with one large single gap will create one track across almost the full width of the tape. A half track head will produce a track nearly half the tape width and a quarter track head will create a track a little less than a quarter of the tape width.

The different number of tracks were developed, just as were the different speeds, as a means of economizing on tape. The half track machine allows you to record on only the top half of the tape; at the end of the tape the reels are interchanged, thus inverting the tape and presenting the unrecorded portion to the top. The tape can then be recorded over the entire length a second time.

Some machines incorporate two quarter track gaps in the record and playback heads which quadruple the playing time of the tape. One is able to record in both directions with the top gap, then repeat the process by switching to the lower gap.

For stereo recording two separate tracks have to be available at the same time. This is achieved by having record and playback heads with either two half-track gaps (upper and lower) or two quarter track gaps. The latter arrangement allows the tape to be used in both directions in stereo.

Naturally, as the two signals being fed to the stereo record head are not identical, a duplicate set of electronics for both record and playback is necessary.

Advantages and disadvantages

Full track. Often used in broadcasting and recording studios. Maximum use of the tape provides the best possible dynamic range with little chance of small faults in tape manufacture becoming apparent.

Half track. Best compromise providing twice the playing time.

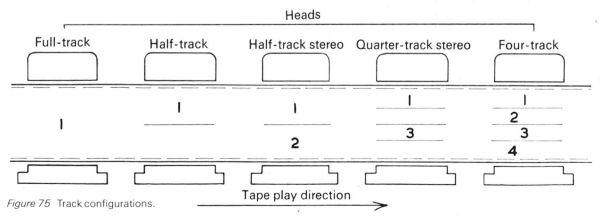

Figure 75 Track configurations.

59

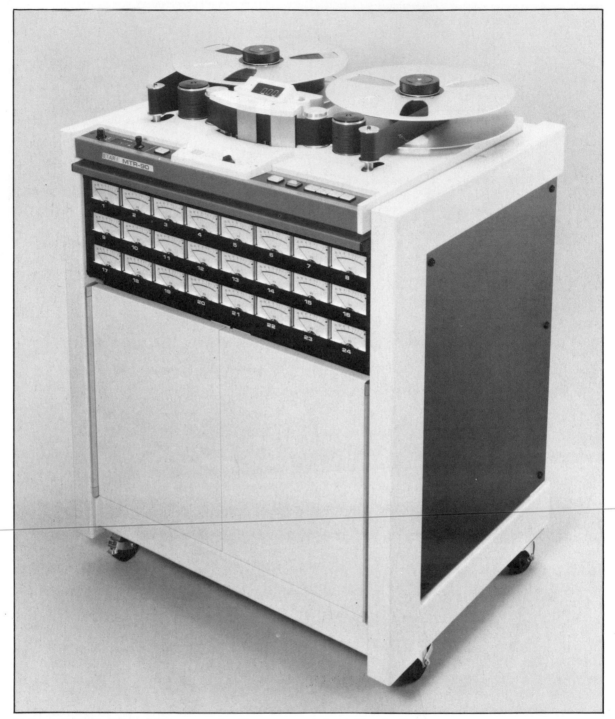

Photograph 12 Otari 24-track 2″ tape recorder. *Photo courtesy Industrial Tape Applications.*

Twin track. Two half tracks providing stereo. Most machines have a switch available for cutting out the lower track thereby making the recorder convertible to half track mono.

Quarter track. Allows more playing time but with such narrow tracks that particles of dust or imperfections in the tape will be noticeable as a fault in the recording. A minute speck will lift the

Photograph 14 TEAC A3440 four-track ¼ in tape recorder. *Photo courtesy R.E.W. Ltd*

Photograph 13 Revox PR99 Professional twin-track ¼ in tape recorder. *Photo courtesy F.W.O. Bauch Ltd*

tape momentarily away from the head, causing a 'drop out' in the reproduced sound. The slower the speed of the tape the more likely it is that this will happen. The other drawback of such a narrow track is that it tends to limit the dynamic range the tape will accept.

Quarter track stereo. Sometimes misleadingly called 'four track stereo', this provides two stereo signals. The same comments as for quarter track apply.

N.B. When preparing tapes for replay in a performance we need to be able to insert coloured leader tapes as cue markers and, if necessary, we must be able to alter the content of sections of the tape. Therefore we only record in one direction, whether it be mono or stereo and whatever the track configuration.

Multitrack recording

In order to achieve a number of separate yet synchronous sound tracks, recording studios have developed multitrack tape recorders. Using tape 2 in. (50 mm) wide, up to twenty-four separate tracks can be recorded either all together or one at a time (photograph 12). (There are even thirty-two track machines in existence.) The need for such machines was created by the pop music world where groups record their backing tracks first, adding the voices when the music is to their satisfaction. Having achieved the backing track and first layer of voices, they can then 'track on' the lead singer, more voices, a string section or a symphony orchestra if they can afford it.

There are also machines on the market which provide four tracks on standard ¼ in. (6 mm) tape. These can be useful for recording and creating special effects. However, the problems previously mentioned with quarter track stereo recording also apply here.

The tape

The tape used on standard recorders is ¼ in. (6 mm) wide and is produced in varying thicknesses. It consists of a plastic-based film coated with particles of iron oxide, which, through various complicated processes, are given a form similar to that of minute needles (i.e. a length of approximately 0·04 thousandths of an inch).

61

This iron oxide is incorporated into a lacquer which is applied to the base film. The coating process is an extremely critical technique and must produce a layer of constant thickness on the base material. At the same time, the needle-shaped iron oxide particles are magnetically orientated in the lengthwise direction of the tape, which improves the electro-magnetic properties. It is most important that the iron oxide is magnetically stable, ensuring retention of the quality of the recording even after long storage or repeated use.

The coating is then polished, giving the tape a non-abrasive, mirror-smooth surface. This treatment further improves the intimate contact between the tape and the magnetic heads, which in turn improves the high-frequency response. Abrasive effects and drop-out are almost eliminated and wear of the magnetic heads is reduced.

Electro-acoustical properties

The electro-acoustical properties of a tape cannot be assessed on the basis of the tape alone, because they are influenced by the characteristics of the recorder. Any evaluation, therefore, must be made by comparing the tape to be tested with a standard reference tape. The results obtained, in the same operating conditions, are compared with the known results of the reference tape.

With these factors in mind, we will attempt to explain the most important electro-acoustical properties.

Sensitivity. This is the measure of the signal intensity obtained from the tape that has been recorded under specific conditions. A high-sensitivity tape retains a stronger magnetization than a low-sensitivity tape under equal operating conditions and on reproduction will give a higher output voltage. A high-sensitivity tape, therefore, requires less playback amplification, thus giving a better signal-to-noise ratio and greater dynamic range on playback.

Frequency response. A frequency response test shows if the tape can reproduce the high and low frequencies equally well as in the middle range. Here also, the value is given in relation to that of the reference tape. Manufacturers line up their tape machines to suit the frequency response characteristics of a particular type of tape and best results will be achieved with the recommended tape.

Harmonic distortion. This is the amount of distortion occurring on playback. Extraneous harmonics are produced during the recording process, and these overtones, which were not present in the original signal, are given as a percentage of the total signal. Harmonic distortion increases the more the tape is magnetized and can become objectionable.

Print-through

The adjacent layers of a tape wound on reels have an undesirable tendency to exchange their magnetism and this effect, known as 'print-through', increases with the length of storage time. Today it is possible to produce tapes which have such low print-through that it is barely noticeable.

Modulation noise

This noise signal is caused by irregularities in the coating or impurities and dust on the surface of the tape.

Reels and spools

The tape is wound on to a spool and thus becomes a reel of tape. The spools generally range in size from 3 in. (75 mm) in diameter up to 7 in. (175 mm). Some machines will accept a spool size of $8\frac{1}{4}$ in. (206 mm). Professional tape recorders handle the large $10\frac{1}{2}$ in. (263 mm) spools. Larger spools are available in two types: either with the European 'ciné' centre or with the NAB (an American standard spool centre commonly used throughout the world for professional equipment) which requires a large centre hub on the machine.

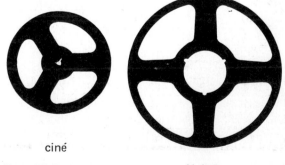

ciné

Figure 76 Spool standards.　　　　N.A.B.

Which tape speed for which purpose?

15 i.p.s.
The speed normally used in recording studios for the best dynamic range and frequency response.

7½ i.p.s.
This speed gives an extended dynamic range and is therefore most suited for Hi-Fi music recordings. In addition, this speed will also facilitate editing.

3¾ i.p.s.
The most popular speed. The frequency response at this speed is excellent and the amount of tape required is kept within a reasonable limit.

1⅞ i.p.s.
The loss of high frequencies must be taken into account, although speech can be very satisfactorily recorded at this slow speed.

15/16 i.p.s.
A speed as slow as this is only suitable for lengthy dictation or for the recording of conferences, where the main factor is a very long recording time without interruption.

		Spool Diameter cm/in.		Tape Length m/ft.	
		cm	in.	m	ft.
Standard Tape For use with semi-professional and professional machines.		13	5	180	600
		15	5¾	270	900
		18	7	360	1200
		22	8¼	540	1800
		28	10½	720	2400
Long Play Tape A general purpose tape of high quality.		8	3	65	210
		10	4	135	450
		11	4½	180	600
		13	5	270	900
		15	5¾	360	1200
		18	7	540	1800
		22	8¼	810	2700
		28	10½	1080	3600
Double Play Tape High quality tape with twice the playing time of SP tape. Specially suitable for four track recording.		8	3	90	300
		10	4	180	600
		11	4¼	270	900
		13	5	360	1200
		15	5¾	540	1800
		18	7	730	2400
Triple Play Tape Treble the playing time of standard play tape. Specially suitable for recordings of long duration and for portable machines.		8	3	135	450
		9	3½	180	600
		10	4	270	900
		11	4¼	360	1200
		13	5	540	1800
		15	5¾	730	2400
		18	7	1080	3600

Playing times at a glance

Length m	ft	15 i.p.s. 38 c.p.s.	7½ i.p.s. 19 c.p.s.	3¾ i.p.s. 9·5 c.p.s.	1⅞ i.p.s. 5 c.p.s.	15/16 i.p.s. 2·375 c.p.s.
45	150	1·87 min.	3·75 min.	7·5 min.	15 min.	30 min.
65	210	2·75 min.	5·5 min.	11 min.	22 min.	45 min.
90	300	3·75 min.	7·5 min.	15 min.	30 min.	60 min.
135	450	5·5 min.	11 min.	22 min.	45 min.	90 min.
180	600	7·5 min.	15 min.	30 min.	60 min.	120 min.
270	900	11 min.	22 min.	45 min.	90 min.	180 min.
360	1200	15 min.	30 min.	60 min.	120 min.	240 min.
540	1800	22 min.	45 min.	90 min.	180 min.	360 min.
730	2400	30 min.	60 min.	120 min.	240 min.	480 min.
1080	3600	45 min.	90 min.	180 min.	360 min.	720 min.
1280	4200	53·75 min.	107·5 min.	215 min.	430 min.	860 min.

Figure 77 Table of speeds, playing times, types of tape and spool sizes.

Tape thickness

Because of its robustness, ease of handling (especially when editing) and its inherent quality standard play tape is used whenever possible in the theatre.

However, a number of thinner tapes have been developed which allow for more tape, and therefore a longer playing time, per reel. These are as follows:

Long play. One and a half times the playing time of standard play tape. A good general purpose tape for non-professional work.

Double play. Twice the playing time of standard play tape. Particularly suitable for domestic quarter-track machines as the suppleness of the tape allows for maximum contact with the heads. It must be handled with care as it is more easily damaged.

Triple play. Treble the playing time of standard play tape. Suitable for recordings of long duration where quality is not critical. Often used on portable machines with small reel sizes. This tape is even more prone to damage.

The operation

Having chosen our tape, speed and track configuration we now arrive at the stage of making a recording. Let us assume that we are making a monaural recording on a half-track machine at $7\frac{1}{2}$ i.p.s. (19 cm/s) using standard tape. The signal to be recorded is coming via a mixer at line level and could therefore originate as one or a number of microphones, tape machines, disc units, etc.

Connection

The mixer is connected to the line input (sometimes labelled 'Radio' 'Auxiliary' or 'Music') of the tape recorder. We have previously ascertained that there is a correct impedance matching and that the interconnecting lead is correctly wired for a balanced or unbalanced system, whichever is applicable. If we were recording with a microphone straight into the machine then it would obviously be plugged into the microphone socket. Here again, impedances and balancing must be watched.

Loudspeaker monitoring

It is necessary when recording to be able to hear as well as see via the meter what is going on to the tape. A simple way of monitoring is to connect an amplifier and loudspeaker to the mixer. However, with this method one is hearing the original signal before it is recorded. A better method is to connect an amplifier and loudspeaker to the playback head and thus monitor the signal a fraction of a second after it has been recorded. With professional equipment both options are available and simply by flicking a switch one can compare the original with the just-recorded signal.

Most machines are equipped with a monitor headset socket. This will suffice if a loudspeaker is not available. Indeed, a headset is preferable when recording in the same room as the microphone in order to preclude feedback and unwanted echo effects from the playback head.

Meter monitoring

Although an aural quality check is necessary, the recording meter must dictate the input level adjustment, which is made via the Record Gain control.

The rules are very simple: if the signal supplied to the recording head is too low, the playback will have to be amplified to such an extent that all the background noise inherent in both the tape and the recording/playback process will also be amplified. This is described as a poor signal-to-noise ratio. Alternatively, if the signal supplied to the recording head is too high, the result will be an 'overloaded' or badly distorted recording.

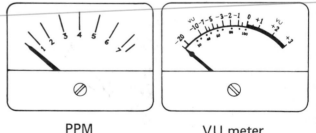

PPM
peak programme meter

VU meter
volume indicating meter

Figure 78 Meters. PPM Peak programme meter: an accurate way of measuring the electrical nature of an audio signal. VU Volume indicating meter: a cheaper device measuring overall loudness, that does not display all the peaks of the electrical signal.

The listening level is adjusted at the playback stage. One should never attempt to make a *'quiet'* recording. A correct recording is ensured if the loudest signals, or peaks, are near the maximum level shown on the meter, but it is as well to check the manufacturer's handbook for their recommendations.

N.B. When dubbing from one machine to another it is essential that the machine originating the signal is also set up so that the meter is 'peaking' correctly.

Tone controls

The tone controls on most tape recorders only affect the playback. Recordings should be made 'flat' and any necessary tone correction or filtering coped with either in the mixer or at the playback stage.

The recording

1 The tape is on the machine with the full spool on the left and the free end of the tape wound two or three times around the take up reel on the right.

2 The 'coated' side of the tape is facing the magnetic heads.

3 The speed adjustment is set.

4 Any track-selection is set.

5 The tape counter is set at zero. (A note should be made of the material to be recorded with the number on the counter each time the tape is stopped. This provides quick access to any 'take' of a particular recording and will considerably speed up the recording and editing processes.) Be warned that tape counters on different machines will probably not be compatible.

6 The tape machine is in the 'Record' mode. Some machines have to be switched to Record as a safety measure to prevent accidental erasure.

7 The Record Gain is set for optimum level on the meter.

8 Press Record/Play and you are away.

A few hints which might make life easier:

Make it a habit to let the tape continue for several seconds with the Record Gain turned down at the end of each recording. This will make editing easier. It is also particularly important when making a recording on tape which has already been used, as it will erase any existing material and provide you with a quiet pause.

At the beginning of each recording start the machine and leave a few seconds before cueing in and fading up the signal to be recorded. This allows the tape to attain an even speed and keeps any clicks or noises from the starting action well clear of programme material. This also helps editing. Always preface each recorded item with a verbal identification (e.g., Cue 6 – Take 3) and keep a corresponding list.

Label and keep careful records of all recorded material.

Keep a close check during recording that the levels are neither too low nor too high and make gentle adjustments as necessary.

All fading in and out at beginnings and ends of cues must be done slowly and smoothly. The background noise of a recording, whether the actual room acoustic or noise from the tape itself, becomes much more apparent if it comes in or breaks off abruptly.

When recording with a microphone in remote locations, it is a good idea to record a stretch of room acoustic on its own without altering the record level set up for the session. This can be useful for splicing-in pauses which might become necessary at a later date.

Handle the tapes as little as possible. Grease from fingers attracts dirt.

Keep tapes well clear of magnetic equipment (transformers, magnets, ribbon and dynamic microphones, etc.).

Microphone recording technique

This is the most difficult of all recording operations since so many external influences can affect the result. First make sure that the microphone is so placed that it will not pick up any mechanical sounds from the tape recorder itself. Ideally, the microphone should be in an acoustically treated room separated and soundproofed from all the recording equipment, i.e. a recording studio. If this is not possible then a quiet room with the minimum of external noises should be found. The room should have as little reverberation as possible. If there are curtains they should be drawn to help shut out external noise and deaden reflected sounds within the room itself. Carpets also have a good deadening effect. If such a room is not available it should be possible to rig up a tent or some screens covered in heavy material to surround the microphone on three sides.

In a situation which is acoustically too live it is obviously preferable to use a directional microphone rather than an omnidirectional which will pick up reflected sounds from all angles.

The microphone should be placed at a suitable distance from the sound source. A distance of one foot (300 mm) is ideal for most speech conditions, although some quiet speakers might need to be as close as five or six inches (125–150 mm). With such close techniques there is a danger of breath noise or 'popping' which is an explosive effect on the diaphragm. This can be remedied either by placing the microphone slightly off axis to the speaker or by using a wind-shield (or pop-gag). This is either a sock or a small cage containing foam rubber or some similar substance which absorbs the shock waves of air. As the name implies they are also used for outside recording to minimize wind effects. The only drawback with a wind-shield is that it slightly impedes the higher frequencies.

If the speaker is too far from the microphone the 'body' of the voice is lost by an apparent diminishing in bass response, and the ratio of the direct sound to its reflections becomes poor. If you wish to achieve a distant effect, use a reasonably close-microphone technique but keep to the dead side of the microphone.

For stereophonic recording most engineers use a pair of crossed directional microphones. For larger recording sessions (particularly in orchestral broadcasting) additional 'fill-in' microphones may be placed to highlight certain sections. These are then added to one or other of the stereo channels via a mixer. Two separate microphones may, of course, be used, but the farther apart they are the wider the acoustic separation becomes. The result is a 'hole' in the middle of the stereo image. In fact, the recording becomes two-track and is no longer true stereo.

In recording studios stereo is created artificially within the mixing desk. Each instrument is separately miked, the recording (mixing) engineer being responsible for balancing the sound. Each microphone is then routed via a 'pan' control to stereo left, stereo right or anywhere in between. In this way the engineer has complete control over his stereo picture. A similar technique was used in the theatre for the London production of *Jesus Christ Superstar* which we shall be discussing later.

Faults and maintenance

Sometimes results do not quite measure up to expectations. If the quality of the reproduction does not seem to be as good as it could be, the cause is not always a defective recorder or recording tape: it can be the fault of the operator. Silly things can happen, like under or over-recording, placing the tape on the machine with the oxide away from the recording heads, selecting the wrong tape speed or overlooking a faulty connection.

Figure 79 Temporary recording tent.

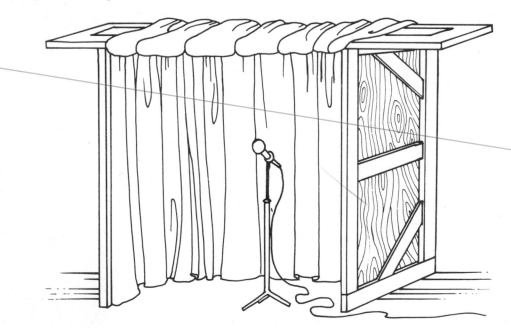

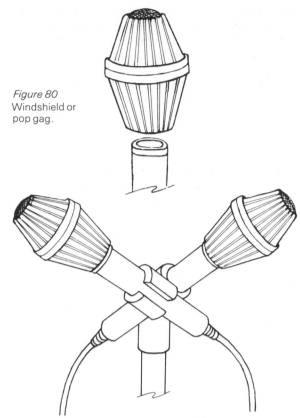

Figure 80
Windshield or
pop gag.

Figure 81 Crossed stereo pair of microphones.

Dust and dirt can also cause trouble with both the tape and the machine. To avoid the possibility of drop-outs caused by dirt tapes should always be stored in their boxes.

No reproduction. Tape incorrectly threaded. Faulty connection to monitor amplifier/loudspeaker. Internal loudspeaker switched off. Wrong track selected. Machine not in correct playback mode.

Inadequate erasing. One of the main causes is a faulty alignment of the magnetic heads, i.e. the erasing track does not fully cover the recording track. (This may also be the reason for unsatisfactory reproduction.) It could also be caused by faulty tape-guides, insufficient contact between the tape and the erasing head, a weak and defective oscillator, or an open or short-circuited erase head.

Two tracks blend into each other (cross talk). This results from incorrect positioning of the heads or faulty tape-guides which cause the tape to move up and down when passing the heads.

Damaged tapes may be the result of too high a tape tension, faulty brakes, badly aligned or dirty tape guides.

Wow and flutter. These objectionable variations in sound pitch are an audible sign of malfunction in the tape transport mechanism. They are most commonly caused by: build up of dirt on the capstan, inadequate pressure of the pinch roller, too high clutch friction of the supply reel shaft or a faulty clutch on the other spooling.

Chirping and squealing sounds. These are caused by tape vibrations resulting from defective pressure pads or from an accumulation of dust or dirt. The felt pads should be cleaned or replaced. Finally, it is also advisable to clean the different parts of the tape guides.

Excessive head wear. This can occur if the tape tension is excessively high. Poor quality tapes have an abrasive surface which is also conducive to head wear. Worn heads will affect the frequency response. Defective tape lifters also lead to head wear when fast spooling.

Tape spillage or poor take-up. Bad spooling of the tape on the take-up reel may be caused by incorrect adjustment of either the clutches or the brakes. Tape spillage usually results from incorrect synchronization between take-up and supply reel brakes. Under these conditions, the supply reel continues to feed tape after the take-up reel has stopped. As a temporary measure to avoid tape spillage, the tape may be kept taut by using the hand as a brake on the supply reel.

Erratic response. This is also caused by incorrect tape tension. Inadequate tension results in the loss of intimate contact between the tape and the heads.

Poor high-frequency response. A severe loss of high frequencies is most often caused by a worn head, in which the metal of the pole-piece has worn away, enlarging the head gap. Worn heads must be replaced. If this loss becomes apparent only with old recordings, or with those made on different recorders, it may be because the vertical alignment of the head gap (azimuth) is faulty.

Maintenance. The capstan, pinch wheel, tape guides and all three heads must be examined at regular intervals for the accumulation of oxide dust. Any coating should be wiped off with a soft

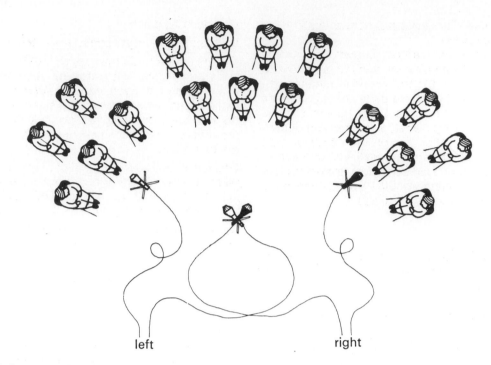

Figure 82 Crossed pair with fill ins.

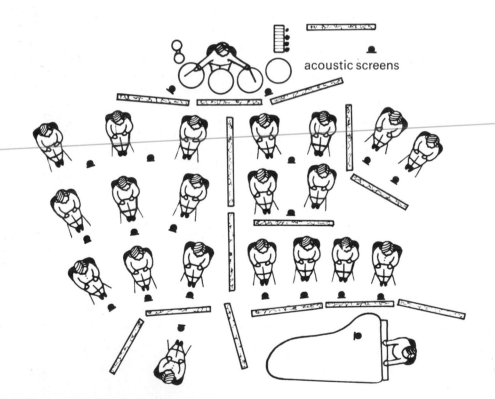

acoustic screens

Figure 83 Artificial stereo with multimicrophone technique.
Each microphone is 'panned' as required at the mixing desk.

piece of cloth slightly moistened with methylated spirits or alcohol.

CAUTION Never use carbon tetrachloride, which even in small quantities will ruin the tape base or cause slippage in the friction drive mechanism. Also remember that these parts should never be scraped with any metallic or hard objects. If you have inadvertently placed a magnetized screwdriver or some other tool on the heads or tape guides they must be demagnetized. Demagnetizers can be purchased from most dealers in electronic equipment and should be used every once in a while to 'demag' the heads.

Editing

When preparing a tape for a show the editing is as important as the recording. It is a very simple process and once the basic rules are known the skill can be developed only with a great deal of practice. Editing performs various functions:

1 Removing unwanted 'takes'.
2 Removing clicks or other noises.
3 Placing all the cues in their correct order.
4 Cleaning up the beginning and end of each cue.
5 Splicing coloured marker tapes between each cue.
6 Building up sound montage effects by splicing together various preselected sounds.
7 Timing: shortening cues by cutting out sections or lengthening them by insertions or additions.
8 Inserting a metallic strip or section of translucent tape before the start of each cue when the tape is to be used with a machine incorporating an automatic stopping device.

Editing kit

There are many different types of editing equipment and proprietary splicing gadgets designed to catch the eye in hi-fi shops, but professionals pretty well unanimously go for the same simple kit:

One splicing block.

One packet of single-edged razor blades.

One pair of unmagnetized scissors. Special brass editing scissors are strongly recommended. Alternatively, a head demagnetizer should be used to ensure that the scissors and razor blade do not become 'magged up'. Cutting with a magnetized instrument will affect the tape and cause a click.

One reel of splicing tape 7/32 in. (approx. 5 mm) wide. It is very important to use this width which is a little less than the $\frac{1}{4}$ in. (6 mm) tape. Do not be talked into buying the $\frac{1}{2}$ in. (13 mm) variety.

Several reels of coloured leader tape. Choose a make which has a matt side suitable for writing on with a ball-point pen.

One white chinagraph pencil.

One stopwatch.

Several empty spools.

In addition to these items you also require a cue sheet giving full details of the order and timings require for the final tape or tapes, and a recording sheet listing everything from the recording sessions.

The first vital step is to make absolutely sure that you know which is the playback head. Unless you have a non-standard machine it will be the one on the right nearest the capstan.

Once you are ready to edit find the beginning of the first cue by playing the machine and pressing the stop button as soon as you hear it. Then locate the exact point by moving the tape smoothly backwards and forwards over the heads, turning the reels by hand. (Practise this a lot, being careful not to stretch the tape.)

When you are sure that the sound is actually at the gap on the replay head, make a small mark with the chinagraph pencil. Do this carefully, to avoid damaging the head. You can then rewind the tape a few inches and run it at normal speed, checking that the mark coincides with the sound. Another method is to put the machine into the Play mode with the pause control held, and to

Figure 84 Splicing block. Emitape block in the UK (EMI Ltd). Editall tape splicer in the USA (Tech. Labs. Inc.).

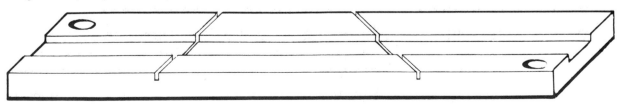

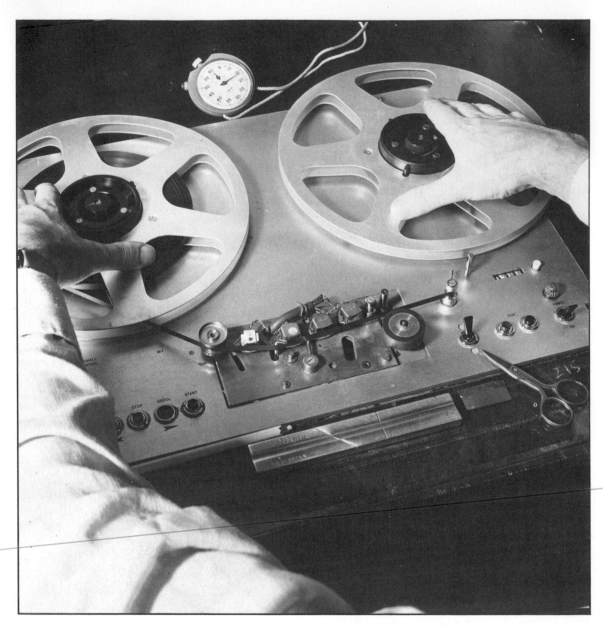

Photograph 15 Locating the cue by hand.

move the tape until the mark centres on the head. When the pause control is released, the sound should start immediately.

Once satisfied that the mark is correct, cut the tape about half an inch (13 mm) away from the mark. CAUTION Always cut on the opposite side of the head to the wanted sound; i.e. if it is the start of a cue, cut on the right of the head, and if it is the end of a cue cut on the left.

Take the wanted end of the tape and place it in the splicing block with the mark at the centre of the 45 degree cutting guide. The 90 degree guide is only used for really critical editing as the join is not so strong and the result may be a click or thump as the tape goes past the heads.

Now cut off a sufficient length of leader tape and place one end overlapping the cutting guide by about an inch (25 mm).

Holding the razor blade firmly at an angle of slightly less than 45 degrees, place the point in the cutting guide and slice the tape gently but firmly across.

Photograph 16 Marking the tape.

Photograph 17 Snipping the tape to the waste side of the mark.

Photograph 18 Cutting in the block the two ends of tape to be joined.

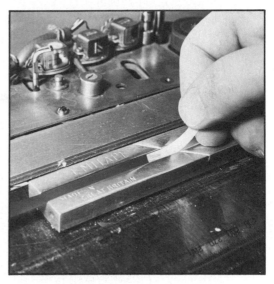

Photograph 19 Positioning the splicing tape.

There should now be two ends neatly butted together with a small end of waste on top which can be removed with a fingernail or the point of the razor blade.

The final step is to cut off about an inch (25 mm) of the self-adhesive splicing tape and lay it very carefully along the groove over the two pieces of tape, making sure that it does not over-lap at the edges. Any overlap can cause the tape to snag and break; it can also contaminate the heads with adhesive material. If you are satisfied with the lay of the splicing tape, press it into position and remove all air-bubbles by rubbing it firmly either with a finger or thumb nail or the rounded handle of the scissors. Having checked that the two pieces of tape still butt and do not overlap, the job is done.

A few hints

1 Always edit the start of cues close to the leader to facilitate quick and accurate cueing-in during a performance.

2 Always leave a little spare tape at the end of each cue to allow for wastage in the event of having to re-edit.

3 When re-editing always leave the leader into the cue intact and pull apart the end of the cue where a split end or a tear will not matter.

4 Use light-coloured marker tape between cues for easy identification under poor lighting conditions.

5 Coloured marker tapes should have the matt side away from the heads so that a cue-number or other written identification can be seen during playback.

6 It is a good idea to insert a completely different coloured marker every so often for quick identification when fast spooling during rehearsals. I would suggest not only between every act and every scene, but also at the end of any particular sequence of cues.

7 Make a 'protection copy' of your final tape in case of disasters.

Automatic stops

Machines incorporating an automatic stopping mechanism are recommended for theatre installations especially where two or more machines might be in operation at the same time. The operator can then concentrate on cueing in his tapes and obtaining the correct sound balance.

The two main ways of effecting an automatic stop are a) with a metallic strip fixed to the tape which hits two electrical contacts placed near the heads, thus completing a switching circuit, and b) by means of a photo-electric cell on one side of the tape and a small light on the other which, as soon as the tape runs out or there is a translucent section, allows the light to shine on the cell and completes a switch circuit.

The first method simply requires an inch (25 mm) of self-adhesive metal foil (Scotch 51) stuck to the inside of the leader tape in a suitable place to stop the machine as close as possible to the next start position.

For the photo-electric cell one can either splice in a short strip of clear leader tape, or remove an inch of coating from the coloured tape itself. This can be done by scraping carefully with a razor blade or, better still, by wiping it off with a cloth moistened with acetone.

Cartridge machines

These machines were developed particularly for use on radio stations for the convenient handling of jingles and commercials, and because they are so easy to handle, they are sometimes used in the theatre, although a separate cartridge is needed for each effect.

The $\frac{1}{4}$ in. (6 mm) tape is contained on a single spool within an enclosed plastic cartridge with the tape exposed at the front like a standard cassette. The spool is actually a turntable with a centre hub around which the tape is wound with the loose end at the centre brought off, threaded round guides and joined to the other end. This creates a contained endless loop. The cartridge slots into a letter box opening in the machine which operates like a normal tape recorder except that the playing time is limited by the length of the tape loop.

The machines are so designed that at the start of each recording a pulse is automatically placed on the tape which, under playback conditions, triggers a relay to stop the machine. Thus if the sound effect runs for thirty seconds but the duration of the tape loop is one minute the

Photograph 20 Stack of three-tape cartridge playback machines. *Photo courtesy Sonifax*

machine will continue for the thirty seconds of blank tape. It will then stop with the start of the effect ready to go again.

Cartridges are very compact, mechanically silent and extremely accurate in operation. But there are drawbacks. For example, it is not possible to perform the speedy edits that are often required during rehearsals; one always has to go back to the original conventional tape master for editing purposes and then transfer back to the cartridge. And most machines have limited rapid spooling facilities; often it is only possible to fast run forward at double speed. This can mean a wait of half the playing time of the entire cartridge in order to set back (or rather forward) to the beginning. Under strained rehearsal conditions this can be a serious drawback. This lack of spooling ability is also inconvenient with cues of indeterminate length where with a conventional tape machine one can fade out at any point and quickly spool on to the next leader.

For continuous background sounds of indeterminate length (wind, rain, birds, etc.) the endless loop cartridge is, of course, ideal.

Despite these disadvantages I feel that as cartridge machines develop they will increasingly be used in theatre control rooms, perhaps eventually replacing reel to reel machines altogether.

10
The control position

It is as important for the sound technician to hear what the audience is hearing as for the lighting switchboard operator to see what the audience is seeing. It can even be argued that with a complicated sound balance it is much more important. For whereas lighting levels when plotted will remain the same for every performance, sound levels will vary. The number of people in the auditorium, even the clothes they are wearing (whether lightweight or heavy and absorbent) will have an influence. The amount of humidity in the air also has an effect. When one is working with microphones the changes can be quite dramatic. Every performance will need a slightly different balance. A particular artiste may be 'giving' more or less or he may be at a different distance from the microphone; or the orchestra may be playing louder or softer, and so on.

It is therefore of the utmost importance that a permanent sound control position is centrally placed within the auditorium. Ideally, it should be a room at the centre rear of the stalls or circle. (The central position is particularly vital for balanced stereo.) It should be soundproofed to the auditorium but have a very large window, which opens easily and quietly, with an unrestricted view of the stage and orchestra pit.

The mixing desk should either be very narrow back to front or be placed sideways on to the window. This will allow the operator to listen close to the auditorium and not be confused by the acoustics of the room in which he is sitting.

For balancing a multi-microphone setup it is essential for the operator to be within the acoustic environment of the auditorium where the sound from the stage combined with the sound from all the loudspeakers plus the natural reflections from walls, ceilings and other surfaces can be assimilated. Particularly for coping with stereo the mixing desk must be centrally placed and not more than half to two-thirds of the way back from the stage.

An alternative plug-in point in the auditorium with all the necessary microphone lines and tie-lines to power amplifiers, etc., will facilitate the movement of a portable mixer from the control room as required. It also means that for productions not requiring such a critical balance the mixer, tape decks, etc. may be placed in the auditorium for rehearsals and then moved back to the control room for the public performances.

I personally abhor the idea of a permanent sound control sited slap bang in the middle of an auditorium unless the theatre is permanently given over to staging big music shows. In a theatre with a more varied diet the auditorium control will be unused for a great deal of the time and it will constitute both an eyesore and a

Figure 86 Typical control room positions.

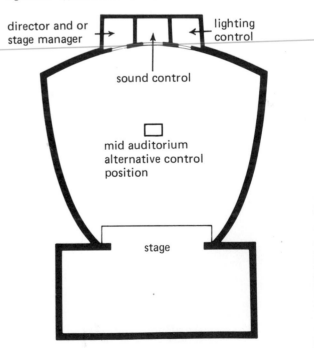

director and or stage manager

lighting control

sound control

mid auditorium alternative control position

stage

significant loss of revenue from a prime seating position.

Monitor loudspeakers should be provided for recording, editing, lining up and checking cues, etc. Under live performance conditions, however, these monitors can be no substitute for listening to the real thing. We are dealing not only with a balance between loudness and softness, live action and electronic sound, but a balance between many widely spaced loudspeakers. Unlike a recording studio or radio station we are working in three dimensions. And there is the added complication of always bearing in mind the differences in perspective from various seating positions within the auditorium, i.e. the front row of the stalls and the back row of the balcony.

The control room should have space for the mixing desk, one or two turntables, two or more tape machines and a certain amount of storage. There should also be adequate silent ventilation.

Being the nerve centre of the sound system, all permanent wiring will terminate here. It is recommended that high level and low level lines be brought to separate plug panels. This is a flexible arrangement which also allows broadcasting or recording organizations to share the facilities.

There should be a single phase main supply complete with a mains switch and indicator lamp. A generous supply of standard 13 amp (15 amp in US) 3-pin sockets should provide for all permanent installations as well as any extra equipment which may be required. It is essential to have a good earth (ground).

Part 2

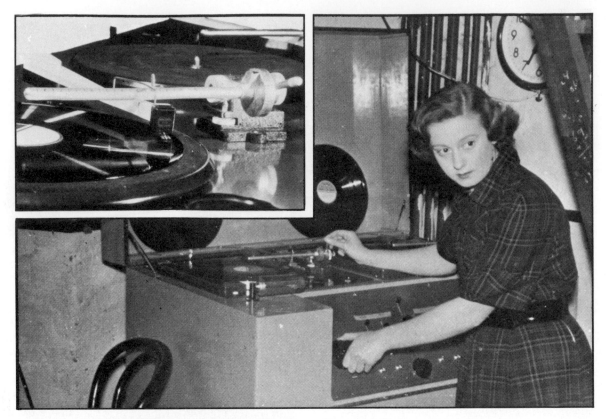

Photograph 21 A panatrope in use.

Photograph 22 Close-up of groove locator and pick-up arm lowering device for a panatrope *(inset)*.

Photograph 23 Taped sound effects at Theatre Royal, Drury Lane in 1957. *Photo courtesy Stagesound (London) Ltd*

11
Sound effects

Their use and creation

In the 1950s when I first became involved with theatre sound, as a stage manager at that time, the use of 78 r.p.m. sound effects discs was still prevalent. The sounds were selected from the fairly basic libraries that were available and then transferred to disc. Usually only two or three items were recorded on each single-side to allow for maximum flexibility during mixing. Music was still obtainable on 78 r.p.m. commercial discs since the new long playing record (at that incredibly slow speed of $33\frac{1}{3}$ r.p.m.) was only just being introduced.

The turntable units were rugged affairs, incorporating large valve amplifiers and loudspeaker switching. Each pick-up arm had a lowering device and some form of patent groove-locator. In the UK, these large gramophones were called 'panatropes' and instead of 'sound cues' stage managers used to write 'Pan cues' in their prompt scripts (photographs 21 and 22).

As an assistant stage manager I have worked with six turntables and upwards of thirty discs, all boldly numbered for quick reference. This method of working was very convenient during rehearsals because it allowed the director to call for any combination, sequence and balance of effects. Everything then depended on the skill of the operator. It is interesting to note that the BBC and other broadcasting authorities, with their fast turnover of programmes, still use sound effects discs for the same reasons.

In 1957, during the last scene of *Brouhaha* at the Aldwych Theatre in London, Peter Sellers, playing the Sultan of an impoverished Arab country, stood alone on stage shouting directions at a number of foreign ships which were supposed to be arriving through the auditorium bringing his people aid. Each instruction was followed by a sound effect of, say, a ship's siren, two ships colliding, men shouting, a ship going aground, a ship sinking, etc. During one short page of script there were twenty or more sound cues using four turntables and a large collection of discs. An added complication was that Mr Sellers, who was not actually known for keeping to the script, on more than one occasion deliberately gave the wrong line – paused – listened – then gleefully pronounced 'Aha, that caught you out!', knowing that off stage confusion reigned with discs flying in all directions. We eventually learned to cope with this situation by filling in with strange strangulated noises into a microphone while hurriedly rearranging the turntables.

Soon after this era of the panatrope it became the practice to rehearse and open a show using discs. Once the show was set and looked likely to run, it was all transferred to tape, which was easier, more accurate to operate and, even more important, more durable. Lacquer discs had to be renewed about every four weeks in order to maintain a reasonably scratch-free quality.

This transitional stage lasted some eight to ten years. At the beginning of the 1960s tape was firmly established in London's West End theatres and disc was only used for playing the National Anthem and scene-change music in those theatres already possessing a panatrope.

The use of sound

Sound effects may be used for a variety of reasons:

1 To establish (a) locale (b) time of year (c) day or night (d) weather conditions
2 To evoke atmosphere
3 To link scenes
4 As an emotional stimulus
5 To reproduce physical happenings: spot cues like cars arriving, babies crying, clocks striking, elephants falling out of trees, etc.

Background effects. Let us take background and atmospheric sounds first. Just pause for a moment and listen . . . I guarantee you are now aware of a whole spectrum of background noises of which you were not fully conscious a moment ago. These are the reassuring and comfortable sounds of life, of people, of things going on.

I am not, however, advocating a continual racket of birds, bells, traffic, radios, etc., running throughout the play. Far from it. Much thought must go into a good background sound track which should, as in real life, register for the most part only on the subconscious level.

In the theatre we have the tremendous advantage of being able to add to and subtract from the background at will; at one moment strengthening a dramatic pause, at another adding to a confusion, thereby giving depth, life and atmosphere to the whole.

A sudden silence or absence of sound can be just as disturbing as a sudden loud noise. This artifice was used to great effect by Peter Hall in his original London production of *Cat on a Hot Tin Roof*. The hot still atmosphere of the deep South was created by using a combination of continuously cheeping crickets and various croaking frog noises with occasionally, during a pause, the harsh squawk of a bird.

The method was, for example, to start a scene with a cricket chirping slowly and repetitively out on the verandah, then when the action was under way very subtly to add some deeper frog noises; a couple of pages later these would be supplemented by the high-pitched and continuous sound of cicadas. Having built up the background over quite a long period in order to achieve total acceptance by the audience, dramatic moments could be heightened by merely subtracting one or more of the elements. At one moment I had two types of cricket and three different frog sounds all going at once until, in the middle of the last line of a tense exchange, they all abruptly disappeared. The ensuing pause was electric.

Although there must have been well over seventy sound cues in that production, including plantation workers singing, a distant church bell, an offstage party, children shouting and several radio sequences, many friends who saw the show were unable to remember sound effects at all. That kind of total integration of effects in a production is the essence of a good sound track.

One of the real cliché effects for creating tension is the heartbeat, and under the right

circumstances it really does work. We have noticed even in our own sound effects department that when working with music or effects which have a slow rhythmic beat everyone tends to work more slowly than if the beat is fast. The pulse rate changes. This phenomenon can be applied to an audience.

In a production of *Macbeth* I once used a very low frequency drumbeat during the scenes leading up to the battle. It started at a little below the speed of a normal heartbeat and was played at a very low level, with the gain being increased imperceptibly over a long period during which the speed of the beat was also gradually increased, the idea being that it would carry the audience's pulse rates with it. During some final frenzied activity on stage a few moments before the start of the battle the drumbeat which was by now quite loud and fast was suddenly cut. There was a pause . . . the audience were on the edges of their seats . . . then crash! trumpets, shouting, swords clashing and all hell let loose.

This sequence used the increasing heartbeat effect, the heightened pause and the shock of a sudden loud sound.

It often happens that a continuous background sound creates a distraction. This is especially true in a large theatre where intelligibility is a problem. In all too many places of entertainment one has difficulty in hearing the proceedings because of the hum of an air-conditioning plant or the rumble of traffic. Because this low frequency sound is constant it tends to be discounted, but the effect is of an aural barrier between the actors and the audience.

To run a wind or rain effect, for example, throughout an entire twenty-minute scene at a fixed volume level is seldom a good idea. Maybe it is supposed to be raining but it is not necessary to hear it all the time. When it rains in real life we hear it usually when it starts (change of background) and then only become aware of it spasmodically, particularly during pauses in concentration.

In a theatrical situation the rain would either be brought in suddenly to denote a downpour or would be faded in under dialogue some thirty seconds before it was actually required in context. The audience should register the fact that it is raining and then turn their concentration back to the action (if they do not, then we are all in trouble). The level can now be adjusted so that the effect is gently lost under the scene. In other words, we are assisting the concentration process and moving the focus back to the actors. The rain should then occasionally be brought back to be registered during pauses. The reasons for bringing it back are as follows:

1 Because the text calls for it.
2 Because the director wishes to remind the audience of the world outside.
3 Because the scene requires punctuation.

An obvious place to bring back an effect is when someone enters or leaves the stage setting; not only does this action relate to the world outside but it is usually a punctuation point in the scene.

A sensitive use of background sound can add an interesting and important dimension to the setting.

Photograph 24 Professor Lowe recording traffic sounds in Whitehall, London, on a disc-cutting machine (1923). *Inset:* machine for recording the commentaries of BBC reporters in the field during World War II.

Spot effects. Specific spot effects can also do a great deal to help atmosphere. They should, however, be used sparingly and always to some purpose (the aforementioned three reasons). They should be cued-in accurately at every performance just as a film sound editor will precisely position his various voice, music and effects tracks. Good spot effects can assist the actor by giving him another element against which he can react. For example, a scene with a period setting inside a house: at a suitable moment the distant sound of a horse and carriage or a street seller shouting his wares is heard. The actor, without necessarily even pausing, gives the merest glance towards the window and the reality of the situation is immediately enhanced.

Commercial recordings. Most of the everyday sounds of weather, traffic, birds, animals, aircraft, bells, people, etc. can be obtained on commercial recordings. However, these recordings are limited both in the range of available sounds and in the duration of the tracks. They are aimed primarily at the amateur movie maker who seldom requires lengthy effects.

Tape loops. It is possible to lengthen an effect by recording it on to tape and making a continuous tape loop of it by splicing the beginning of the sound on to the end. The loop is then placed on to a tape machine, ensuring that sufficient tension is maintained by running it round some smooth heavy object (such as a microphone stand), played back and recorded on to a second tape machine. It is hazardous to use tape loops during a performance.

To avoid an unpleasant hiccoughing effect it is essential to ensure at the beginning and end of the loop that the content of the sound and the recording levels are identical.

Short loops are seldom satisfactory because their repetitive pattern makes them recognizable as such. This can, however, sometimes be used to advantage: a slow tolling bell, for example, can be made to ring rapidly by making up a loop of a single strike to the length required. If the dying away reverberation is required to complete the effect, then the last note from the original is recorded and spliced on to the end. Other rhythmic sounds of machinery, drum-beats, ghostly breathing, footsteps, etc., can be created in this manner.

It is also worth experimenting with playing loops backwards. For example, a cymbal crash beginning with the reverberation, building up to the initial percussion then cutting back to the reverberation can form the basis of an interesting effect.

With a very lengthy background effect even a long loop can become repetitive. The answer here is to make up two identical loops and play them back out of sync. on two tape machines. After recording the first loop for a while 'cross-fade' to the second to break up the rhythm.

N.B. When cross-fading always establish the sound you are bringing in before losing the original. Do it by listening and checking the meter and not by watching the positions of the faders. The object is to avoid a dip or hole in the programme.

Location recording. Given a portable tape recorder of sufficient quality many natural sounds can be captured. But, be warned, this is not as easy as it would appear. Let us take a few examples:

1 *Birds in the wild*. First find your bird, then get near enough to make a recording, then persuade it to sing.

2 *Animals in the wild*. The same applies but can be more dangerous!

3 *Surf breaking*. On an open beach if there are no people or birds in the background then there will probably be a wind to upset the microphone. (A windshield is a must for most outside recording.) Surf recorded too near is unnatural because only one wave appears to be breaking, but when recorded at too great a distance it sounds like hiss and extraneous noises are difficult to avoid.

4 *Wind*. The main problem with wind is that one has to be sheltered from it in order to be able to record it. Light winds are almost impossible as they hardly register on the meter, therefore the signal-to-noise ratio is bad. When a light wind is played back and amplified in a theatre it is not usually recognizable as such. A strong wind often creates unwanted side effects like rattling shutters, singing telegraph wires, etc.

5 *Traffic*. It is difficult to find good town traffic free from the other sounds associated with urban life.

6 *Aeroplanes*. Get near enough, then stop all the birds and traffic in the vicinity.

7 *Vehicles*. It is relatively easy to record a car or motorcycle, assuming you find a deserted place

Photograph 25 Recording footsteps in the dead of night on tape. Recording van *c.* 1960. *Photo courtesy Stagesound (London) Ltd*

in the dead of night. The difficulty comes in the unending combinations of starting – running – stopping – stalling – reversing, fast – medium – slow, well – badly, interior – exterior, road surface – gravel surface, large engine – small engine, sports – saloon, ancient – modern, doors – horns.

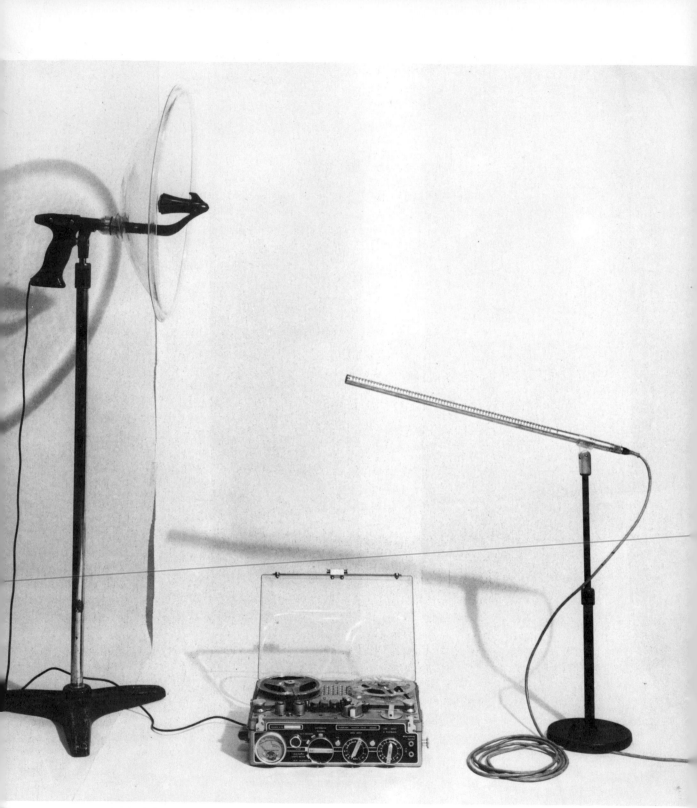

Photograph 26 Modern battery/mains professional Nagra
tape recorder with Sennheiser gun microphone and Dan
Gibson parabolic reflector microphone.

8 *Church bells.* The problems of recording church bells and clocks are very basic: outside the church there are too many extraneous noises, and inside the church the sounds of the ringing mechanism are discernible.

Despite what I have just said location recording of effects can be both fun and rewarding. The requirements are a good battery operated tape recorder with a pair of headphones, a directional microphone with an efficient windshield and patience. It is a matter of personal preference but some people use an ordinary cardioid, some a hypercardioid or rifle and others insist that the best results are obtained by means of a parabolic reflector (photograph 26). This is merely a rigid dish, or parabola, which collects sounds (rather like cupping your hands behind yours ears). The microphone is fixed to a clamp in the centre of the dish and points into the dish. One of the drawbacks of the reflector is that unless one has an enormously large dish made of the right type of material only the high frequencies are collected. Hence the extensive use of parabolas for bird recording.

Simulated effects. Certain sounds can be successfully simulated in front of a microphone with the added advantage that extraneous noises can be eliminated completely. Here are a few suggestions:

Rain. Method one: take 15–20 dried peas and let them roll back and forth over a fine-meshed wire sieve directly above the microphone.
Method two: make a chute about 12 inches (300 mm) long of grease-proof paper, place the microphone underneath and pour down a constant trickle of castor (grain) sugar.

Wind. Pull a length of silk across two or three wooden boards. The strength of the wind can be increased or decreased by varying the amount of drag. For wind in the trees agitate a handful of old recording tape in front of the microphone.

Thunder. This can be achieved by breathing gently on the microphone; preferably not an expensive ribbon microphone.

Artillery fire. Method one: a short percussive breath on the microphone.
Method two: burst a paper bag while recording at 15 i.p.s. (38 cm/s) and play it back at 3¾ i.p.s. (9·5 cm/s).

Waves. Take two brushes and move them in opposite directions across a long sheet of metal.

Water lapping. Agitate the surface of some water in a plastic bucket and record the sound of the water lapping against the sides.

Rowing boat. Dip a piece of wood rhythmically into the water and make a rusty hinge or door squeak in unison.

Fire. Crush cellophane paper in front of the microphone. A matchbox being crushed will add another dimension. A pan of sizzling fat is also effective.

Ship's siren. Blow across the neck of a bottle half filled with water; the less water in the bottle the deeper the sound.

Comic steam train. Take two wooden blocks covered with sandpaper (glasspaper) and rub them together.

Hoofbeats. Take two halves of a coconut shell and either strike them together or drum them upon a plaster wall. If you cover them with cloth you can imitate hoofbeats on a soft surface.

Footfalls. In the forest: rhythmically crush a handful of old recording tape in front of the microphone.
In the snow: do the same with a small bag of flour.

Bird's wings. Small bird: let a small piece of card flutter against an electric fan.
Large bird: rhythmically swish two pieces of bamboo cane in front of the microphone.

Jet plane. Run a hairdryer or vacuum cleaner near the microphone and make it howl by restricting the exhaust.

Gun shot. Strike a table or a leather chair seat with a rule or cane.

A telephone voice. Method one: speak into a small plastic or earthenware cup.
Method two: plug some headphones into the microphone input and speak into them. If the impedances are reasonably correct the headphone diaphragm corresponds in performance to the cheap microphone in a telephone.

Ordering effects from a sound library

In order to save yourself time, money and general heartache a comprehensive and detailed list should be compiled before you approach a library. The director will say what effects he requires but it is up to the sound man to interpret these in practical terms. First you must plan how many cues on how many tapes you will require.

If the sound track is at all complicated then at least two playback units will be required. Place all the important spot cues on one tape (assuming that there is no danger of overlapping) and all the general backgrounds on another. This is not only more logical in operation but in the event of a deck failure all the vital cues are still available.

Any cues of indeterminate length where there is danger of running into the next effect should be kept on the second or third tape. Always allow extra running time if in doubt as it is a simple matter to prune the tape in rehearsals.

First make a list of cues in the order required on the reels required with their timings. The library technician, who knows nothing about your particular production, will also need a detailed description of each effect. It is no good specifying 'church clock strikes four': is it small, large, town, country, with Westminster chimes, with simpler chimes, without chimes, near, distant, fast, slow, high, low?

You may also wish to specify a different coloured leader tape between certain cues for ease of location in rehearsals. And you must certainly specify the tape speed and the track configuration.

It was difficult to know what to do with some requests we have received for sound effects. For instance, one stage manager wrote ordering 'five minutes of almost recorded silence – like you get in the country'. A dear lady replying to our request for more specific details such as the duration of her cues and the required tape speed ended her letter with '. . . and as for the speed of tape, I think fairly slow'. One customer took our plea for 'as much information as possible' to heart. We have on file his letter requesting five cues of pigs grunting and/or squealing: it goes on for four closely typed pages. We not only had a good idea what the entire play was about, but knew how many pigs were in the sty, what their age range was, their sex, how they felt about the possibility of food, how they felt about the possibility – then probability – of death by the knife, how some panicked when the assassin entered and some remained calm, and so on and so forth. I am also very fond of the letter from a vicar staging an amateur production in the church hall; he wanted 'the sound effect of a cock crowing (*thrice*)'.

Mono, twin-track or stereo

Because one is usually putting a single sound on to a single loudspeaker, theatre recordings are more often than not monaural. But there are exceptions. Theoretically with loudspeakers placed widely apart at both sides of a proscenium arch stereo music recordings should not work. The loudspeakers are supposed to be within an angle of not more than 30 degrees and equidistant from the listener. However, I have found that in most cases music is definitely enhanced by being recorded in stereo.

Stereo can also be useful for providing breadth and perspective to crowd, battle, traffic, sea effects, etc. Moving sounds like cars, aeroplanes and trains can, of course, be recorded in stereo, but will be fixed in their timing. It is much more flexible to have the same mono sound on twin tracks fed separately to two loudspeakers. Then, by adjusting the relative gains, the effect can be moved from one loudspeaker to the other at will.

Twin tracks may also be used for two different continuous effects of indeterminate length; for example, rain on one track and wind on the other. This would leave a second tape machine free for spot effects.

Mock stereo effects can be made up on twin-tracks for synchronous playback. For example I once created a good 'theatrical' sea effect by recording waves crashing on to the beach on the upper track and deep sucking undertow noises on the lower track. In the theatre the crashing of waves from loudspeakers on stage was followed by a quieter undertow sound within the auditorium. This gave the effect of water advancing and retreating. Incidentally, the wave was made up from a constant heavy waterfall with sharp increases of level and treble for each crash; and the undertow noise was several loops of various water effects at half and quarter speed. Real sea recordings did not sound half as convincing.

A similar technique was used in *Othello* at the Old Vic in London, 1963, when the director requested a rapid tolling bell which was somehow to build into an insistent mind-tormenting noise. So on one track there was an ordinary bell which began the sequence and on the other was a short loop of some of the reverberation of the same bell played backwards. This loop produced an unpleasant rising stabbing sound. It was gradually faded up during a period of intensive action on the stage until, at its height, it had taken over from the original bell. Thus the bell was 'transformed' into a surrealistic effect.

"TITLE OF PRODUCTION" - MUSIC AND EFFECTS

CUE	TIMING	TAPE A	TAPE B	TAPE C	DESCRIPTION
1.	30"	Curtain Music			Disc: LP 3012 Side 1 Band 2 from start of theme after 20 sec. INTRO.
2.	3' 00"		Crowd - (Happy)		Approx. 500 talking, shouting in town square.
3.	12"	Crowd Cheer 1			Big cheer for popular leader (Same crowd as 2)
4.	5"	Crowd Cheer 2			Bigger cheer
5.	4' 00"			Crowd (Angry)	Same crowd - verging on riot.
6.	5"	Crowd Shout 1			Angry shouts of protest.
7.	10"	Crowd Shout 2			Same with booing and jeering added.
8.	15"		Police Sirens		2 or 3 modern British police cars arrive. (No blades or sirens)
9.	8"	Gun Shots			Machine gun (2sec) then 5/6 sporadic pistol shots.
10.	5"	Explosion			Car petrol tank blows up.
11.	6"	Ambulance			Ambulance arrives with siren and squealing tyres.
12.	2' 00"	Scene Music			Disc: LP 3012 Side 2 Band 1 from start.
13.	6' 00"		Birds		2 or 3. English countryside. Hot summer afternoon.
14.	15"	Dog			Farm dog (Collie?) barks at stranger.

Figure 87 Typical working list of music and effects.

A very convincing thunder effect was achieved for another production by recording thunder crashing on one track and rumbling on the other. In the theatre the initial crash was played on large loudspeakers high up in the auditorium followed by the rumble fading away on loudspeakers on stage. The feeling of perspective and distance was remarkable.

Examples of the creation of recorded effects

At this point it is worth looking at a few more practical examples of the creation of sound effects, the problems encountered and the techniques used to solve them.

The Battle of Trafalgar

At Madame Tussaud's Waxworks Exhibition in London there is a life-sized and faithful reconstruction of part of the lower gun deck of HMS Victory at the height of the Battle of Trafalgar. In the orlop deck below is the famous tableau of the death of Lord Nelson. On the gun deck there are lighting effects, flashes, smoke and even the smell of tar and cordite. The six synchronized sound tracks include the roar of cannon, the shouts and cries of men, a falling mast, cannonballs crashing through timber, musket fire, naval commands, return fire from the enemy, bugles blowing 'cease fire', etc. (photographs 27 and 28).

When we were asked to create the sound of Trafalgar (in 1968) we were lucky enough to have the cooperation of the then captain of the Victory, the ship being in permanent dry-dock at Portsmouth. About a dozen naval ratings were pressed into becoming our guncrew for the afternoon and, complete with shouted commands from an authentic gun-drill of the period, we were able to record the massive lumbering cannon being loaded, run out and aimed.

Later the Royal Navy Gunnery School, who after a slow start because of red tape and insurance problems became more than enthusiastic,

actually fired several rounds using one of Victory's guns which stands on the quay beside the ship. The correct loading, aiming and firing drill was carried out; there was a drummer 'beating to quarters' and the Navy had even gone to the trouble of providing papier mâché cannonballs.

As this was possibly the last time that one of these guns would ever be fired we made sure that we were well covered for equipment. The plan was to use different types of microphones at varying distances from the gun to obtain a selection of perspectives.

My colleague, Tony Horder, and myself positioned ourselves very efficiently with our headsets on and our best microphones and equipment carefully placed and ready. But there was one very old EMI-L2 tape machine left over with an equally old and battered Grampian moving coil microphone. So I set the record control at almost nil and asked a willing helper to take it a little way off, point the microphone in the general direction of the cannon and switch the machine on before the bang. Needless to say this was the most effective recording we obtained. It was used in the final programme as the main explosions of nearby guns, while the other recordings provided a whole spectrum of cannon fire for the general background.

The day preceding the session on board Victory we actually went to sea in a yacht to record sounds of timber creaking, rope through tackle, canvas flapping and water running against timber. We also went on board Foudroyant which is the oldest wooden warship still afloat.

All this is the fun part of location recording. But because of the various hazards previously discussed we ended up with many reels of tape of interesting atmospheric sounds, but very few clean effects. And it was at this point that the work really began. After days of sifting through the tapes the basic sounds finally came from the following sources:

Gunfire: Location HMS Victory
Gun being run out. Location HMS Victory
Gun orders: Studio with hoarse friends (aided by a little alcohol).
Shouts, cries, screams: Studio with hoarser friends (aided by a lot of alcohol, and later drastically edited).
Other orders: Studio
Bosun's call (whistle): Studio

Photograph 27 Firing one of the 50lb cannons of HMS Victory. The recording equipment and engineers are masked by the smoke. *Photo courtesy Portsmouth and Sunderland Newspapers Ltd*

Photograph 28 A section of the 'Trafalgar' exhibit at Madame Tussauds. *Photo courtesy Madame Tussauds, London*

Ropes, tackle, etc.: Fly gallery in an empty theatre

Musket fire: Library muskets plus a crackerjack firework, which sounds remarkably similar.

Sea sounds: Library

Timber creaking: Squeaky chair at quarter speed

Ropes creaking: Squeaky door at half speed

Thumps and crashes: Wooden boxes, heavy weights, chairs and tables hurled around the studio. The result carefully edited and played at various speeds either forwards or backwards depending upon which sounded more interesting.

Mast falling: A bit of creaking from a library effect of tree-felling, into more creaking from breaking a piece of wood in the studio (half speed), into a selection of carefully edited thumps and crashes from previous session.

Enemy ship alongside: A really deep thump for the initial impact followed by a scraping sound made by a large wooden sliding door. The door was slightly warped and made a marvellous noise, especially when played back at half speed.

Enemy cannonball: A sharp crack and splinter of wood recorded in the studio, edited on to a rasping-scrape made by dragging a wooden crate filled with heavy weights along a concrete floor, edited on to general crashes and thumps. The finished effect, lasting only about three seconds, gives the impression of a heavy lump of metal bursting through the wooden side of a ship and crashing along the deck. A few shouts and screams complete the picture.

Fire crackle: Library

Running feet: Bare feet running on the wooden deck of a ship were actually recorded on board *Foudroyant*. This was meant to be the fire party rushing to deal with a small fire. Unfortunately bare feet did not sound very dramatic and a library effect (with boots) was used.

Nearest gun: When a large gun is fired the force of the explosion makes it leap backwards. Naval guns of the period were fitted with heavy chains to restrain this vicious recoil. To recreate as authentic a sound as possible we recorded some chain being whipped tight, and edited on to this a particularly hefty thud recorded on *Victory* when they were heaving one of the cannons into position. These two effects were mixed with the best cannon sound. The resulting sequence is of an almighty explosion with the clink of the restraining chains as the gun leaps backwards followed by a heavy thud as it comes crashing down on to the deck.

So although tremendous time and effort went into trying to record the real sounds, they were mostly used for reference. A good 75 per cent of the finished sound track had to be fabricated.

Henry V

Another interesting example of making up a complicated composite effect was for John Barton's production of *Henry V* for the Royal Shakespeare Company at Stratford Upon Avon in 1966. In that season the repertoire included all of Shakespeare's historical plays in sequence. These included so many fights and battle scenes that by the time we reached the first battle in *Henry V* every trick in the book had been pulled. It was therefore decided that the battle of Harfleur should be recreated in sound alone with a darkened stage and no actors or scenery. In fact the idea does spring directly from the text. At the beginning of the play the Chorus addresses the following lines to audience:

Piece out our imperfections with your thoughts:
Into a thousand parts divide one man.
And make imaginary puissance;
Think, when we talk of horses that you see them
Printing their proud hoofs i' th' receiving earth;
For 'tis your thoughts that now must deck our kings . . .

Given this lead we went to work to produce a battle in the mind. First to collect the ingredients. Guy Woolfenden, musical director of the R.S.C., had created what he called his 'sword noise'. This had backed up all previous fight sequences in the season and so it was decided to incorporate it in order to maintain style. The sword noise was a particularly unpleasant and penetrating metallic sound made by bowing with violin bows on cymbals. I had some good arrow swishes recorded with a bamboo cane and repeated in a tightly edited sequence to sound like a flight. We also had a copy of what has become accepted as standard arrow noise from Laurence Olivier's wartime film of *Henry V*. Incidentally, he once told me that this 'authentic' flight of arrows was actually made by looping an elastic band round the needle of one of the studio's big old-fashioned gramophones and twanging it. (Not to be recommended on our modern and more delicate equipment!) The sound which came out of the loudspeaker was a marvellous twangy-swishing effect of hundreds of archers firing in volleys.

Other ingredients immediately available were some very good screams and shouts recorded with the actors, stock crowd effects, sword clashing recorded with the actual prop swords, horses neighing, thundering hoofbeats and various French and English trumpet calls and flourishes specially composed and recorded by Guy Woolfenden.

It was decided to make the start of the battle as realistic as possible and then, as the director put it, to 'go nasty'. The end of the sequence would meld back to normality with the lights and the actors and the resumption of the play.

Two things were missing: a tension-getting sound preceding the battle to be building during the Chorus speech, and some unreal and nasty arrow noises. The first was manufactured by recording a continuous bowing on a tam-tam (large oriental gong) which, rather like running a wet finger round the rim of a glass, builds and builds the more you bow. Played back at a quarter speed the effect was of a deep singing roar growing relentlessly in pitch and intensity.

The 'nasty arrows' were eventually created at about 4.30 in the morning by viciously scraping piano strings with a coin. The resulting metallic screeches rising in tone were played backwards to obtain descending notes, and were then tightly chopped together to match up with the bamboo cane flights of arrows.

Our four minute battle when complete used four tape machines; one for the tam-tam effect and three for the specific sounds. These three tapes were carefully timed with prerecorded fades and blank coloured leaders inserted when pauses or speaker switching were called for. Even so, the sound operator had to memorize the many volume settings and loudspeaker changes throughout the sequence.

The pattern of events was broadly as follows: tam-tam building imperceptibly under Chorus speech; then during last line of speech (' . . . eke out our performance with your mind') thundering hoofbeats can be heard approaching from upstage centre; at the end of the speech the lights fade out on the lone figure centre stage, and the hoofbeats build to a crescendo; suddenly there is a flight of arrows loud from the rear of the auditorium and the scream of a horse in agony on stage; then immediately, filling the entire theatre, the ferocious impact of two armies meeting head on with the clash of arms, fearsome shouts, horses, bugles, arrows, and all hell let loose; the real arrows gradually turn into metallic arrows and the screeching sword noise takes over from the battle effects; the tam-tam, running throughout, has by now built up to a high-pitched whine; when everybody in the audience has their teeth well and truly set on edge the metallic horror sound in the auditorium fades down leaving a realistic battle noise on stage. Thus the focus is brought back to the action.

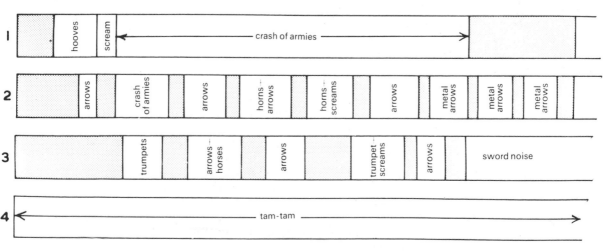

Figure 88 Diagram of the four timed effects tapes for the battle in *Henry V*.

Blitz

In 1962 at the Adelphi theatre in London there was a musical which was a sound man's dream. Written by Lionel Bart (of *Oliver* fame) it was set in wartime London during the worst period of bombing. Aptly enough, the show was called *Blitz*.

As far as I can ascertain it was the first West End production to have a specially designed and built sound effects mixing console. This was fairly basic by today's standards but seemed very daring at the time. It consisted of three sets of remote starts and gain controls for the tape machines, switching of any combination of tape machines to any combination of four main 'group' faders (each controlling a 100 watt amplifier), and fourteen loudspeaker circuits with individual on/off switches and selection to any one of the amplifiers.

The research for the show was extremely interesting as much of the sound track had to be genuine archive material. We used BBC recordings of wartime news bulletins and radio programmes, Lord Haw-Haw broadcasting propaganda from Germany and some extracts from Churchill's famous speeches. From Pathé news and other film libraries we obtained genuine wartime recordings of the Blitz itself.

But, as is usual, most of the finished tracks had to be fabricated in the interests of a good 'clean' tape. For example, the film recording of a German bomber was very good and very exciting, but unusable because of the background and surface noise. A substitute was created by taking a more modern aeroplane recording and slowing it down until it matched the sinister pitch.

The climax of the first act was a full-scale raid on London. This started with a distant air raid

Photograph 29 One of the stage managers of *Blitz* cueing by radio.

92

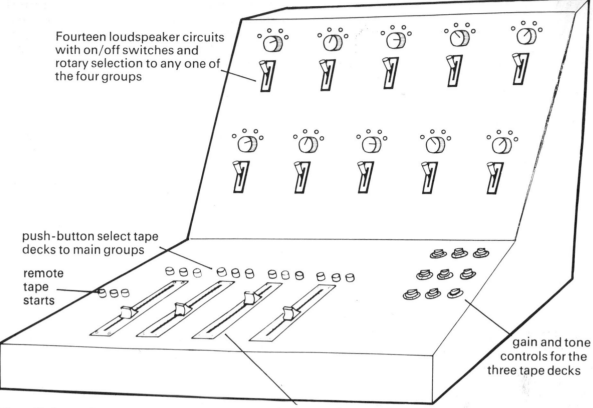

Fourteen loudspeaker circuits with on/off switches and rotary selection to any one of the four groups

push-button select tape decks to main groups

remote tape starts

gain and tone controls for the three tape decks

Figure 89 Sound effects mixer built for *Blitz (1962)*.

four main group faders

siren echoed by one closer, then another and then one in the auditorium. Next came distant anti-aircraft gunfire followed by nearer gunfire and the drone of enemy aircraft. From that point on it built up into a cacophony of bombs, guns, aircraft, buildings falling down, fire engines and ambulance bells. At its peak the four 100 watt amplifiers managed to top a thirty piece orchestra playing flat out.

The lighting effects, with flame projectors, searchlights, smoke bombs and flashes, were handled by Richard Pilbrow and we carefully worked out our sequence of flashes and bangs so that they would not only coincide but come from the right area of the stage.

I used a similar technique to that used later in *Henry V* in that one tape consisted of air raid siren into general blitz and the other two were air raid sirens into an assortment of spot effects. The general background was played through three large loudspeakers incorporating 18 in. (457 mm) bass units on stage, and the others were switched frantically around so that an aeroplane would appear audience left, a bomb would drop

up stage right, an ambulance down stage left, a bomb up centre, ack-ack down stage right, a building collapse up stage left, and so on. Throughout all this the orchestra was playing, the stage setting was constantly changing, and the actors were rushing about in general confusion putting out fires, taking cover and rescuing people with ladders from second storey windows.

There was one other interesting innovation in that show. The basic stage setting consisted of two 30 foot (about 9 m) steel towers spanned by a steel bridge nearly the width of the proscenium arch. Not only could this bridge go from stage floor level to thirty feet up, but the entire four ton motorized unit could track from the back of the stage to the front. As if this were not enough of a stage manager's nightmare, there were also four two ton steel structures representing three storey buildings which were capable of moving freely about the stage. Each one measured approximately 24 feet (7·5 m) high with a base 5 ×.10 feet (about 1·5 × 3 m). The units were battery powered with the controls set in a small camouflaged cabin in the centre. The stage managers responsible for these juggernauts could, with the aid of a few push buttons and a steering wheel, drive them forwards or backwards. And they could also revolve the entire structure about them.

Take all these free-ranging pieces and add a great deal of fixed-position flying scenery and lighting, plus a cast of nearly forty people, and it is obvious that the strictest technical control is necessary. Again as far as I have been able to discover, this was the first West End show to use a radio system for the technicians. The complexities of the production called for two technical stage managers working in unison. It worked out as follows: stage manager A was positioned on the non-working side fly gallery with a microphone and radio transmitter (photograph 29). From this vantage-point he could operate the massive bridge, making sure that the other mobile units were not in the way. He gave verbal cues and general instructions to the four drivers via individual radio receivers, and similarly cued all the flying. Stage manager B was in the traditional prompt corner position with the prompt script, giving all the lighting, follow spots and special effects cues via cuelights and a normal loudspeaker paging system. He was also equipped with a radio receiver in order to be able to synchronize with stage manager A, while he in his turn could hear stage manager B via a paging loudspeaker on the fly gallery.

All in all, it was a show which relied somewhat heavily upon sound (and I have not even mentioned the reinforcement system).

Loudspeaker placement

When placing effects loudspeakers on a stage one must ensure that they are in the correct location for the illusion required, that they are facing the audience and that they are not behind anything which is not acoustically transparent.

Illusion of sound source. In a large auditorium of a conventional proscenium theatre only the first few rows will be conscious of whether the sound is coming from upstage left or upstage right. However, because the angles become more obtuse, downstage positions are more critical. The 15 degree horizontal angle of directivity of the human ear is a good rule of thumb to follow. Since the ear is not so discriminating in a vertical plane it might be more convenient to mount the speakers above stage level.

If a sound is meant to be coming from a prop radio, television, etc., on stage, every effort should be made to place a small loudspeaker either in the prop or built in to the scenery nearby. If this is not practical then the loudspeaker used should be in a line with the audience, behind and slightly to one side of the prop.

Facing the audience. It has been previously stressed that the higher frequencies provide crispness and clarity. And as high frequencies are directional and do not travel round corners it is essential to mount loudspeakers so that they are facing the audience. Again because high frequencies are directional this will assist the audience to locate the source of sound. If a loudspeaker is on one side of a stage but pointing at only one section of the audience that section will hear a clear sound from an obvious source. The rest of the audience will hear, in varying degrees, a blurred sound from no distinct source.

Problems of masking. In almost every instance loudspeakers on a stage have to be masked from the audience, and this is where compromises may have to be made. With a little forethought and some cooperation from the set designer, however, it is usually possible to find a satisfactory solution.

A definition of 'acoustically transparent' is a perforated material which is at least 50 per cent open. Gauze (or scrim) is all right, and some open weave hessians (burlap) of the non-hairy variety are passable. All brands of loudspeaker material are, of course, ideal. Scenic canvas is not acceptable, and painted scenic canvas is even less so. Drapes or heavy curtain materials are to be avoided at all costs.

When arranging for a hole to be made in the scenery for the loudspeaker remember that it need not be the size of the entire cabinet. Ideally, all of the cone (or cones) should be free. However, as long as the high frequency section is completely open it might be acceptable to mask, say, a third of the bass unit.

I once did a play with a particular musical effect which sounded perfectly all right when played during a sound rehearsal, but always sounded dull and muffled during the dress rehearsals. The reason for this puzzling phenomenon was eventually discovered. An elderly actor wearing a heavy and voluminous robe was using the loudspeaker as a resting place between entrances. On another occasion I had similar trouble from a party of 'nuns'. But this time I was forewarned and took immediate steps. The loud-

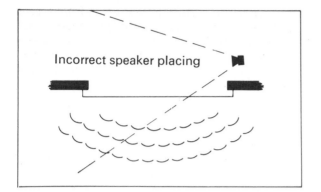

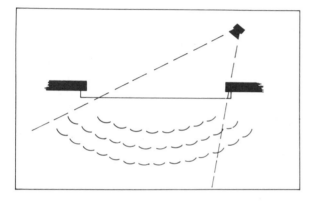

Figure 90 Effects loudspeakers should face the audience.

speaker was suspended off the ground to above head height.

Setting levels

If the control position is properly placed within the auditorium then the setting of sound levels is purely a matter of discussion between the operator and the director. The sound man will note the director's wishes and balance the sound with the action accordingly.

If the control position is backstage or in an enclosed box then the matter becomes more complicated. In this case it is important that the sound operator is able to equate what he is hearing with what is going on in the auditorium. He should therefore, as a first step, set up a selection of quiet cues so that they are only just discernible in the auditorium. He should then go back to the operating position to judge the difference.

When working from backstage one is likely to be near a loudspeaker and it will probably be found that an effect which seems quite loud is hardly audible out front. So when plotting levels note the actual setting where the sound first

becomes audible to the audience. Thus the cue might read fade from '2½–5' rather than '0–5', in which case the cue will appear on time rather than a fraction late.

Level setting should always be carried out with the correct stage settings in case there are problems of masking loudspeakers or of very absorbent or reflective surfaces.

It is also pointless trying to judge a balance unless the theatre is quiet. Arrange a time when all the noisy people (carpenters and lighting men) have gone to lunch.

Finally, it is worth remembering that when the auditorium is full of people you can probably afford to bring all the sound levels up a touch, since bodies in clothes tend to absorb sound.

Plots or cue-sheets

There are no rules about how one should make out a plot or cue-sheet but there are rules regarding the content. A good plot should:

1 Be clear and logical to follow.
2 Tell you what to do next (whether it be a preset or a cue).
3 Indicate the state of the equipment at any given point.
4 Be as precise and concise as possible.

And it should be all these things before the final dress rehearsals.

Some people prefer to put everything down in columns; for example, Cue – Effect – Tape – Gain – Loudspeaker – Notes. The 'notes' column is used for alterations in tone setting, any specific remarks about changes in volume levels, tricky speaker switching, etc.

I usually like to use a different colour ink for each tape deck and a third very definite colour for all presetting of controls. Presets should be plotted as carefully as the actual cues. In the excitement of a first night it is sometimes difficult to work out whether or not it is safe to, say, switch a speaker on or off on one output channel while an effect is still running on another.

An alternative method is to make a basic cue-sheet consisting of a simple diagram of the control layout leaving space for the cueline and notes. This system requires a separate sheet for every cue but it has the advantage of speed in plotting. It is also very easy to change. Each sheet is a complete record of the state of all the controls at that point. The disadvantage is when one comes to a long sequence of complicated manoeuvres.

Personally I prefer a variation of the first method. I prepare neatly photocopied blank sheets ruled out in columns and insert them between each page of a script in a ring binder. I like to have a script because a sound operator should take his own cues except when technical problems of synchronization make a cue from the stage manager necessary. It is not possible to place a sound into the action of a play with any kind of feeling if you are doing it second hand.

The columns in my cue-sheets vary with the equipment in use and the complexity of the show. If, for example, three tape decks are concurrently in use a great deal of the time I will certainly plot their starts, stops and level changes in separate columns. This will provide an immediate visual indication of what should be happening with each deck. Alternatively, if the production calls for complicated manoeuvring and routing of mainly one tape machine with a second being used only occasionally for general background effects, then the cuesheet would be tailored accordingly. In this instance the group output faders and the loudspeaker switching would feature heavily in the columns.

On a long running show the plot will become unnecessary after a number of performances but I would strongly advocate preparing a short-hand version on a single sheet to be always at hand. Just as an actor can fluff a line on the hundredth performance a technician can suffer a similar blank.

I also use a number of abbreviations and signs when plotting to keep the instructions concise. Some of these are standard music notation and some have been evolved from my own experience.

⌢	music notation for a pause
<8	music notation for growing louder
>2	music notation for growing softer (The number is added to denote a gain setting control.)
SNAP 6	bring gain smartly to that level
0–6	start at 0 and bring smoothly to 6
3–6	start at 3 and bring smoothly to 6
Slow 3–6	start at 3 and fade slowly to 6
Fade	fade effect smoothly out
Slow fade	fade effect slowly out
CUT	Cut the effect
Sp	Loudspeaker
Mc	Microphone
T/T	Disc turntable
Ch	Channel

Figure 91 Cue sheets. Two methods of plotting the same sequence.

	CUE	EFFECT	TAPE	GAIN	SP.	NOTES
	PRESET: TAPE A on Ch.1 / TAPES B+C on Ch.3 / SP 3 - Ch 1 SP 4-5 - Ch 3					
1	CUE FROM S.M.	CURTAIN MUSIC	A	6	3	
2	TABS UP	CROWD	{B / A}	2<5 / FADE	4/5	FADE UP WITH LIGHTS
	PRESET: TAPE A on Ch 3 / SP 3 off					
3	".... VICTORY FOR US ALL."	CHEER	A	3<8	4/5	BUILD AS K ENTERS
4	"BUT ONLY, MY FRIENDS, IF......"		A	>0		
5	AS HE RAISES HIS HAND	CHEER	A	3<10	4/5	QUICK BUILD
6	R LEAPS ON ROSTRUM	ANGRY CROWD	{C / B}	QUICK 0<6 / FADE	4/5	
7	"IT IS THE TRUTH. THE TRUTH."	SHOUT	A	7	4/5	DROWN LAST LINE
	PRESET: TAPE A on Ch 1 / TAPE B on Ch 2 / SP 2 - Ch 1 / SP 6 - Ch 2					
8	"..... AND DEATH MUST BE A PART."	POLICE SIRENS	B	2<7	6	
9	WHEN SIRENS STOP	GUN SHOTS	A / C	8 / <9	2	BUILD CROWD DURING SHOTS.

	CUE	TAPE A	TAPE B	TAPE C	NOTES
	PRESET: TAPE A on Ch 1 / TAPES B+C on Ch 3 / SP 3 - Ch 1 SP 4-5 - Ch 3				
1	CUE FROM S.M.	CURTAIN MUSIC 6			
2	TABS UP	FADE	CROWD 2<5		FADE UP WITH LIGHTS
	PRESET: TAPE A on Ch 3 / SP 3 off				
3	"..... VICTORY FOR US ALL."	CHEER 3<8			BUILD AS K ENTERS
4	"BUT ONLY, MY FRIENDS, IF...."	>0			
5	AS HE RAISES HIS HAND	CHEER 3<10			QUICK BUILD
6	R LEAPS ON ROSTRUM		FADE	ANGRY CROWD 0<6	QUICK SWELL
7	"IT IS THE TRUTH. THE TRUTH"	SHOUT 7			DROWN LAST LINE
	PRESET: TAPE A on Ch 1 / TAPE B on Ch 2 / SP 2 - Ch 1 / SP 6 - Ch 2				
8	"..... AND DEATH MUST BE A PART."		POLICE SIREN 2<7		
9	WHEN SIRENS STOP	SHOTS 8		<9	BUILD CROWD DURING SHOTS

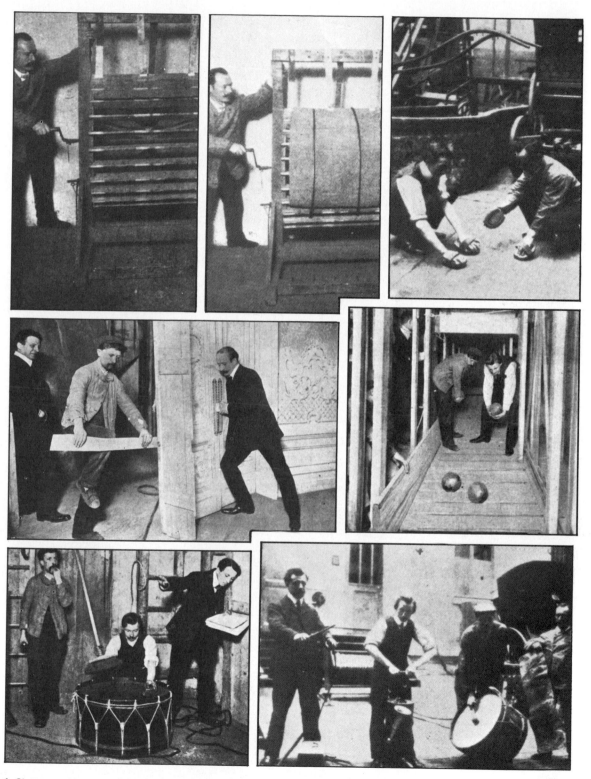

1 Clatter machine – revolving framework of wooden ribs against fixed metal springs.
2 Wind machine – cloth covered frame which brushes against steel springs.
3 The galloping of horses.
4 The crack of a forced door.
5 Thunder rumbling understage.
6 A steam train with two types of brush on a drum and a whistle.
7 A storm – siren wind, thunder drum and metal thunder sheet with electric-spark lightning.

Photograph 31 A reconstruction of creating the effects backstage for a fifteenth-century mystery play.

Live and mechanical effects

Certain sounds will always be more convincingly produced 'live' or manually. For various reasons either the microphone is unable to capture the essence of the sound, or the loudspeaker is incapable of reproducing it. For example, a pistol shot is always much more effective with a blank cartridge in a real gun. Even a good thwack on a leather chair seat with a cane can have more immediacy than a recorded gun shot. And door bells, phone bells, door chimes and door knockers are usually more easily done live. Glass and crockery crashes are also better with the real thing.

To achieve a really loud explosion which will make the audience jump out of their seats there is no substitute for a 'bomb'. This is literally a large firework, obtainable from lighting equipment hire companies, which is set off by connecting it to a mains supply and throwing the switch. The bomb must always be suspended in a large galvanized tank with a wire mesh cover. This 'bomb tank' should be placed understage or somewhere where the actors and technicians are not liable to be at the moment of detonation. Since it is a very short sharp explosion it is often desirable to back it up with a taped effect for added realism.

The best rain effect I have ever heard in the theatre was actually rigged for visual reasons. A perforated water pipe was suspended horizontally about 10 feet (3 m) high behind a window in the set. Below the window, masked from the audience, was a long canvas trough with a runaway at one end. The idea was to side-light the falling drops of water and let the audience actually see the rain. The bonus for us was that the sound the water made hitting the canvas was superb. Later we tried to record it, but it sounded totally unconvincing when reproduced electronically.

An effect I would very much like to experience is of one of the old thunder runs. Theatres such as the Bristol Old Vic still have these long gently sloping wooden chutes running down from the flies. The effect, which apparently rumbled and shook the entire building, was achieved by letting large solid iron cannonballs roll down the chute. Extra vibrations were created by ridges at irregular intervals which made the cannonballs jump.

The Moscow Arts Theatre on a visit to London some years ago achieved a similar effect by rolling heavy weights around in the wings. They also brought with them two very realistic rain machines, one for light rain and one for a downpour. The first was a wire-sided wooden drum on edge with revolving paddles inside which scooped up and let drop fragments of cartridge paper. The stagehand turning the paddles could produce either a continuous or undulating swishing sound. The other machine was a smaller revolving drum with three sets of spaced ridges. As the drum revolved each ridge in turn came into contact with three fixed strips of heavy leather. Each strip of leather was lifted and then allowed to 'thwack' back. This produced an effect of heavy drops of rain falling at whatever speed the drum was revolved. The two machines together in a carefully rehearsed sequence were spectacular.

One of the most famous of all sound effects was for *The Ghost Train* by Arnold Ridley. First produced at the St Martins Theatre in London in 1925, it is still a firm favourite with repertory and amateur companies. I can do no better than quote the actual stage directions as they appear in French's acting edition of the script:

The Ghost Train

1 tubular bell (E flat).
1 garden roller propelled over bevel-edged struts screwed to stage, 30 inches apart.
1 18-gallon galvanized iron tank.
1 thunder-sheet.
Air cylinders (obtainable from British Oxygen Co., Wembley, or local agents).
1 bass *rope* drum and pair of sticks.
2 side-drums.
1 small padded mallet (auctioneer's hammer).
1 large padded mallet (for beating tank).
1 medium mallet.
1 wire-drum brush.
1 milk-churn.
1 pea-whistle.
1 train whistle (for mouth).
1 whistle on cylinder.
2 electric or hand-driven motors.
2 slides cut to give shadows of carriage windows of train.
2 flood arcs on each side *of stage*.
1 tin amplifier to steam with a counterweight placed in its mouth.

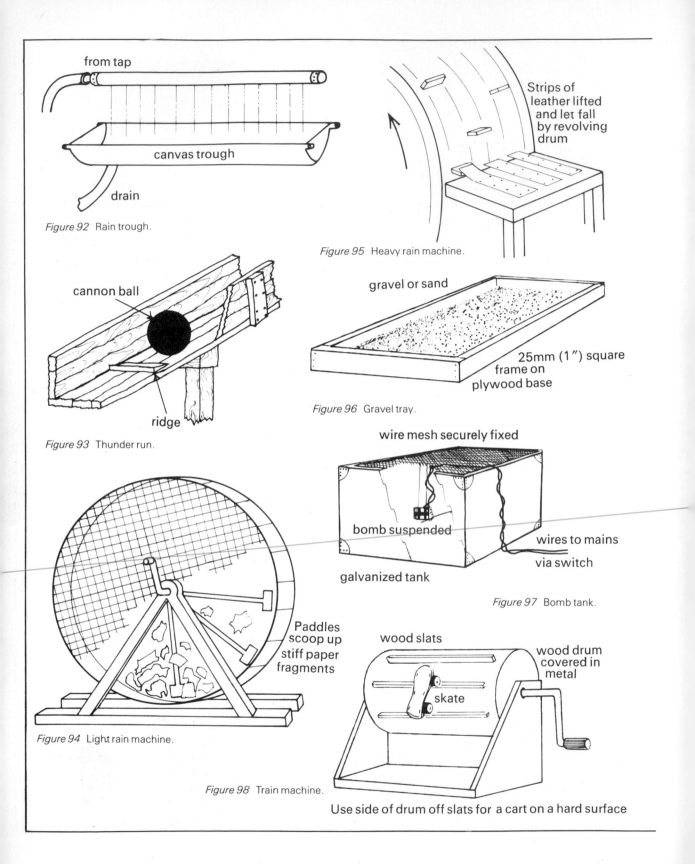

from tap

canvas trough

drain

Figure 92 Rain trough.

Strips of leather lifted and let fall by revolving drum

Figure 95 Heavy rain machine.

cannon ball

ridge

Figure 93 Thunder run.

gravel or sand

25mm (1") square frame on plywood base

Figure 96 Gravel tray.

wire mesh securely fixed

bomb suspended

wires to mains via switch

galvanized tank

Figure 97 Bomb tank.

Paddles scoop up stiff paper fragments

Figure 94 Light rain machine.

wood slats

wood drum covered in metal

skate

Figure 98 Train machine.

Use side of drum off slats for a cart on a hard surface

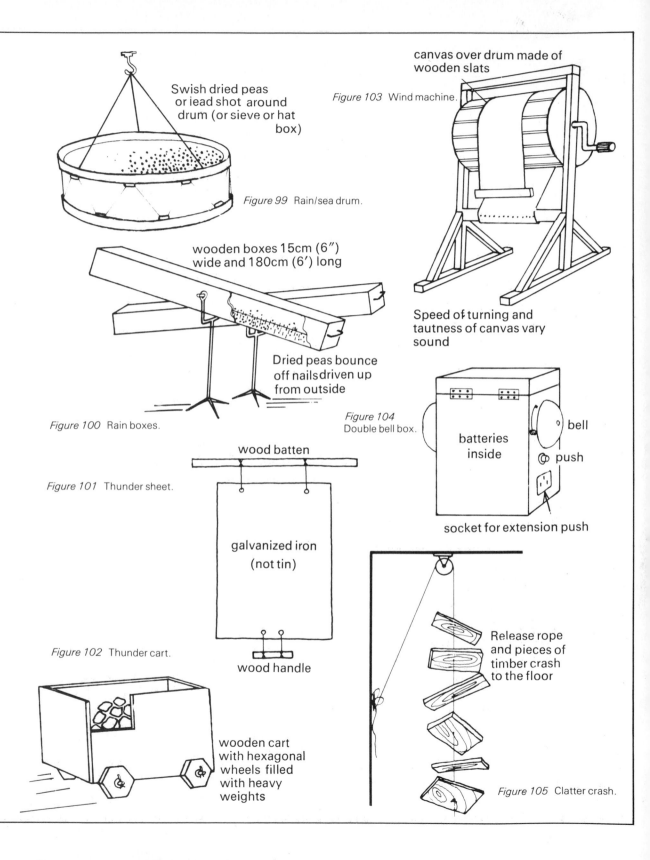

Swish dried peas
or lead shot around
drum (or sieve or hat
box)

Figure 99 Rain/sea drum.

canvas over drum made of
wooden slats

Figure 103 Wind machine.

Speed of turning and
tautness of canvas vary
sound

wooden boxes 15cm (6″)
wide and 180cm (6′) long

Dried peas bounce
off nails driven up
from outside

Figure 100 Rain boxes.

Figure 104
Double bell box.

batteries
inside

bell

push

socket for extension push

wood batten

Figure 101 Thunder sheet.

galvanized iron
(not tin)

wood handle

Figure 102 Thunder cart.

wooden cart
with hexagonal
wheels filled
with heavy
weights

Release rope
and pieces of
timber crash
to the floor

Figure 105 Clatter crash.

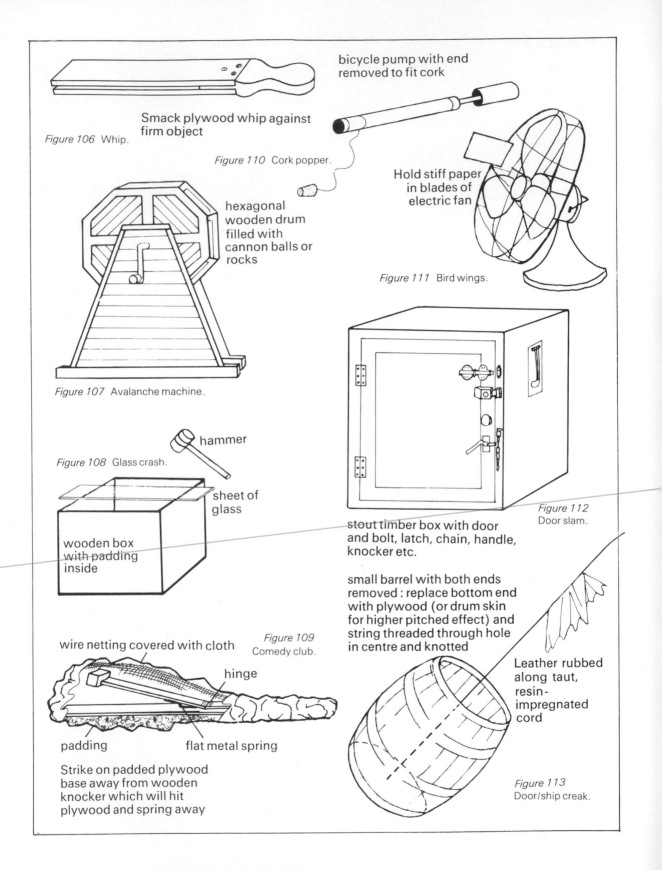

Smack plywood whip against firm object

Figure 106 Whip.

bicycle pump with end removed to fit cork

Figure 110 Cork popper.

hexagonal wooden drum filled with cannon balls or rocks

Figure 107 Avalanche machine.

Hold stiff paper in blades of electric fan

Figure 111 Bird wings.

hammer

Figure 108 Glass crash.

sheet of glass

wooden box with padding inside

Figure 112 Door slam.

stout timber box with door and bolt, latch, chain, handle, knocker etc.

small barrel with both ends removed : replace bottom end with plywood (or drum skin for higher pitched effect) and string threaded through hole in centre and knotted

wire netting covered with cloth

Figure 109 Comedy club.

hinge

padding

flat metal spring

Strike on padded plywood base away from wooden knocker which will hit plywood and spring away

Leather rubbed along taut, resin-impregnated cord

Figure 113 Door/ship creak.

To work first train

Screw whistle into nozzle of cylinder.
1 man sits astride this and another cylinder with amplifier ready to work (A).
1 man stands by roller (B).
1 man stands by tank with large padded mallet (C).
1 man stands by thunder-sheet (D).
2 men stand by motors (E).
2 men stand by floor arcs with slides focused on exterior of windows (F).
1 man stands by with wire brush and small side drum (G).
1 man stands by bass drum (H).

On the rise of the curtain the Stage Manager hits the tubular bell twice with small padded mallet. When Stationmaster lights gas, C and H beat on tank and drum gently, gradually increasing in volume. Then E and G start, followed by D. Finally A starts air release, and as the total volume of sounds increases, B starts to pull his roller over the struts as rapidly as possible, gradually slowing. When noise is at its height, all *stop dead* except A, who continues to blow off air. While train is in station, Stationmaster shouts 'All change!' 'All change!' while C repeatedly beats milk-churn with its lid. He stops as Stage Manager blows pea-whistle. A gives two sharp blasts on his whistle (H has carried his bass drum to O.P. (R) side of stage while train is in station). Stage Manager then grasps medium padded mallet and beats second side-drum (which should be fairly slack) 1 beat. Then another beat, then another, gradually increasing in pace and diminishing in volume as train is supposed to leave station. *Simultaneously, and keeping in time with him,* D gives a shake to sheet, A gives puff of steam, B gives beat on tank, E works motors and B starts roller. H also does roll on drum. These effects should be carried on until noise of train dies away in the distance in an indistinct murmur. As train leaves station F slide their slides across the window in turn, gradually increasing in pace to give the effect of the train lights passing the waiting-rooms. *The whole success of the Effect depends on each unit being together and the rhythm preserved.*

To work second train

In this train it is necessary to have three cue lights fixed so that all the effects men can see them. The switches should be in prompt corner. When the Stage Manager blows whistle for train in distance C and H start as in the first train, E then starts with G, then D joins in. When Peggy says 'It's coming! It's coming!' and runs to Charles, Stage Manager should switch on his first cue light. This should bring A with steam, and other effects, except B, to nearly forte. When Julia turns to run up to window, he switches on second cue light. This should bring in *all* effects double forte, including B and A's whistle. When Julia throws bottle through window, an amber flare followed by flash-box, on P.S. (L) window, fractional pause, then amber flare and flash-box through O.P. (R) window. When Julia falls, bring curtain down. At end of first picture switch on third cue light. On this, all effects must *stop dead.*

To work third train

Only A, B, E, G and H are required for this train. B works his roller over the bare stage in this effect and *NOT* over the struts.
When Teddie shoots at Price in doorway, the Stage Manager blows his train-whistle (mouth), H starts gently on drum, giving beat of a train puffing up hill. A and G keep time with him. The sound gradually increases until Teddie exits. When it comes up to forte but still maintains its steady beat B joins in. When Teddie re-enters, the train rapidly dies away to silence.

12

Sound reinforcement

Acoustics

Before discussing electronic sound reinforcement a few basic facts about acoustics might be helpful. The rules of acoustics are simple, but the situations and factors affecting them are very complex.

The object of theatre acoustics is to project the sound of the performance out to the entire audience and to have it arrive everywhere with similar characteristics of spectrum and intensity and without excessive reverberance. This ideal state of affairs is for many reasons extremely difficult to achieve. For instance, except in the case of a solo performer, the sound source can be anywhere in the stage area. We may also be dealing with a number of sources at the same time. Furthermore, the sound from these sources will arrive at the listener's ear having travelled by many different paths.

Apart from a certain amount of direct sound most will reach the listener by being reflected off ceilings and walls and even floors; in fact, off all surfaces, to a greater or lesser extent. In a badly designed auditorium sound may reach the listener after having been reflected back and forth across the auditorium several times. This is why most good auditoria combine various features for combating multiple echoes, such as non-symmetrical walls, absorbent rear walls, curved boxes, convex balcony fascias and sloping ceilings.

Reflections within the stage area must also be taken into account. The hard brick walls of an empty stage will set up undesirable multiple reflections, and the relatively small area of the proscenium opening will allow only a minor percentage of the energy through. A box set, on the other hand, will help to project the sound into the auditorium. If the fly tower above the box set is full of scenery and drapes this will absorb a great deal of energy, but it will also help to eliminate unwanted reverberations. So the pros will outweigh the cons.

Sound will continue to be reflected around in an enclosed evironment until it is absorbed.

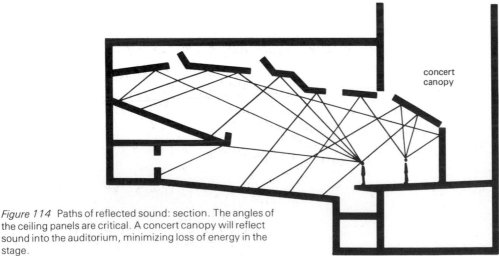

Figure 114 Paths of reflected sound: section. The angles of the ceiling panels are critical. A concert canopy will reflect sound into the auditorium, minimizing loss of energy in the stage.

concert canopy

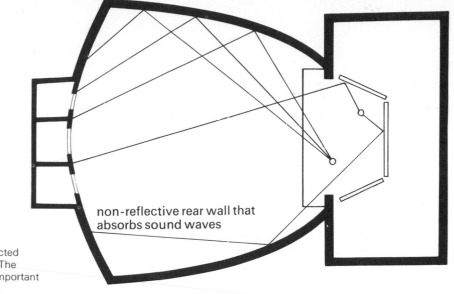

Figure 115
Paths of reflected
sound: plan. The
walls are as important
as the ceiling.

non-reflective rear wall that
absorbs sound waves

Smooth hard surfaces like plaster, brick, concrete, plywood and metal will reflect efficiently and absorb little. Scenic materials will reflect in proportion to their stiffness and hardness; a painted canvas backdrop, for example, will assist the projection of sound, while a heavy velour backdrop will not (although it will reduce the 'bathroom effect'). Most theatres built for plays and musicals are moderately live, i.e. they have a large area of hard interior surface, and they are often excessively reverberant when the house is empty. Cinemas are acoustically designed for listening to loudspeakers and are therefore usually non-reverberant.

All auditoria have their own *resonant characteristics* in that certain frequencies will resonate more than others. The different surfaces in an auditorium will have varying effects on the frequency spectrum: absorbing some frequencies more than others, and reflecting some frequencies more than others. These variations in absorption/reflection (coupled with the overall reverberation time) are what gives an auditorium its own individual sound or resonant characteristic.

Loudspeakers also have their individual resonant characteristics and if these should coincide with those of the auditorium, thereby perhaps doubly accentuating a range of frequencies, the result can be disastrous. In this instance 'room equalization' is a possible cure and is discussed later in the chapter.

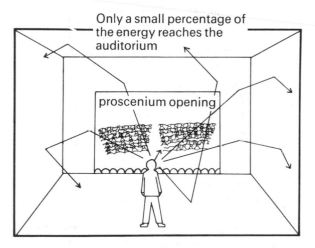

Only a small percentage of
the energy reaches the
auditorium

proscenium opening

Figure 116 Reflections and wastage of energy within an empty stage.

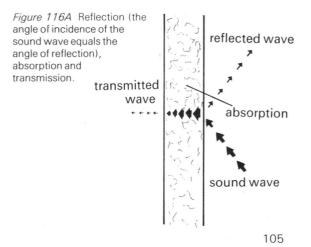

Figure 116A Reflection (the angle of incidence of the sound wave equals the angle of reflection), absorption and transmission.

reflected wave

transmitted wave

absorption

sound wave

Masking noise from air-conditioning and other mechanical services can present a significant barrier to audibility and has to be taken into account when designing an auditorium. Care has also to be taken to isolate the auditorium acoustically from adjacent noisy areas such as foyers (lobbies), rehearsal rooms, green rooms, etc.

Intermittent noise from external sources can also be a serious distraction and although it is sometimes difficult (or too costly) to protect totally against the odd passing police siren or low-flying aircraft, one should not expect to hear such things as paging announcements to public areas or the bar staff washing up the glasses after the interval.

Sound reinforcement or public address?

The terms Sound Reinforcement and Public Address are difficult to define; partly because of a lack of universal agreement on their usage, and partly because the two forms of amplification tend to overlap.

Public Address systems were originally, as implied, functional systems for addressing the public where quality of sound was secondary to the clear transmission of information. They were installed in such places as railway stations, churches, sports stadiums, conference halls, etc., and, later, theatres.

A significant improvement in quality did not come about until the explosion of the pop music scene during the 1960s. A new breed of high performance sound equipment was developed so that recording artistes like the Beatles and the Rolling Stones could present themselves in concert to vast audiences. And although an announcement system in a railway station is a far cry from a sound installation for an open air rock concert, they are both referred to as PA systems (Public Address). And they do, in fact, have one major factor in common: for in each case a person at one end of the system is in close proximity to a microphone producing at the other end an obviously amplified sound, although in a Sound Reinforcement system the microphone is not necessarily near the performer and the aim is to present the listener with an amplified yet, hopefully, natural sound.

Unfortunately, and to complicate matters, modern musicals more often than not call for a combination of the close and the distant microphone techniques to produce a louder than natural sound—in other words a cross between Reinforcement and Public Address. This requirement has arisen because on the one hand audiences, having become used to the electronic sound of broadcasting, films and pop concerts, are less prepared to concentrate in the theatre than was once the case. And on the other hand modern equipment and techniques have made it possible to provide a bigger sound for a live performance.

Another factor is that composers, knowing that a sound system will be available, feel freer to write orchestrations which once would have been appropriate only in a recording studio. And they are encouraged by many theatrical producers who (mistakenly) equate loudness with excitement. It also has to be said that the style of acting has changed: a large percentage of actors have either lost the art of projection or are content to rely upon the sound system to reach the audience at the back of the room.

Loudspeaker placement

Whether we are dealing with Reinforcement or PA somewhere has to be found for the loudspeakers, and their positioning and angling are critical. The basic requirements are that they should be sited as *near to the stage* as possible to maintain the illusion of the sound coming from the actors; they should be on the *audience side of the microphones* to minimize acoustic feedback; and they should be *angled to provide direct sound to every seat in the house*.

The ideal would be to have some large full-range loudspeakers slap bang in the middle of the front of the stage. Behind the screen in a cinema this is possible (see photograph 32), but in the theatre there might be complaints from the actors. The alternatives are either to raise the loudspeakers above the proscenium or to have them at the sides of the proscenium.

Which is best?

Well, in theory a single sound source in the centre above will give the 'cleanest' sound, as the number of sound paths and therefore the chances of unwanted reflections have been reduced to a minimum. Furthermore, the sound source is not in close proximity to any one section of the audience. So, bearing in mind the fact that

Photograph 32 The five bins and horns installed behind the cinema screen at the Queen Elizabeth Hall, London. *Photo courtesy Vitavox*

the ears are less discerning in the vertical plane as opposed to the horizontal, this could be our first choice. (Figure 117).

One of the drawbacks to this solution is that often there is a siteline cut-off from overhanging balconies. If there are seats in the house where it is not possible to see the top of the proscenium the people sitting there will not receive direct sound. And these are the areas which normally require the most help from a sound system.

A solution might be to add some small loud-speakers to 'fill-in' the dead areas. (Figure 118). But if this is attempted it will be necessary to incorporate some form of *electronic time delay*; otherwise, because electricity travels faster than airborne sound, the audience at the back would hear the sound from the nearer 'fill-in' loud-speakers a fraction of a second *before* the main

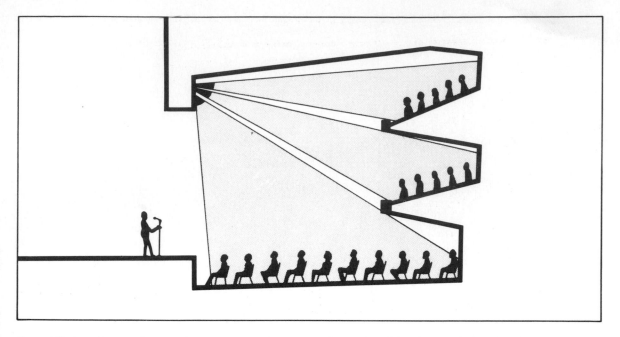

Figure 117 A small array of loudspeakers above the proscenium will, in theory, provide an even distribution with the minimum of unwanted reflections.

loudspeakers and the natural sound from the stage. This can be a disconcerting effect, certainly destroying the realism and often actually hindering intelligibility.

With a correctly calculated delay the natural airborne sound from the stage will reach the audience a fraction of a second *before* the electronic sound. The effect then is similar to that of direct sound being naturally reinforced by reflecting off an acoustical design ceiling (figure 119). The delayed sound can be surprisingly loud without sacrificing realism because the human brain always registers the initial sound received as being the source.

Loudspeakers on a delay line are also used as a means of increasing the general level of re-inforced sound. Here they might be placed a third or halfway back on the side walls of an auditorium where, being farther away from the microphones than the proscenium loudspeakers, more sound before feedback can be obtained (figure 120).

Acoustic feedback or *howlround* is caused by the signal from a loudspeaker being picked up by a microphone, going round through the system and out of the loudspeaker again *ad infinitium*. The beginnings of feedback are characterized by a zing on the end of each word. Unless the micro-phone level is checked this builds into what is called a ringing sound. And this, in turn, will build into a howl or scream.

The frequency of the feedback tone will depend upon many factors: these include the characteristics of the microphone and the loud-speaker, the resonant characteristics of the environment and the position of the microphone in relation to the loudspeaker; for example, the feedback tone produced with a microphone behind a loudspeaker will tend to be of a low frequency in contrast with the high notes produced in front.

Sound reflecting off walls, ceilings and balcony fronts back to the microphone can be a prime cause of feedback. For this reason we tend to use loudspeakers with directional character-istics so that the sound is delivered to where it is required and reflections back to the microphone from walls and balcony fronts are kept to a minimum (figure 121).

So an overhead loudspeaker array in an auditorium might consist of one or a number of bass units (which will not be very directional) plus some mid and high frequency reproducers which *will* have directional properties. They may be radial or multicellular horns chosen for a particular pattern of dispersion, or could be specially designed enclosures housing cone loudspeakers. In a large auditorium it will be necessary to incorporate short-throw and long-throw loudspeakers with different directivity

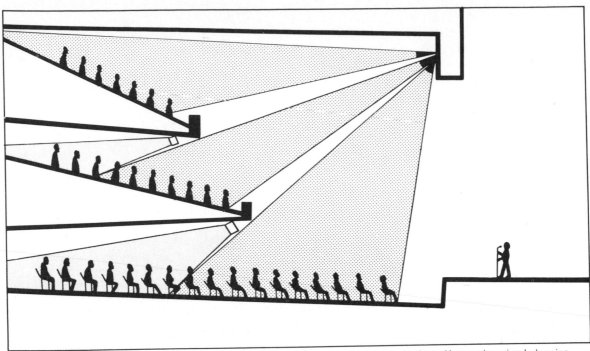

Figure 118 Small fill-in loudspeakers fed via electronic time delay can cover the areas shadowed by overhanging balconies.

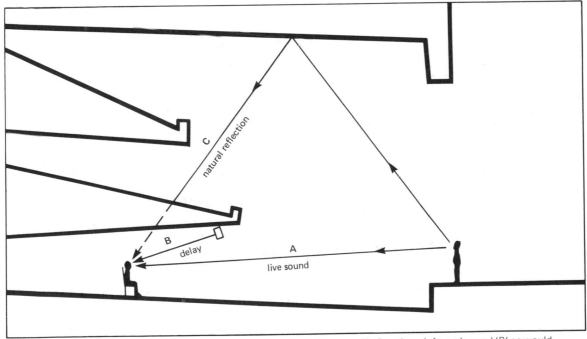

Figure 119 The live sound 'A' should reach the listener a fraction of a second before the reinforced sound 'B' as would a natural reflection.

patterns for covering the front and rear seating areas.

If stereo is required then two loudspeaker arrays will be necessary. Taped music and reinforced live music will sound more realistic, but it could adversely affect vocal reinforcement because the number of sound paths has been doubled and therefore a lack of clarity may be caused by the additional reflections and time delays. Some larger installations therefore employ a stereo system for music plus a central mono array for vocals. In this way vocal clarity is maintained (figure 122).

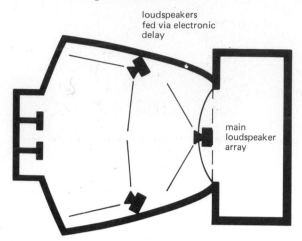

Figure 120 The more sound before feedback the greater the distance from the loudspeakers to the microphones.

Figure 121 Loudspeakers with directional characteristics minimize unwanted reflections from walls, ceilings and balcony fronts.

However, there is a major drawback with a pure overhead loudspeaker system – especially in a large theatre – in that the sound becomes divorced from the stage and the sound 'image' will be hovering about in mid-air; its exact whereabouts depending upon the relative loudness of the live and amplified sound. In my opinion, therefore, a properly engineered system will include some lower side-fill loudspeakers which will, when correctly balanced with the overhead array, bring the image down to the same plane as the performers. I shall expand upon this topic when discussing the O'Keefe Centre for the Performing Arts in a later chapter.

Placing loudspeakers above and in front of the acting area is, of course, not always possible or even desirable. On aesthetic grounds a lump of loudspeakers suspended above an architecturally pleasing proscenium would properly be regarded as an unwarranted eyesore. Or maybe there is a visual cut-off below the balconies and not sufficient funds for the additional fill-in loudspeakers along with their amplifiers and necessary delay equipment.

So, if we cannot go up we must move sideways.

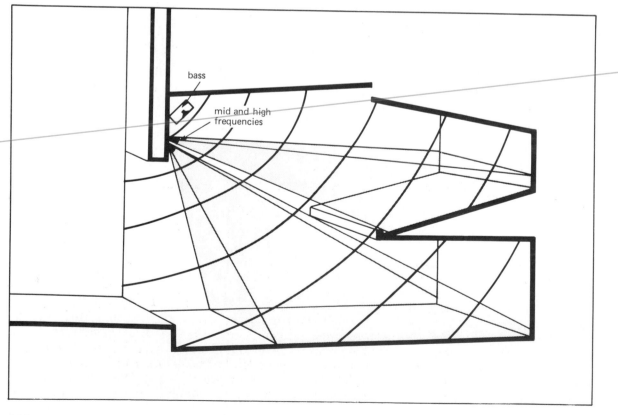

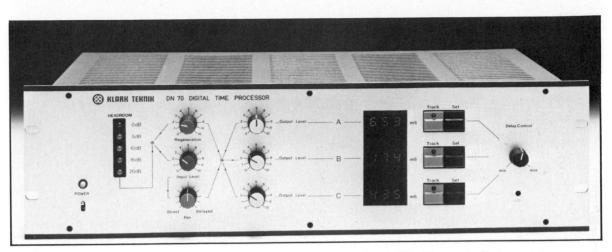

Photograph 33 A digital delay line with 3 outputs, each with variable delays of up to 653 milliseconds. *Photo courtesy Klark-Teknik Research Ltd*

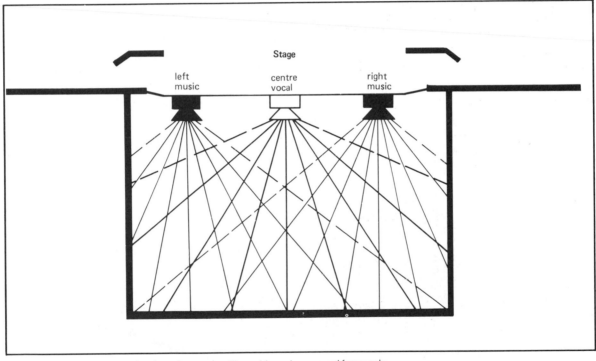

Figure 122 A central mono loudspeaker array will provide a clean sound for vocals.

Loudspeakers suitably placed on the proscenium walls can provide sound to each level of the auditorium with the bonus of stereo thrown in. But there are two possible drawbacks: one is that space is often limited, making it difficult to incorporate loudspeakers of adequate size and performance, and the other is that there is a danger of blasting the front rows of the audience. One answer to this problem is to use a line of loudspeakers in a column giving a slim enclosure and a clearly defined directivity pattern. Line source column loudspeakers were originally conceived for speech reinforcement and their design precludes a great deal of response in the bass frequencies. They are therefore not normally considered where there is a requirement for a full range music reproduction unless bass supplement loudspeakers are incorporated into the system. However, a *good* column (and you get what you pay for) is characterized by a smooth

111

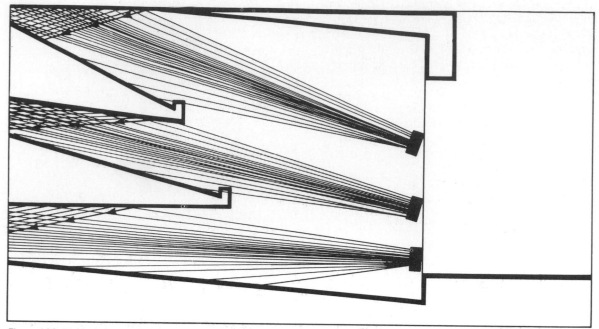

Figure 123 Vertical placement of column loudspeakers, taking advantage of ceiling reflections to enhance rear of auditorium.

Figure 124 A low glancing angle with the centre of the beam directed at the rear of the auditorium will provide an even coverage without hot spots.

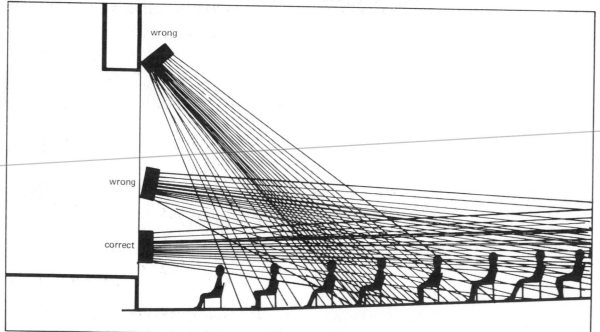

frequency response providing the minimum coloration of sound and, most important, a directional property which is wide in the horizontal plane and narrow in the vertical. This fan-shaped response is, of course, ideal for the coverage of an auditorium.

It is recommended that the columns be placed as low down as possible so as to be essentially in the same plane and as close to the original sound source as possible. For not only does this assist the illusion of the sound coming from the actor, but it also tends to take advantage of any angled ceilings which have been designed for natural reflections (figure 123).

Another reason for keeping a column loudspeaker at a relatively low height is to obtain maximum coverage of sound avoiding 'hot spots'. If you imagine that the signal from a column is a wide flat beam of light, then a complete coverage of the auditorium is possible from a low glancing angle, but as the source is raised the area of coverage is reduced and a hot spot will be created (figure 124).

Now you might imagine that this low glancing angle will result in a far greater level of sound at the front of the auditorium than farther back where it is more needed. But if the column is correctly positioned this will not be the case. It should be placed at a height from which the back rows of the auditorium can see the entire loudspeaker and it should be tilted so that these people are in the centre of the focus of the beam. Thus the front of the auditorium will benefit from only a small part of the total energy, but the farther back one goes the more one comes into range until the entire output of the loudspeaker (plus any natural reflections) are being received. Just like the beam of light, one person can sit near a spotlight below the beam and be lit by a general glow whilst another person further back has the light focused fully upon him.

It is difficult to aim a column loudspeaker accurately by eye. There is, however, a simple method requiring two people, a torch and a mirror. Attach a small mirror to the centre of the front of the column. From the desired position aim a torch at eye level into the mirror. Then tilt the column until the reflection of the torch is visible in the mirror. But although this is accurate it does not take into account any effects of reflection or absorption arising from the natural acoustics. This is where *ears* come in.

By turning up a few empty channels on the mixer with plenty of mid and treble added it is usually possible to obtain a reasonable level of hiss. A person moving around the auditorium will quickly discover where the signal is strongest and where it drops away. The point at which the two beams cross is also very striking and should, naturally, be in the centre of the auditorium. By swaying from side to side in this position one is extremely aware of moving from one loudspeaker to the other. If they are wired out of phase then the sensation will be most unpleasant, and the fault should be remedied immediately.

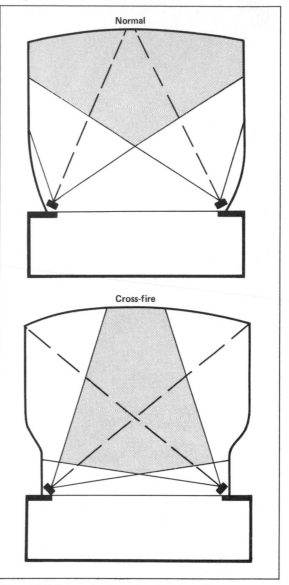

Figure 125 Column loudspeakers in a cross-fire arrangement tend to produce an uneven coverage.

It is important to remember that the audience are seated. Therefore if the angles are correct for the back row the hiss will drop away sharply as you stand. I find that it is a great help to cup both hands behind the ears when concentrating on hiss levels. I discovered some time ago that my colleagues, well used to seeing me running up and down the aisles with hands behind the ears and an intent expression upon the face, now standing, now crouching and generally bobbing about from side to side, have christened the operation 'Doing Rabbits'.

In the horizontal plane the loudspeakers should be swivelled so that imaginary lines from the centre of each pair of columns do not quite meet. Loudspeakers are normally mounted in a 'cross-fire' arrangement only if this is dictated by architectural restrictions; because, as can be seen in figure 125, the rear auditorium coverage is not so good and the intensity of the coverage at the front increases the likelihood of feedback. If the facilities are available, loudspeaker angling is more accuratley carried out with the aid of a pink noise generator (which provides a wide band hiss) and a sound pressure level meter.

If there is a loud orchestra in the pit the

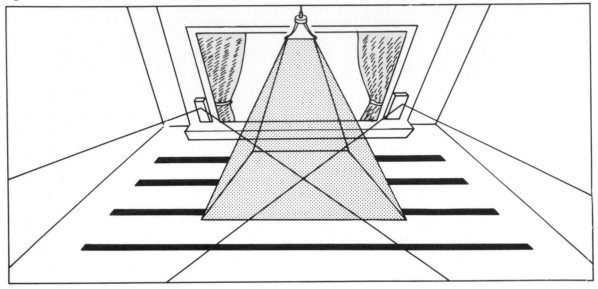

Figure 126 Centre-fill above helps to shift the image from the side loudspeakers towards the centre.

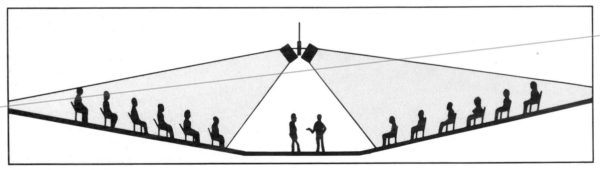

Figure 127 For arena theatre a central loudspeaker position often works wonders.

Figure 128 Loudspeakers placed towards the perimeter of the acting area will be less prone to feedback.

audience near the stage may need a good deal of help from the sound system and additional loudspeakers will be needed to fill in the dead triangle at the front of the stalls. An overhead central column or horn loudspeaker is often very effective because it not only provides the additional centre-fill required, but it moves the apparent sound source towards the centre; so that people sitting at the front become less aware of the side loudspeakers (figure 126). If this solution is not possible then two additional (and maybe smaller) columns mounted on the proscenium walls will do the trick. Either way it is necessary to adjust the signal strength of these fill-in units carefully so that they blend in with the overall system and do not cause feedback.

With a *distributed loudspeaker system* directivity is no longer such a critical factor. For while it remains necessary to have loudspeakers in the proscenium zone, or relatively close to the performers, in order to provide a source reference, other loudspeakers around the auditorium fed via delay lines can do most of the work in their immediate areas. Hence, it is possible to utilize reasonably small full frequency range loudspeakers (e.g. studio monitors) which in a non-distributed system would not be capable of providing an even coverage of the auditorium.

The placement of loudspeakers for Theatre in the Round (or Arena Theatre) is seldom entirely satisfactory. The obvious answer is to provide a central cluster (figure 127); good dispersion from a point source. But for microphone work sometimes the feedback threshold is unacceptable, in which case the loudspeakers have to be sited more towards the perimeter of the stage (figure 128). However, the steeper angle will make an even coverage more difficult; so it might be necessary to use a greater number of loudspeakers. A certain amount of experimentation is recommended to find the best compromise. Incidentally, the distributed loudspeaker format for arena theatre can be useful for the replay of sound effects as it provides possibilities for localized sound as well as general coverage and travelling effects.

Amplifiers

In the more traditional form of theatre acoustic conditions will often make it necessary to drive the first balcony loudspeakers harder than the main floor (stalls) loudspeakers in order to provide a similar listening condition. The best

place to make permanent level adjustments of this nature is at the amplifier. It is therefore desirable to have separate amplifiers for each floor level of the auditorium.

Additional amplifier channels will be necessary for monitor loudspeakers in the control room and stage monitor loudspeakers for artists' foldback. If working in stereo then the same number of *twin* channel amplifiers or *twice* the number of single channel amplifiers will be required. The use of twin amplifiers usually constitutes a saving in both price and space.

Preset gain panel

A preset panel with lockable gain controls is one way of ensuring that the correct sound balance throughout the sound system is maintained once it has been set (figure 129). With all the amplifiers set to maximum output and the level of the signal driving into each amplifier determined at the preset panel it is possible to interchange like amplifiers in the event of failure without fear of upsetting a critical balance. The gain controls on most amplifiers, if fitted at all, are not calibrated accurately enough for this purpose.

Setting optimum levels

A simple method of balancing an auditorium without the use of measuring equipment is as follows:

First ensure that the output from the loudspeakers at each floor of the auditorium is balanced left to right. This can easily be ascertained by putting hiss through the system and listening to each pair of loudspeakers in turn.

Next, we need to establish the operating level of the mixer and set the input gains. For this a microphone in a central position at the front of the stage is required. Then, with *all the amplifiers turned off*, fully open the microphone channel on the mixer and set the input gain so that the meters show the mixer is working well within its capability with the loudest expected noise; e.g. get someone to shout at the microphone. Leave the microphone channel open at this setting for it has now become our reference for testing the feedback threshold of the loudspeakers.

Having decided which area of the auditorium is likely to require the greatest amount of amplification (probably the first balcony) turn on the corresponding amplifiers and bring their levels gently up to the threshold of feedback . . . then back off the levels until the system is completely stable even when a loud sound is presented to the microphone.

Go through the same process with the next most important area for amplification (perhaps the stalls) and so on; always adding to what has already been set.

Having achieved the optimum potential level before feedback a thorough listening test should be carried out. With an assistant on stage speaking at a constant level into the microphone, adjusted at the mixer to provide only subtle reinforcement, all parts of the theatre should be visited. It might be found that the acoustics on one floor are so good that the relative amplifiers can be reduced in gain. This will improve the stability of the system and provide a little in hand for boosting another section of the auditorium; a little less in the balcony, a little more in the stalls, etc.

Of course, if you have access to a Sound Level Meter this is a great asset as it speeds up the process and makes it more accurate.

Room equalization

The performance of any loudspeaker is affected by its acoustic environment. Within the overall spectrum certain frequencies will be accentuated by reflecting off hard surfaces and other frequencies will be absorbed.

With pink noise through the system (this is a broad band hiss which contains equal energy per octave band width) an instrument called a Spectrum Analyser (photograph 34) could read a response in the auditorium similar to that shown in figure 130. (Note the peaks – or increased gain – at 500 Hertz and around 4,000 Hertz) ... whereas the same loudspeakers measured under ideal conditions might produce a much smoother response, as indicated in figure 131.

Sound systems therefore often incorporate Graphic Equalizers (photograph 35), which are really a form of sophisticated tone control, to iron out the peaks and troughs so that the performance of the loudspeaker in the auditorium can be made to resemble its performance under ideal conditions. So in our example if the 500 Hz and 4kHz bands are attenuated this will produce a more natural sound in this particular acoustic setting. And there is an additional benefit in that the accentuated frequencies, the peaks, can be a prime cause of feedback so the introduction of a Graphic Equalizer not only makes the system sound smoother and more pleasant to the ear, but it increases the feedback threshold.

Setting Graphic Equalizers correctly can be a lengthy business requiring readings of pink noise taken with the Spectrum Analyser at many locations throughout the auditorium to obtain the best average response.

Even so, having done all this you are well

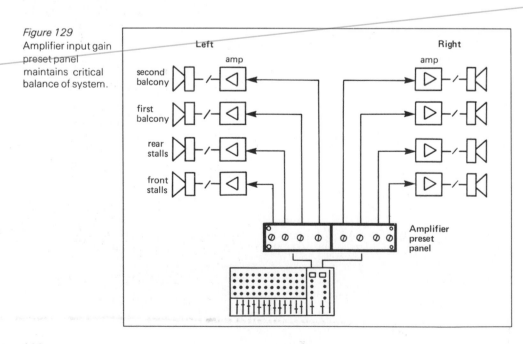

Figure 129
Amplifier input gain preset panel maintains critical balance of system.

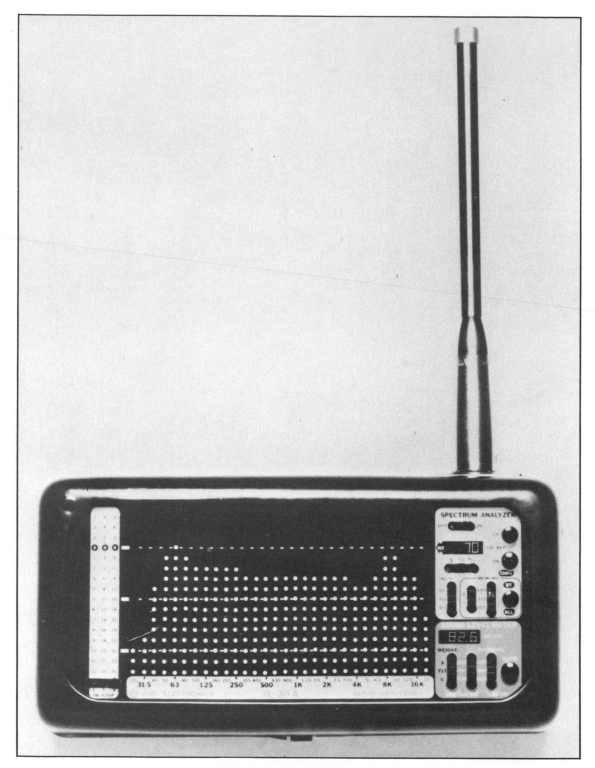

Photograph 34 Spectrum analyser and sound pressure level meter with LED display of frequency content. *Photo courtesy F. W. O. Bauch Ltd*

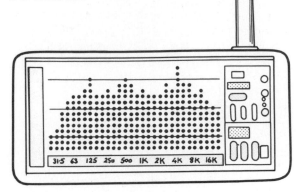

Figure 130 Typical response shown on spectrum analyser measuring pink noise in an auditorium.

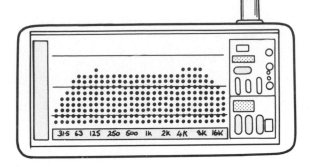

Figure 131 Typical response of the same loudspeakers measured under ideal conditions.

advised to sit down quietly and *listen*, and if you do not like what you hear, *change it*.

A cautionary tale: in 1967 I was involved with the design of a temporary 50 channel sound installation in the London Palladium for a season of international stars including such august names as Bing Crosby, Julie Andrews, Rosemary Clooney and Sammy Davis Jnr.. All went well and everyone seemed very pleased with our efforts until we came to the final star of the season. He was a very well-known American recording artiste who had his own sound designer and normally travelled with his own equipment. However, it was decided that what was already *in situ* was suitable for their requirements and we agreed to let them use our system and do with it as they wished.

The first thing the visiting sound designer did was to produce his spectrum analyser and set to work taking readings and making adjustments to the graphic equalizers which, I have to admit, we had originally set up by ear. In order to produce a so-called 'flat' response some of the frequency bands on the equalizers were drastically changed and the result to my ears was of a much harder sound than our more tentative approach had achieved. This could well have been because he was getting rid of some severe notches shown on the analyser but, at the same time, creating peaks on either side of the notch not measured by the analyser because they fell between the frequency bands. However, once he was happy with the system we all went home and left him to get on with the show.

The point of the story is that the following morning the press were unanimous in their condemnation of the Palladium management for having provided this renowned American singing star with such a second-rate sound system. I have often noticed that, as far as most people are concerned, bad or inadequate sound is the fault of the equipment whereas bad lighting is the fault of the designer.

Photograph 35 Dual channel 30-band third octave graphic equalizer. *Photo courtesy Klark-Teknik Research Ltd*

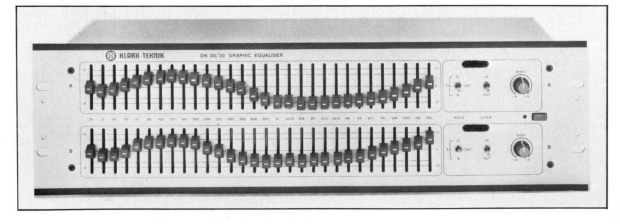

Control equipment

The mixer

There are many mixers available on the market to suit different applications within various price brackets. The basic workings of a simple mixer and most of the additional facilities found in the more comprehensive mixing desks were discussed in detail in Chapter Five.

The mixer is the heart of any sound system and, as such, should be as flexible as possible in operation and of a sufficiently high standard of technical performance not to introduce noise (hum or hiss) into the system and, at the other end of the scale, not to create distortion when being driven hard. In other words a theatre mixer must be flexible, noise-free, and able to handle a very wide dynamic range.

Limiters and compressors

These are devices, originally designed for recording studios, which can electronically control sound levels. A limiter can be set so that extremely strong signals which might cause an amplifier or a mixer to overload, resulting in distortion, are automatically reduced. In other words, one can set a ceiling on the peaks. However, a word of warning, the limiter must be of extremely good quality and design, and must even then not be overdriven, otherwise the unit itself will introduce distortion.

Photograph 36 Signal processing modules for plugging into rack mounting or portable main frames. The range of modules includes equalizer, expander/gates, pan effects, compressor/limiters, etc. *Photo courtesy Audio and Design (Recording) Ltd*

Photograph 37 Close-up of compressor/limiter module. *Photo courtesy Audio and Design (Recording) Ltd*

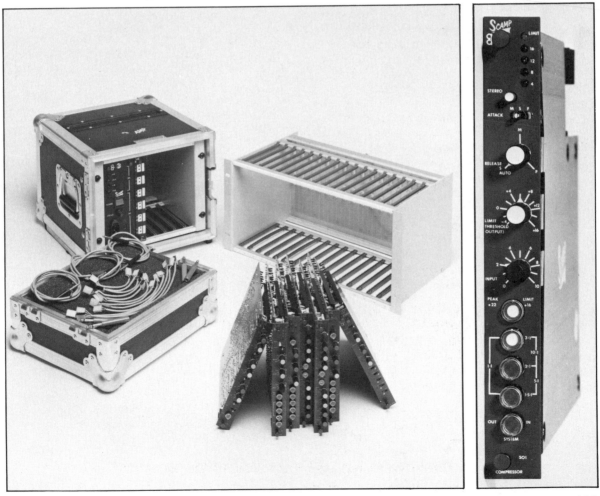

A *limiter* may be 'patched' into one channel of the mixing desk to help to cope with the upper end of the dynamic range of a vocalist or a musical instrument. Limiters may also be patched into sub-groups for limiting a number of channels associated with, say, a drum kit or a brass section. They are also incorporated in some systems between the output of the mixer and one or a group of power amplifiers. In this instance their purpose is to protect the amplifiers and loudspeakers from being overdriven.

A *limiter/compressor* is a device which not only limits the peaks but boosts the lesser signals. So all the signals become compressed between a predetermined floor and ceiling. This is a tricky piece of equipment to use with live amplification as it is prone to pull the signal up into feedback. However, if a vocalist has poor microphone technique, it can be a very useful tool.

Anti-feedback devices

Audio experts are constantly researching new ideas for obtaining a dramatic increase in gain before feedback and there are some devices on the market which certainly help towards that aim. One such unit is called a *frequency shifter*. As the name implies it will shift the entire frequency content of the signal up or down by some four or five Hertz (more than this and the 'key change' becomes noticeable). By this means any critical frequency peaks in the source sound are not exactly reproduced. Thus, instead of a peak at, say, 1,000 Hz, being amplified to create one big potentially disastrous peak at that frequency, there would be two smaller peaks – one at 1,000 Hz and one at 1,005 Hz.

A system correctly set up with graphic equalizers as we have already seen will produce a flatter overall response, thereby creating more stability. But sometimes there still remain one or two specific frequencies where the system tends to take off. In this instance one might introduce a *notch filter* or a *parametric* equalizer both of which have very precise control over spot frequencies. As long as one is dealing with a very narrow band width troublesome frequencies can be attenuated without the effect being noticeable to the listener.

Microphones

In a reinforcement system where the requirement is for maximum pick-up with minimum potential feedback we deal almost exclusively with directional, or cardioid, microphones. It might reasonably be thought that the more live microphones there are scattered about a stage the better will be the general pick up. In practice the opposite is true.

Rule one is to have as few microphones live at any one time as possible. When working close to the feedback threshold each time the fader is opened on another channel there is a significant loss in potential acoustic gain. In other words, *all* the microphone levels have to be pulled back in order to accommodate the additional microphone.

It has been calculated that each time the number of open, or live, microphones is doubled 3 decibels of gain-before-feedback is lost. Notice in figure 132 the difference between say, using four and eight microphones; those three dB could very well be the difference between hearing and not hearing.

Another reason for economy is that the greater the number of microphones the less clear will be the sound. Take, for example, two live microphones with a performer closest to microphone A. The effect will be as follows: microphone A will pick up the voice signal, some reflections of that signal from the floor, walls, etc., plus a certain amount of whatever ambient noise there might be (perhaps an orchestra, other performers, scenery being moved, etc.). Microphone B will pick up less of the original signal in ratio to the ambient noise and the signal plus any reflections will be received a fraction of a second

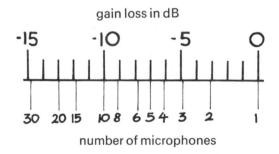

Figure 132 Gain loss in dB using multiple microphones.

later. Thus the combined effect of the two microphones is to produce an increased level of ambient noise with a voice signal degraded because of the time lags and reflections. Introducing a third microphone will multiply these factors.

So, although there are bound to be a number

120

of microphones positioned around the stage in a Reinforcement System, the aim of the sound operator should be to use as few as possible at any given moment in the performance. And this is where the skill of the operator really tells.

The key is to anticipate the movements of the performer, ensuring that the next microphone is made live *before* it is required. If you think of the microphone pick-up pattern as a beam of light the object would be never to let the performer move into darkness.

The positioning of microphones in the theatre is often a cause of some concern because more often than not the requirement is that they should be unseen. In television even though the studios are acoustically treated and the orchestras are more often than not at some distance from the performers, the sound technician would expect to have a boom microphone at all times within a couple of feet of the actor's head. If this were not possible then the actor would be given a small radio transmitter connected to a microphone hidden in the costume somewhere around the middle of the chest. If neither of these options was open, the voice would be prerecorded and the actors would mime to the tape. A television sound technician would never employ the long range microphone techniques used in live theatre.

Why not? Simply because of the fact that the performance characteristics of microphones deteriorate with distance. This is easily demonstrable by recording your own voice at an ideal 9 inches (23cm) or so from a microphone and then again at a distance of a few paces. The voice will sound thinner with much of the bass content having disappeared. This would be totally unacceptable for normal broadcasting purposes. So how do we get away with it in the theatre? Well, for a pop concert or a rock opera there is no substitute for the close microphone technique combined with the correct choice of loudspeakers for a full bodied sound. But if we are dealing with Reinforcement then the audience will be hearing a large percentage of live sound from the performers. The Reinforcement is mainly to increase intelligibility and we are therefore dealing mainly with the higher frequencies.

Float (or foot) microphones

The most obvious and usually most important position for Reinforcement microphones is along the front edge of the stage, being directly in the firing-line between the actors and the audience. We call microphones in this position 'foot mics' or, more commonly in the UK, 'float mics'. (This is because all theatres once had lights in this position called 'footlights', which were originally known as 'floats' because they consisted of lighted wicks floating in wax.)

It used to be the object of every sound engineer to raise the float microphones as near as possible to the source of sound; that is, the actor's head. And many battles were fought with set designers, producers and directors vis-à-vis their unsightliness as opposed to the importance of audibility (Photograph 38). But in the late 1960s some American engineers were testing out a large installation and discovered that one of the microphones appeared to perform more efficiently than all the others. Upon closer inspection they were surprised to find that the microphone in question had fallen from its stand and was resting on the floor.

Subsequent experiments with test equipment produced the explanation that when a microphone is raised in the air it will receive direct sound plus reflections from the floor; these reflections will not only make for a less clean sound but the short time-lag will mean that certain groups of frequencies will arrive at the microphone out of phase with those of the original signal. This produces a cancelling effect in those frequencies. Thus the quality of sound is impaired. If the microphone is placed at floor level the direct and reflected sound waves arrive at the microphone at almost the same instant producing a tighter sound with no audible cancellation effect (figure 133). And there are additional benefits in that the floor acts as a radiator; while it collects sound waves from the stage on the one hand it shields the microphones from the orchestra pit on the other.

Lowering the microphone does not noticeably increase the pick-up of *airborne* foot noise. After all, if the microphone is raised by twelve inches a footfall two feet upstage will only make a difference of a couple of inches. And the difference decreases the further back you go.

Transmitted foot noise is catered for by correct shock mounting to isolate the microphone from floor vibrations. There are on the market shock mounts especially designed for float microphones. One of these takes advantage of a particular type of condenser microphone which can incorporate a swivel adaptor between the

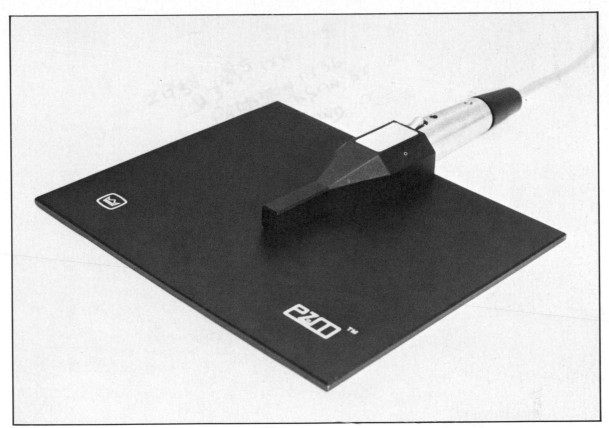

Photograph 38 Photo showing old system of microphones along the front of the stage mounted as high as possible. Note the riser microphone through the trap in the stage floor. Performer: Ben Lyon.

Figure 133 Direct and reflected waves reaching a microphone on a high stand will be out of phase, thereby cancelling out certain frequencies.

Photograph 39 Pressure Zone microphone. Small moving coil microphone designed to take advantage of the fact that as a sound wave approaches a boundary (such as a wall, table or floor) there is formed at this boundary a pressure zone 4 or 5 mm deep within which the direct signal and its reflection from the boundary remain in phase and therefore add coherently. *Photo of microphone from HHB Hire and Sales by C. Wass*

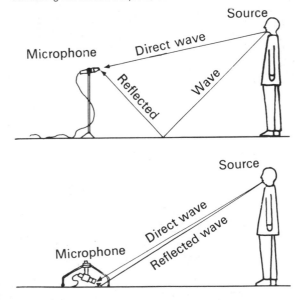

preamplifier body of the microphone and the capsule (figure 134).

But an ordinary microphone base standing on a piece of foam rubber all held in place by two rubber straps secured on either side will perform the same function (figure 135). To be effective the stand must support the microphone so that the capsule is about $\frac{1}{8}$" away from the floor. The angle should be between 30 and 45 degrees.

For an even coverage across the stage the float mics should be set on about 5 ft. centres. Certainly not more than 6 ft. apart. An odd number of microphones is recommended as it allows for a central position; often the most useful.

Float microphones should cover at least the first 15 ft. of the acting area and will normally be useful for another 10 ft or so. But this will depend

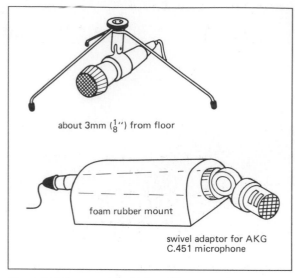

about 3mm ($\frac{1}{8}$'') from floor

foam rubber mount

swivel adaptor for AKG
C.451 microphone

Figure 134 Two specially designed float mounts.

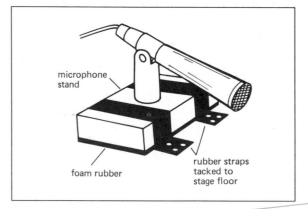

microphone
stand

foam rubber

rubber straps
tacked to
stage floor

Figure 135 Makeshift shock-absorbent mounting for a float microphone.

upon the size of the theatre, the positioning of the loudspeakers, and the acoustics.

Suspended microphones

In figure 136 you can see that in the front section of the stage only the float position is of any use. Microphones from above would be farther away from the performer and more likely to pick up orchestral sounds from the pit. In position B, further up stage, the performer is equidistant from the floats and a possible overhead microphone; which is best? Well, the overhead microphone is farther away from the loudspeakers and should therefore provide a greater level of sound before feedback. It is also farther away from the orchestra pit – another possible advantage.

However, hopefully, the actors will be projecting their voices forwards into the audience and not upwards into the flies. So the answer would be to try both and make the decision on a listening test. Positions C and D would almost certainly be more successfully covered by an overhead microphone.

Because overhead microphones normally have to be at least 18 ft. above the stage it is necessary to use a very directional 'shotgun' microphone. But if, as in position E, the microphone is within 7 or 8 ft. of the performer a shotgun might become too directional; whereas a normal cardioid, while not producing such a hot spot, will almost certainly provide a better sound quality.

The hyper-cardioid gun microphone is usually and most successfully employed in the theatre in this overhead position. It should be suspended a few feet down stage of the actor and aimed roughly at his feet. The microphone will then pick up the voice *plus* some vital reflections from the stage floor. Tone controls will need to be adjusted to give as clear a sound as possible while trying to match the different sound of the float microphone .

Guns are sometimes used from the sides in a more horizontal plane but this has to be thought about carefully as actors have an unfortunate tendency to move about and turn their heads. It is natural for a voice to become less clear when the speaker has his back to the audience (and the float mics), but it is not natural for the voice to recede merely because the actor turns or moves from left to right.

Radio (or wireless) microphones

If an important solo artiste in a musical cannot be heard it is not necessarily the fault of the reinforcement system. It is often a combination of many factors: sometimes it is simply excessive choreography producing a breathless actor facing away from the microphones, or it might be over-heavy orchestrations, an acoustically unsympathetic stage setting, or just a lack of good microphone positions.

The simple way out when faced with this situation is to give the actor a personalized radio (or wireless) microphone. The kit comes in two or three parts, the microphone and transmitter, which can be separate or integrated, and the receiver. The receiver with its aerial (or antenna) simply plugs into an input on the mixer like an ordinary microphone.

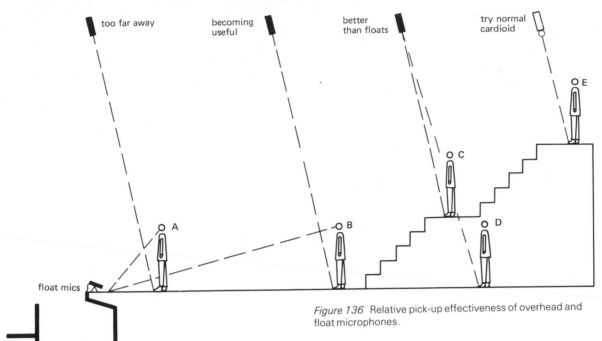

overhead shotgun microphones

too far away

becoming useful

better than floats

try normal cardioid

O E

O C

O A

O B

O D

float mics

Figure 136 Relative pick-up effectiveness of overhead and float microphones.

With the separate microphone the transmitter pack, tuned to the same frequency as the receiver, is secreted somewhere in the actor's clothing. The associated microphone should be fixed so that it remains in a central position, approximately 4 in. (100 mm) below the chin. It is vital to ensure that the head of the microphone is completely exposed or, at most, covered by only a thin piece of material. And it is worth bearing in mind that some radio microphones are susceptible to interference from static electricity generated by materials such as silk, etc. Clothes can also make unfortunate rustling noises against the microphone unless it is firmly fixed.

The microphone will be of the omnidirectional variety, providing a general pick-up to cope with all the head movements. Since it is so near the source of sound there are unlikely to be serious feedback problems. There will, however, be unwanted pick-up problems when an actor wear-

Figure 137 Angling a shotgun microphone.

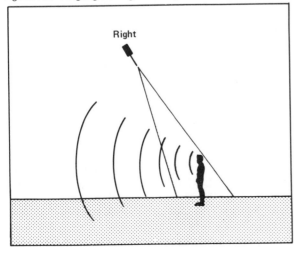

Right

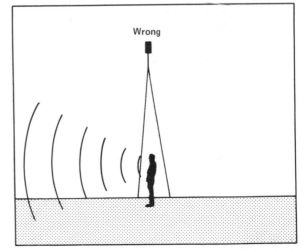

Wrong

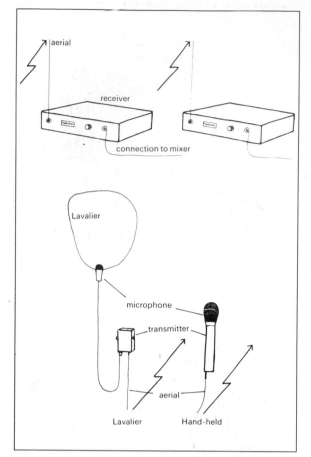

Figure 138 Radiomicrophone systems.

ing a radio microphone comes into range of one who is not. Here the skill of the sound operator will tell in deft yet subtle adjustments of gain.

In Great Britain where the Government exercises a strict control over radio frequencies and a radio transmitting licence is required, the number of microphones it is safe to use within the band of allotted frequencies is limited. Each microphone operates on its own frequency, and when dealing with quantities in excess of four or five there is the ever-present danger of inter-action.

In countries where the licensing laws are a little more lax there is another problem; the likelihood of a hotel paging system or a radio taxi service sharing your frequency. It is not unknown for per-formers to find themselves suddenly doing a double act with a police patrol car.

One of my favourite radio microphone anecdotes arose from the rehearsals of *Joseph and the Amazing Technicolor Dreamcoat* which was in a theatre backing on to where *Godspell*

was playing. In *Joseph* we actually had six radio microphones, so were using up most of the frequencies available.

In the middle of our first sound rehearsal there suddenly appeared beside the mixing desk a breathless and ashen-faced stage manager from the theatre next door. Apparently Joseph's voice was being picked up on the *Godspell* system. Although I pointed out that a touch of the Old Testament might not come amiss in his show, he failed to see the humour of the situation and we were forced to change to another radio fre-quency.

Diversity systems: Even when a transmitter is in close proximity to a receiver, antenna 'drop-outs' can occur due to reflections causing phase cancellations. The diversity system virtually eliminates this problem by employing for each transmitter two antennae with two receivers which automatically switch to the stronger of the two signals.

Distribution amplifier: It is possible for a number of receivers operating on different fre-quencies to share a single antenna. However, a distribution amplifier is necessary to compensate for losses in signal strength.

Riser microphones

Although microphones rising out of the stage floor are no longer in fashion they are sometimes required, especially for cabaret and night-club work. They can be mechanically operated by means of a hand-winch or an electric motor. The more sophisticated motorized risers can be made to stop at any height and they will also disappear smoothly and silently through the stage floor, closing the trap afterwards. With any riser it is essential to mute the microphone while the mechanism is in operation.

Hand-held microphones

For the cabaret or concert performer and for some musicals hand-held microphones are called for. They may be either radios or con-ventional microphones with trailing leads. If the musical backing is on stage it will be necessary to use a very directional microphone (hyper-cardioid) and one which is designed to be used close to the mouth. Both of these factors will help exclude orchestral sounds and allow the voice to

Figure 139 Less chance of feedback from a monitor loud speaker with a directional microphone.

predominate. This type of microphone will have a built in 'windshield' or 'pop-gag' to stop explosive breath sounds. Other microphones designed for close work under less stringent conditions – either on a stand or in the hand – will be straightforward cardioids with, perhaps, optional windshields for use as necessity dictates. Some performers find a very directional microphone difficult to handle because one can so easily move 'off-mike'.

The directional properties of the microphone become even more significant if the performer is using monitor loudspeakers with a foldback signal of his voice plus whatever else he wishes to hear from the orchestra. You can see in figure 139 how easily feedback can result with a non-directional microphone.

Amplifying musical instruments

There are differing techniques for amplifying musical instruments, but most of these employ a directional microphone placed as near the source of sound as possible; e.g. near the bridge of a violin, the bell of a wind instrument, the struck surface of a drum or cymbal, the loudspeaker of an electric guitar or organ, and so on.

There are available *contact microphones* which are actually attached to the sounding-boards of instruments like pianos, harps, and double basses, where the microphone reacts to the vibrations of the sounding-board. The main advantage is the exclusion of pick-up from other

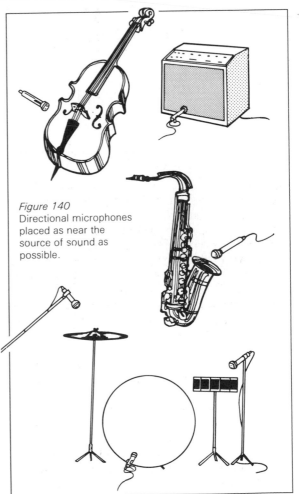

Figure 140
Directional microphones placed as near the source of sound as possible.

instruments. But some people feel that the reproduction is not always faithful to the original.

With electronic instruments there is an excellent way of ensuring a 'clean' sound. This is with the use of a little plugging unit called a *direct injection box*. This box accepts the feed at the preamplifier stage from the guitar or keyboard and splits it two ways: one into the instument's own amplifier in the normal way, and the other straight into the mixer. So a microphone is not used at all. The signal is directly injected into the mixer. Some instrument amplifiers have an output suitable for sending a direct signal to the mixer.

There are also *microphone inserts* of different types especially designed to be inserted into various wind instruments. The object again is to obtain as clean a sound as possible. But no matter what microphone technique is employed the procedure of balancing the orchestra remains unchanged.

In order to obtain a good overall sound it is necessary first to concentrate on individual instruments and then on individual sections of the orchestra. For instance we might take the string section and first listen to the violins, adjusting the tone controls as necessary and, perhaps, adding some reverberation. (By the way, always start a session with the tone controls in the zero position, or flat). When each violin is sounding good and they are balanced one with another, switch them off and carry out the same operation with the violas, then the cellos, and then the double bass. Having set the internal balances within the string section, listen to them together and set an overall balance.

When the complete string sound is to your satisfaction move on to the brass, woodwind, drums, percussion, etc., gradually building up the orchestra until all the sections are balanced. Solo instruments – piano, harp, organ – can now be blended in, plus backing vocals and finally the lead singer or singers.

If certain instruments are being amplified in an orchestra pit for a show which has sound reinforcement the same principles apply, but one is usually trying to give a boost to the weaker instruments whilst maintaining a natural sound overall. Here the use of *stereo* is a very important factor, for if one sees and hears the violins in the left-hand side of the pit it can be very disconcerting to have an amplified violin sound coming from the right-hand side of the auditorium. Moreover, this effect will be most noticeable when the microphones are receiving the greatest level of sound from the instruments, for when the instruments are playing quietly proportionally less sound will be coming from the loudspeakers. Therefore as the dynamic range, the loudness, changes the 'sound image' will constantly appear to be moving from left to right and back again. (Alternatively, if the loudspeaker installation consists of an overhead array – as discussed earlier – the 'sound image' will appear to shift up and down.)

Wherever there is live amplification *feedback* is the omnipresent enemy. Its occurrence may be minimized, as we have seen, by the correct choice of equipment and the way it is set up. But the ultimate responsibility lies with the Sound Operator.

A good operator will make good use of the rehearsal period for experimentation to find the best combinations of microphones and tone settings, and the thresholds of feedback. Every major change to any of the controls will have been plotted in detail so that at any given point in the show it is immediately clear which microphones should be in use. It is essential to have this basic information to preclude major errors during the stress of a live performance.

But the essence of good sound balancing is to use one's ears. Meticulously follow the plot so as to get the correct fader to its prescribed setting at the right moment and, once it is there, listen and be ready to adjust.

Figure 141 Direct injection.

Figure 142 Microphone insert.

Photograph 40 Shure SM 17 miniature dynamic omnidirectional microphone specially designed for use with acoustic stringed instruments. *Photo courtesy Shure Electronics Ltd*

A plea. Do not become a knob twiddler. The best engineers do 99 per cent of their knob twiddling during rehearsals and, perhaps, the very initial stages of the first public performance. After that their concentration is reserved for the main faders and the attainment of that elusive perfect balance.

Company. This musical (with music and lyrics by Stephen Sondheim) was first produced on Broadway in 1970 and later transferred to London. It was, incidentally, the first time an entire American show – cast, sets, costumes and all – was air-lifted across the Atlantic. Only the sound and lighting equipment were English.

As the cast were scheduled to arrive only three days before the first public preview, leaving very little time for technical experimentation, I flew to New York to prime myself with the problems before they arrived.

Jack Mann, the American sound expert, had carried out an extremely impressive job on a very tricky show. And I was able to benefit not only by his intimate knowledge of the production but by the very good rig which he had evolved during the pre-Broadway tour.

The orchestra was large, twenty-four, for a small cast musical and included two electric guitars and an electric organ. Experience has shown that 200 watts or so of sound under the control of three musicians usually makes for headaches (in every sense of the word). The volume levels tend to creep up during a period of performances with the rest of the orchestra trying to compete. And the smallest adjustment of a guitar amplifier can completely obliterate a carefully worked out sound balance.

It is essential therefore that the sound man has a good working relationship with an understanding musical director. And we were fortunate enough on that show to have one of the best. Hal Hastings used to say that he had a method of judging the balance of his orchestra to the stage, and it went like this: 'I reckon it is my job to control the orchestra so that from my position in the front of the pit I can hear all the lyrics from the stage. After that it is up to the sound man.' Nothing could be fairer than that.

The lyrics in the case of *Company* were very important yet often very difficult to get across. Even on the cast album the complex orchestrations and vocal arrangements make it hard to discern certain passages. On stage we had the added complication of a large open skeletal set on several levels with very few microphone positions near enough to the singers to be suitable for the precise pick-up required.

An example of the kind of problem encountered was for the number 'Someone is Waiting'. The leading man starts singing stage centre then walks to a staircase stage left which transports him, still singing, to a 7 foot (2·1 m) level. Moving stage right he now reaches a motor-driven elevator which takes him to a higher level, then on to some more stairs leading down to a second elevator which drops him back to stage level for the final note of the song.

Throughout the number a fairly heavy orchestration was augmented by an off-stage chorus (on echo). And at certain points during the number other members of the cast, widely dispersed around the set, also had to join in.

Single float microphones were used for the beginning and end with a series of gun microphones for the movement around the various levels. The sound operator literally followed the leading man around the set so that at no time were there more than two microphones live for this purpose. The pick-up of the other people on the set was from the nearest float or gun; but strictly on cue as necessary. In this way a 'tight' sound was maintained. The off-stage chorus, watching the musical director via closed-circuit television, posed no problems of feedback, being

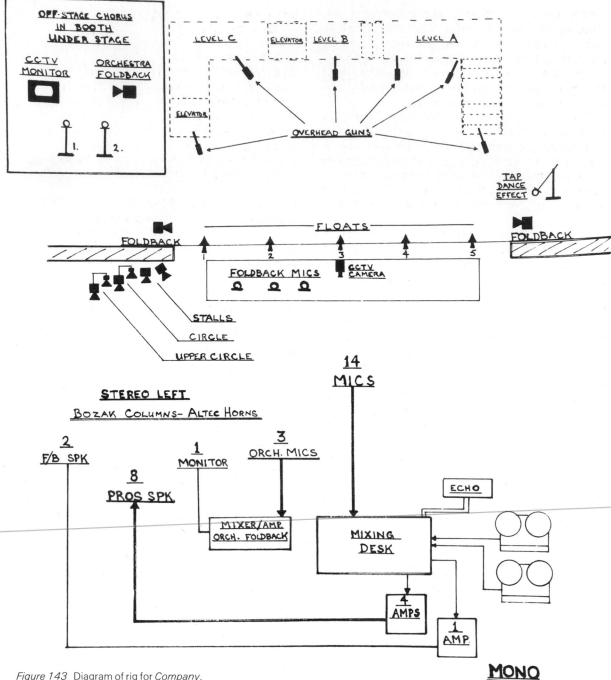

Figure 143 Diagram of rig for *Company*.

well out of the way. But they did pose a problem of balance and clarity. Originally the two microphones for the five singers were positioned in the wings where they could both hear the orchestra and see the conductor. But as many of the backing vocals occurred during scene changes an

alternative position had to be found. Under stage was first tried with the door to the orchestra pit propped open to obtain a view of the conductor. Unfortunately, the microphones picked up the drum kit and brass section almost as much as the singers. So the door had to be closed and the microphones moved to a quieter corner of the understage area. The brick walls and concrete floor created very unpleasant acoustics, so a carpet was laid and heavy drapes hung around the walls. The microphones were omnidirectional and mounted on high stands with one for the ladies and one for the gentlemen.

The gun microphones on stage were on brackets fixed to overhead lighting bars. Each was positioned about 3 feet (1 m) downstage of the required area of pick-up, pointing roughly at the feet of the singer. A great deal of experimentation with tone controls was carried out to equalize the guns to the better quality float microphones.

There was one joke effect of a purposely over-amplified tap dance. In this particular number there were short breaks for single members of the cast to perform short tap solos. The director wanted to overdo the whole thing and bring the float way up. Hoever, this did not have the required effect. So instead the float mikes were killed completely and we had a dancer off stage tapping away on a suitably hard surface some twelve inches (300 mm) away from a directional microphone. The result was extremely comic.

Another interesting effect was achieved when the cast were called upon to sustain a very long note while moving rapidly about the entire set. Not only did they run out of breath but the microphone coverage could not be that good. The problem was solved by recording the note so that the tape could take over as the live voices faded. The sound operator coped with the transition so well that even I could never tell where it happened.

Pippin (1973) and *The Good Companions* (1974). For these productions, both in the same theatre as *Company*, we added microphones in the orchestra pit, not necessarily to make it louder, but to give the composers and orchestrators the balance and presence they required. A string or woodwind section will sound very dead in most orchestra pits and a harp, string bass or piano will often not be heard at all. So some subtle reinforcement with very directional microphones placed as near to the instruments as possible can compensate. However, it is not good enough to leave all these microphones open at set levels throughout an entire show. A balance must be found for each musical item. There will be occasions when certain microphones must be killed because they

are, for example, picking up and over-amplifying a loud brass passage.

For operational reasons it is a good plan to use a sub-mixer for the orchestra. The internal balance can then be preset and brought up on cue with a master fader. It also gives scope for general variations in level during the number.

There is an old lighting trick of fading up that extra bit of light for the end of each song. This is to give a lift which will encourage applause. A similar lift may be obtained with the judicious use of the orchestra master fader.

Billy. At the Theatre Royal, Drury Lane, London, was one of the biggest headaches of all, having an enormous permanent box set made of steel clad in hardboard. Drury Lane is one of London's largest theatres and the set itself was 4 feet (1·2 m) deeper from footlights to back wall than the largest stage on Broadway. From the point of view of acoustics, it was like working on a completely empty reverberant stage. A close microphone technique seemed to be called for, but where to place them?

Gun microphones were of no use because of the height. Most of the staircases and platforms were flat steel motorized units with nowhere to hide anything. The one conventional piece of scenery, a two storey cut-away house on a truck, was seized upon and microphones were set behind the television, amongst the tea cups on the table, over the doorway in the hall and beside the wardrobe in the bedroom. A few more positions were found for 'specials', i.e. microphones specifically placed to do a job in perhaps only one song. After that we had to rely on floats and radios.

The star, Michael Crawford, who was on stage for the entire performance apart from speedy costume changes, wore two radio microphones (photograph 41). A great deal of dancing and acrobatics sometimes made for broken aerials (antennae) or intermittent connections, when the standby would immediately be brought into service. Three other characters also used radios, though not for all their numbers. It depended upon the orchestration, the costumes they were wearing and their position on stage relative to the floats.

One of the numbers was completely on tape with the cast miming. This posed no particular problem except for the transition from live to taped sound. A good signal from loudspeakers on stage as well as from the front-of-house sys-

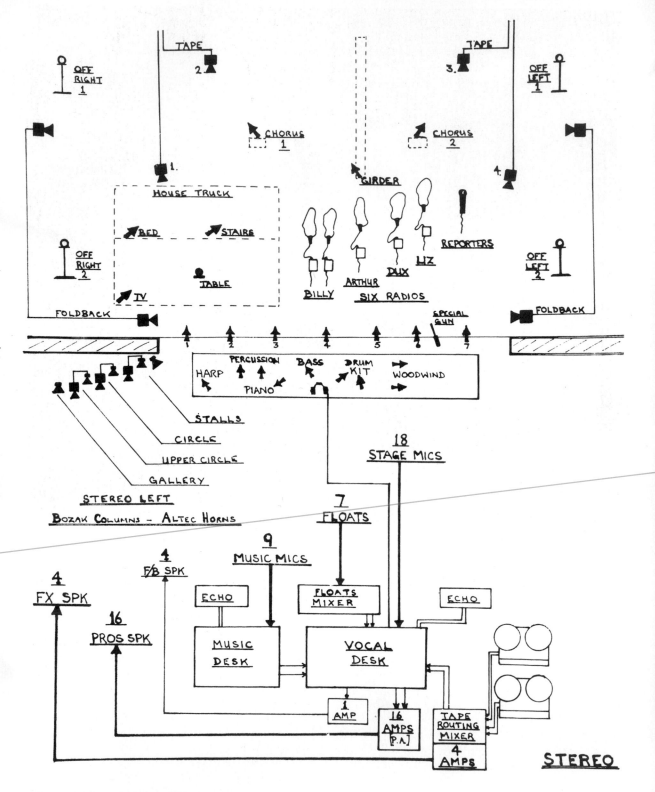

Figure 144 Diagram of rig for *Billy*.

Photograph 41 Michael Crawford, star of *Billy* at the Theatre Royal, Drury Lane, holds his radio transmitter while sound operator, Claire Laver, adjusts the microphone. 1974

tem was required otherwise the sound would have appeared to have a hole in it.

Mixed live and taped sound. In certain shows, particularly large scale revues, it is necessary or advantageous to have all or part of the vocals prerecorded. Keeping the orchestra synchronized with the tape is the essence of this operation. This is done by recording a separate 'click track' giving a very definite and constant beat for the musical director (and sometimes also the drummer) to hear via a headset. It can be very effective to have a recorded choral arrangement from loudspeakers on stage with the live chorus and soloists also singing. The microphone sys-

tem picks everything up and blends it into a whole.

Jesus Christ Superstar (1979). The London production came after the American, the Australian and several European versions. Originally a record album, it was turned into a show with varying degrees of success in different countries. Jim Sharman, who directed an ambitious stage production and a static concert version in Australia, was asked to direct it in England. The musical director, Anthony Bowles, had worked on the Paris production. And they were agreed that musically the concert versions worked best.

They determined, therefore, to produce the show on a set which precluded a great deal of movement and to use a close microphone technique throughout. Even the chorus whenever possible would be on individual hand microphones. With a multi-microphone installation for the orchestra as well it should be possible to obtain a recording studio type of balance.

The problem of the distribution of microphones was resolved by having downstage in the floats three riser microphones which could be lifted off for hand use, plus six other hand microphones (colour coded for easy identification) situated around the stage. Three general pick-up microphones were placed upstage although they were seldom used. There were eighteen hand microphones for chorus use distributed around the upper levels of the set plus two for off-stage choruses.

We had a lot of trouble in the final scene trying to pick up the actor playing Jesus when he was suspended on the cross. Eventually a small black omnidirectional microphone attached to a strip of metal was fixed to the cross so that it stuck out somewhere above his right shoulder. A bass cut and mid lift at the mixing desk compensated for the fact that he was 'off-mike'.

The thirty musicians were split up with the main orchestra in the pit, the rock group in two sections either side of the acting area on stage, and an overspill percussion section in a separate space off-stage. In all thirty-three directional microphones were used for the orchestra plus a direct feed into a line input channel from the synthesizer. With the vocal microphones the grand total amounted to sixty-seven channels.

In order to control and balance such a large installation, a special mixing desk was devised. It was obviously not physically possible to manipulate this number of faders so a certain amount of sub-grouping was incorporated in the design. For example, one channel would control four 'woodwind' microphones. Each microphone had its own preset gain control but one channel fader with equalization, echo, panning, etc. mastered the lot. Certain chorus microphones were also grouped in a similar fashion.

The desk was now reduced to twenty-six main channels, which was still too much for one man

Photograph 42 Jesus Christ Superstar. The loudspeakers can be clearly seen around the proscenium. Two speakers placed overhead on the lighting grid cover the front stalls. The three riser microphones are downstage and the chorus hand microphones are distributed around the ramps above the rock group positions. *Photo courtesy Audio Magazine*

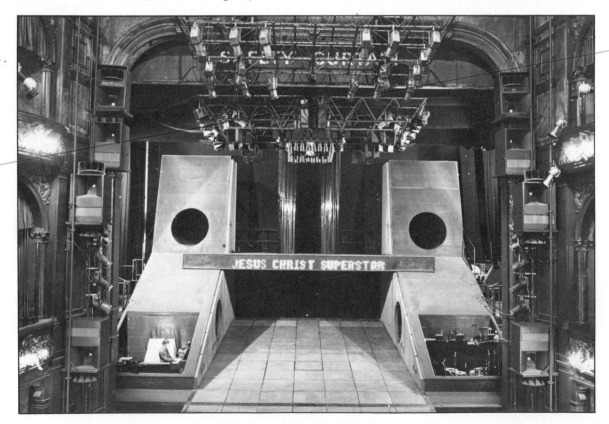

Photograph 43 *Jesus Christ Superstar*. Dave Roberts, one of the two sound operators, adjusts one of the foldback amplifiers positioned under stage. *Photo courtesy Audio Magazine*

Photograph 44 *Jesus Christ Superstar*. Roger Norwood controls the vocal end of the 80-channel Alice mixing desk. *Photo courtesy Audio Magazine*

speakers, as in a normal recording studio, but at the same time making sure that the sound via the speakers enhanced the natural sound of the live orchestra in the auditorium.

In New York they tried covering the pit completely with glass. And the conductor stood in a perspex bubble. This presumably made balancing an easier task but the theatrical and exciting sound of a live orchestra was lost. So the glass had to go.

The musical director was very insistent that *Superstar* should not become for the audience what he termed 'an aural assault course'. The purpose of the sound sytem was to produce a studio quality balance with the added excitement of a live performance. There are very few places where the music is really loud. But there are many places where just the piano or guitars are backing a quiet solo. The final number in Act One ranges from unaided solo voice with quiet piano to close microphone with full strings, brass, percussion, rock group and all. The proper use and control of this kind of dynamic range made *Jesus Christ Superstar* a unique experience.

to cope with. So the desk was split down the middle into voice and music channels to allow for two operators.

The loudspeakers in the auditorium were eight Altec 'Voice of the Theatre' systems with bass bins and horns, plus two smaller units for front stalls fill-in. All the loudspeakers were separately powered to allow for stereo.

The initial orchestra balancing session was under the control of Michael Moor who is a first class studio recording engineer. With his skill and experience he was able to produce the right sound from each instrument to please the musical director, and blend them into an exciting overall sound. He had the unusual task of not only balancing the orchestra through loud-

Since 1976 I have been less involved with shows as my time has been taken up with the design of permanent sound and communications systems. In this period the number of big new musicals produced per year has significantly decreased, largely because of escalating costs making it a less viable risk for commercial backers. But despite these economic strictures the trend for the major musicals which do see the light of day is very much to place more emphasis on the importance of audibility. This can be seen by comparing the relative costs for sound and lighting equipment for a selection of London West End productions over the past few years. It should be noted that the lighting figures do not include the lighting switchboard and dimmers as in the UK these have traditionally been part of the permanent equipment installed in the theatres.

Production	Year	Theatre	Seating Capacity	£ Pounds Sterling Lighting	Sound	% of Total
Cabaret	1964	Palace	1400	4,913	1,357	(21·6)
Fiddler on the Roof	1967	Her Majesty's	1285	5,808	1,382	(19·2)
A Little Night Music	1975	Adelphi	1500	9,920	5,400	(35·2)
Kismet (revival)	1978	Shaftesbury	1300	11,800	10,060	(46·0)
Evita	1980	Prince Edward	1666	32,821	57,600	(63·7)

One of the more interesting shows from an audio point of view has been *Cats* (New London Theatre, 1981) because it was staged with the audience on two levels around two-thirds of an arena stage with the orchestra to one side at the rear. The highly balletic style of this open stage production – which on several occasions called for the cast to perform amongst the audience – necessitated the liberal use of radio microphones and a distributed loudspeaker system.

The designer, Abe Jacob, specified a forty-channel mixer with eight sub-groups and eight output groups. The flexible output arrangement allowed him to mix the orchestral and vocal sounds in varying ratios to different sets of loud-speakers. The main source loudspeakers are two splayed pairs of full range monitors (*Meyer UPA 1*) suspended above balcony level to the left and right at the rear of the stage, plus four similar loudspeakers suspended above and around the acting area; the rear stereo system being mainly for the orchestra and the mono stage system –

Figure 145 Diagram of rig for *Cats*.

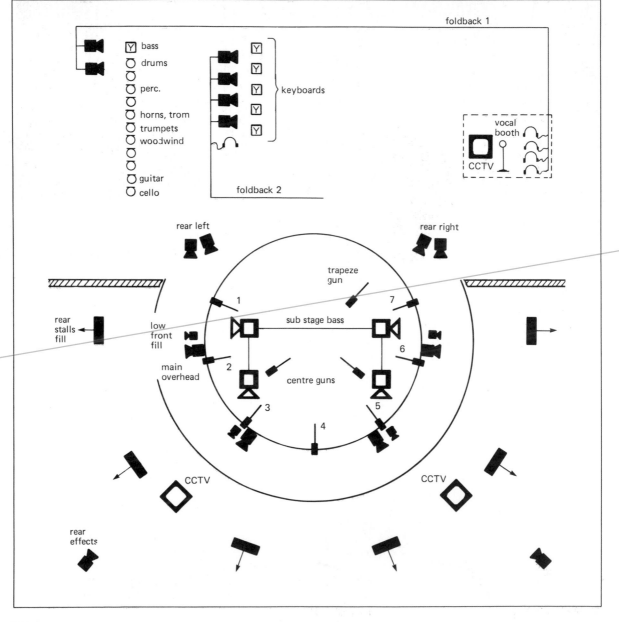

Photograph 45 *Cats* at the New London Theatre 1981.
Photo courtesy Cameron Mackintosh Ltd and the Really Useful Co. Ltd

fed via a short delay – being mainly for vocals, but with a mix of orchestra to add body to the overall sound.

Vocal fill to the rear under balcony areas was provided by six *Electrovoice LR4B* columns suspended on their sides from the underside of the balcony and fed via digital delay. Vocal fill to the front seating area of the main floor was covered by eight small *Auratone 5C* loudspeakers mounted on the front edge of the circular stage.

In order to increase the low frequency content, particularly of the orchestral sound, four bass loudspeakers were placed beneath the stage and fed with a mono signal via a dividing network.

Finally, two *Meyer UPA 1* systems were installed in the rear corners of the auditorium for panoramic and surround-sound effects.

Because of the location of the orchestra and the rear stereo loudspeaker system the cast did not require stage monitors except for one small *Hot Spot* to cover a dead area in the centre at the rear. However, it was necessary to provide monitor headsets to an off-stage vocal booth with the same mix of keyboards and vocals being sent to the bass guitar and drummer who were provided with a *Hot Spot* each. A separate mix of vocals and rhythm section was sent to the keyboards and the musical director.

Closed circuit television monitors were suspended below the balcony so that the cast could catch a glimpse of the musical director for those important cut-offs at the ends of numbers. A third television monitor was installed in the vocal booth where anyone not on stage and not completely out of breath went to sing.

The general microphone pick-up was from seven shotguns suspended above the perimeter of the stage, plus two farther in for centre pick-up and a 'special' up-stage for a particularly important area on the set. All the principals wore wireless microphones with nine systems shared between eleven performers.

The orchestra had a complement of thirteen microphones for acoustic instruments and six direct injection boxes for the electric guitar and the various keyboards.

Sound effects were derived from four NAB cartridge machines and fed into the eight mixer output groups through a quad panorama unit.

The 1981 revival of *The Sound of Music* was a good example of a distributed loudspeaker system for a more traditional stage format. The original intention was to try and create a natural sounding reinforcement, but the Apollo Victoria in London is a very large theatre and once it had proved necessary to provide a substantial amount of amplification for the youngest of the seven Von Trapp children the designer, Julian Beech, decided to use radio microphones for all the principals. For although most of them were well able to be heard with a modicum of assistance from the float microphones it was considered important to maintain a consistency in the style of sound. So nine radios were alloted to the main characters with two more to be passed between those performers who had less solo singing to do.

The general pick-up was mainly from seven float microphones, with two shotguns on the downstage wings for occasional side-fill and three 'specials' on the set. There was also one microphone for an off-stage chorus and a prop 1930s-style microphone with a modern insert.

In the orchestra pit each of the seven strings was equipped with a bridge microphone with stand microphones for the cello and harp. Two general coverage microphones were employed for the brass and woodwind sections just to add a little sparkle to the overture and other non-vocal passages.

The strings were individually miked partly to add some weight to this section of the orchestra and partly as a means of changing the acoustics by adding artificial reverberation. For example, a great deal of echo is used for the Strauss-type waltzes in the ballroom scene whereas very little is evident during the outdoor concert later in the show; although in this scene repeat echo is used very effectively on the prop microphone to simulate an outdoor PA system.

The loudspeaker rig is based mainly upon the *Meyer UPA 1*. Each side of the proscenium there

Photograph 46 Julian Beech at the sound control for *The ...d of Music*, 1981. *Photo by Steve Stephens ...ography Ltd*

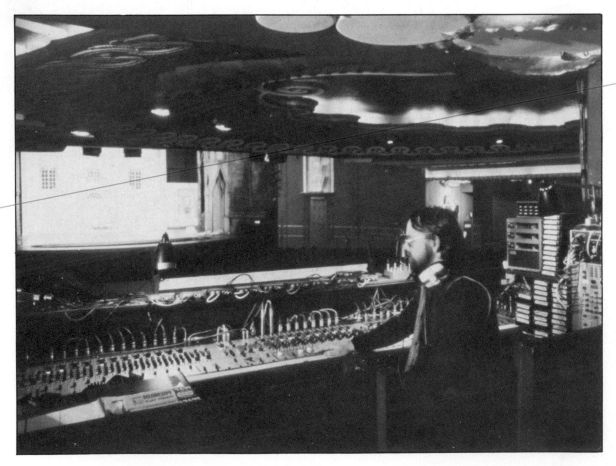

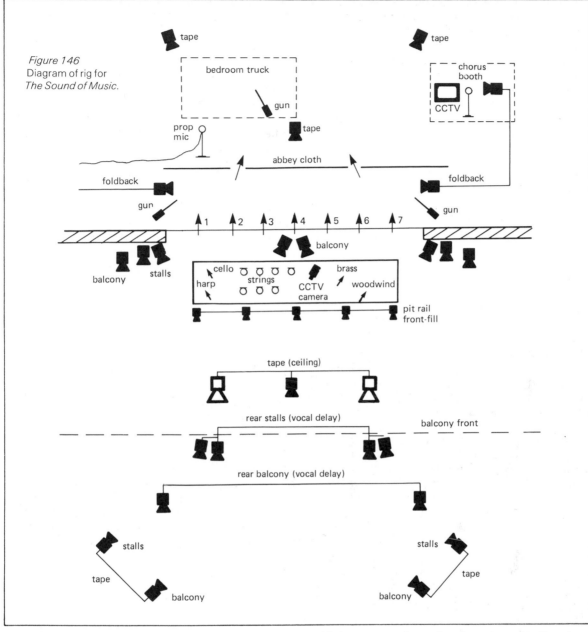

Figure 146
Diagram of rig for
The Sound of Music.

is a pair for the stalls with single units above for the balcony supplemented by a further pair above the centre of the proscenium. Suspended below the high balcony are two more pairs of similar loudspeakers on a delay line, with another pair hanging from the ceiling to boost the rear third of the balcony. Five small *Goodmans* bookshelf loudspeakers positioned along the front edge of the orchestra pit to add a very slight vocal lift complete the reinforcement system in the auditorium. The foldback provision is very basic

with just two column loudspeakers for the stage and one monitor for the off-stage chorus.

Sound effects from NAB cartridge machines are fed through a separate mixer to a system of seven *Bose 800* loudspeakers distributed around the stage and auditorium with two large bass loudspeakers for storm effects mounted in the dome above the centre of the auditorium.

This was a simple, well-planned rig producing an obviously amplified yet evenly controlled sound.

13
Outdoor concert systems

with acknowledgement to Bill Kelsey

When estimating the size of P.A. systems required, the following points should be taken into consideration:

(a) The nature of the music to be played (a 'heavy' rock group obviously requires greater power capabilities than a string quartet).
(b) Any local government restrictions on maximum sound pressure levels.
(c) Anticipated size of the audience.
(d) The budget.

Power and sound pressure levels

As a very rough rule-of-thumb 1 watt per person in an audience of 20,000 or more seems to work remarkably well. The law of diminishing returns applies here – increasing the SPL of a 50,000 watt system by 3 dB requires the addition of another 50,000 watts of power capability.

About another 3dB can be achieved by stacking loudspeakers correctly on top of each other as this tends to concentrate power in the vertical plane, thereby increasing directivity (this directivity factor is sometimes referred to as the Q of a loudspeaker).

Delay towers. However, the odd 3 or even 6 dB will not get you very far with a really large audience, in which case the simplest answer is to use delay towers some 60–70 metres away from the stage with the signal from the main system electronically delayed so as to arrive at the listeners' ears a few milliseconds after the main P.A. signal. Normally two towers are not adequate because if you happen to be standing near to one of them you will be conscious of a monstrous delay between that tower and the one on the other side of the auditorium. It is therefore

suggested, as in Figure 147, that at least four towers are necessary. The loudspeakers would be mounted on a platform some 3–5 metres up in the air so as not to deafen nearby spectators and to afford them a reasonably clear view of the stage.

Multi-way loudspeaker systems

For systems of this size the frequency spectrum would be split three, four, or even five ways with different kinds of loudspeakers specifically designed to handle particular bands of frequencies. Although the trend during the 1970s was to increase the number of ways in a system there is now a movement, brought about by an improvement in the performance of drivers, to return to the three-way configuration.

Early three-way systems were based upon the traditional bass bin and mid/high frequency horn combination but with a tweeter adding some extra 'sizzle' to the top (around 8,000–15,000 Hz). Later it was thought that to require a loudspeaker, particularly a horn, to produce a flat response at high levels from a cross-over point at around 800 Hz up to 8–10,000 Hz was asking a bit much. Equalizers were certainly available to flatten some of the more unpleasant peaks, but these tended to decrease the efficiency of the entire unit at a time when greater sound levels were being called for. It was therefore decided to split this range into lower and upper mid. Cone drivers for the lower mid became very fashionable because horns are generally considered to produce a very hard sound in these frequencies. So we had the bass from about 40–500 Hz with the lower mid up to around 1,500–2,000 Hz, the upper mid to, say, 7,000 Hz and the tweeter going up to 15,000 Hz. It was

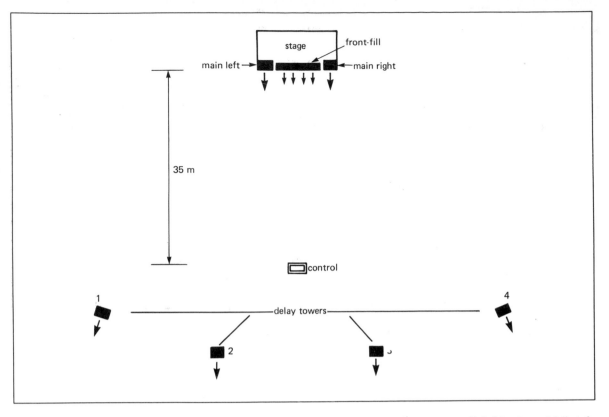

Figure 147 Loudspeaker arrangement for outdoor rock concert with control typically 30–50 metres from the stage and four delay towers.

then but a short step to split the bass frequencies into two to increase efficiency at the lower end of the spectrum. And that gave us the five-part system. Incidentally, a great deal of nonsense is talked about the amount of bass which loud-speakers are supposed to handle. Although many people like to think that their systems go below 40 Hz it is pretty difficult to achieve any power at these frequencies and the physical dimensions of an enclosure which will produce 30 Hz are quite substantial. And it is questionable whether there is any practical application below 40 Hz in a concert system anyhow.

Now that drivers are available which will happily produce a smooth response from 1,000–15,000 handling around 40 watts it makes sense to return to the three-way system. For the greater the number of different types of loudspeaker in a stack the greater the number of cross-over points. And it is at these cross-over points that phasing problems can appear, tending to leave great holes in the response. With such a number of notches or peaks there is a fair

chance that at least one will fall in the middle of a key frequency band.

The phasing problems arise partly because most electronic dividing networks themselves produce severe phase shifting and partly because of the varying path lengths of different types of loudspeaker in a stack. For example, the path length of a bass folded horn loudspeaker is clearly greater than that of a radial horn, and as it is not realistic to place one eight feet farther back in the stack than the other it has to be accepted that where the two path lengths cross over there will be something severely wrong. This is one of the reasons why smaller less efficient bass loud-speakers are favoured by some engineers. They are easy to stack and their path lengths are similar to the rest of the system. True, they will require more driving, but amplifier power is relatively cheap when compared to the cost of trucking – and even the cost of wood.

So, typically, a loudspeaker array might now be split as follows:

Bass	40 up to 500 or 800 Hz
Mid	up to 1,500 or 2,000 Hz
HF	up to 15,000

High frequency loss with distance

It is common knowledge that as you move away from a sound source in a completely flat open environment the signal becomes steadily weaker. In fact, if there are no reflections and no wind or extremes of temperature to affect the sound waves it has been calculated that every time the distance from the sound source is doubled a loss of 6dB will be experienced. For example a sound level measured at 120dB ten metres from the stage would become 114dB at twenty metres, 108dB at forty metres and 102dB at eighty metres, etc. But this is under ideal conditions. Normally, wind, temperature and humidity will make this situation worse – particularly in the higher frequencies.

Engineers sometimes try to achieve a flat response up to 15,000 Hz by adjusting the equalizers at the control position, which could well be some 50 metres from the stage, forgetting that the attenuation in the open air of high frequencies is very severe. Consequently the audience near the stage will be made to suffer with an excess of 15,000 Hz bursting their eardrums.

One of the ways to compensate for the high frequency attenuation, and to relieve the spectators at the front of the audience, is to have very directional high frequency loudspeakers for the rear of the auditorium mounted as high as possible at the top of the stacks. Separate short-throw horns would then be used for the front section, perhaps with acoustic lenses to provide a wide dispersion with a gentle roll off at the edges. It is also quite common, particularly if there is a high stage, to have front-fill loud-speakers below the front edge of the stage. Apart from the fact that the side stacks might be some 10–15 metres apart, the high frequency content from this central source will be a significant factor in combating the blurring effect caused by the artistes' foldback monitors.

Of course, the use of delay towers in the auditorium greatly assists this problem of high frequency loss by decreasing the length of throw.

Separate system for vocals

Splitting the instrumental and vocal content of the sound to different sets of loudspeakers is by no means universal practice although it is simple to achieve and has very worthwhile benefits; for the vocal loudspeakers can be chosen and equalized specifically to suit the vocal require-

ments and a more robust system can be employed for the instruments. After all, it is asking a great deal from a loudspeaker array to cope with bass guitars and drums while, at the same time, handling the much more delicate and subtle sounds of the human voice.

With a large audience most engineers do not bother to mix in stereo because for most of the audience it would be a pointless exercise while to those at the side near the front it would be a distinct disadvantage. In which case the stereo facilites on the mixer are available and can be used to good effect with a split vocal/instrumental system. If the outputs of the mixer are wired with one side to the mono vocal loud-speakers and the other side to the instrumental stacks it is then possible to route each channel proportionately to both systems; e.g. with the pan control fully clockwise a particular channel would be routed fully to the vocal system whereas turning it gradually anti-clockwise would bleed it into the music system.

The control

The mixing console position is normally in the audience 30–50 metres from the main sound system. A typical mixing console would contain 30–50 input channels into 4–8 sub-groups eventually mixing down to a single stereo output. The mixing console would have 6–8 effects sends and insert points on every channel. Most artistes would currently expect all of the signal processing equipment available to them in the recording studio, and a comprehensive sound system would therefore include effects such as harmonizers, reverberation units, repeat echo units, digital delay lines, noise gates, parametric equalizers, compressors/limiters all situated at, and controlled from, the mixing console position. The system would be set up using 1/3 octave graphic equalizers and a 1/3 octave real time spectrum analyser.

We have spoken in this chapter and elsewhere about the dangers of misusing graphic equalizers; compressor/limiters also can be set so that they detract from the end result. They are very useful for controlling certain instruments and, indeed, some voices, from excessive

Photograph 47 Rig for Barclay James Harvest concert on the steps of the Reichstag in Berlin, August 1980. Four delay towers were used for the far audience.
Photograph 47A Part of the audience of 160,000

dynamics and they can be used to good effect on the outputs of a mixer to protect loudspeakers and eardrums alike. But there is a tendency for some engineers to compress to such an extent that there is virtually no variation in the dynamic range throughout an entire concert. This is a pity because the interest and excitement which can be created by both subtle and dramatic variations in sound level are lost. The same criticism can be levelled at broadcast and recording engineers who seem to have accepted that everything must be geared to the very limited dynamic range of the tiny loudspeakers in portable radios. There is also this fallacy about loudness equalling excitement. Loudness equals loudness, which after a while appears less loud.

On the same topic but in a slightly different setting, I was once told in all seriousness by the producer of London's leading theatre restaurant that the excruciating sound level must not drop at any point during the show as the customers would start talking and lose interest in the performance. What faith he must have in his production, I thought – but refrained from utterance.

Stage monitor system

A completely separate system is used to enable the musicians to hear themselves. A separate mixing console with, typically, 20–30 inputs and 6–12 outputs is used in order that each musician can be furnished with his own individual speaker system and his own individual 'mix' (in terms of both 'balance' and equalization). Each output has its own third-octave graphic equalizer and the monitor balance engineer can listen to each musician's mix on headphones via PFL (pre-fade listen). There is usually a stack of cabinets either side of the stage for a general monitor mix, with a somewhat smaller cabinet behind the drummer and several small wedge-shaped monitors for vocalists and lead instrumentalists.

One of the reasons why P.A. systems have not improved dramatically during the past few years is because the on-stage monitoring has become bigger and bigger and louder and louder so that in smaller venues sometimes there is as much equipment for the performers as there is for the audience. Imagine, for instance, the confused sound you would experience if you were a microphone in a pop concert: first you would hear the vocalist, followed a couple of milliseconds later by his wedge monitor, then a few milliseconds later the live sound of the drums, guitars etc. on stage, and a few milliseconds after that the side-fill monitors and then the main system. Multiply this confusion by the number of microphones on the stage, put it all out through the main loudspeakers and it is a miracle that any semblance of the original sound is reproduced at all.

The future

Loudspeakers are, and always have been, the weakest link in the sound system and any major developments in the future hopefully will be in this area. It is, however, largely true that there have been no dramatic improvements in loudspeaker technology since the 1930s and there seem to be no major developments in the foreseeable future. It is safe to assume that mixing consoles will become more complex and, perhaps, digital with microprocessor control, the number of external effects will increase and there will be a general move to make everything more compact in an attempt to offset rising transportation costs.

14

Permanent sound installations

Evolution

In this final chapter I should like to discuss some permanent sound installations which have been specifically designed for various new theatres in Great Britain. The post-war boom in theatre building in this country got under way during the early sixties. Not surprisingly, sound was, at the start, very much an 'also-ran'. Architects, on the whole, spent the majority of their budget on the fabric of the building, leaving a relatively small percentage for technical facilities. And it was usually decided to spend that money on stage mechanics and lighting. Lighting was then very much in vogue, with lighting designers at last being accepted as necessary rather than as a luxury. Great interest was also being aroused by the new smaller and more flexible electronic switchboards.

Nonetheless, a breed of very cost conscious sound consoles evolved, usually incorporating two tape decks with auto-stop and remote start facilities, plus two disc replay units, because tape was still not entirely trusted or understood by some of the older theatre technicians. The console might include a separate very basic microphone mixer (with overall treble and bass controls if you were lucky). The tape decks, turntable and microphone mixer with their associated gain controls would each be switchable to either or both of two output channels feeding into two power amplifiers. Loudspeakers operating via 100 volts line would be switchable to either of these amplifiers. Tone controls were minimal, sometimes only appearing as treble and bass boost and cut at the two output stages. All gain controls tended to be rotary as the range of cheap linear faders available today had yet to be introduced. Photograph 48 shows a typical example of one of the more ambitious consoles

of the era. Photograph 49 shows a departure from this format in a 'desk' designed by the author in 1962 for the Old Vic theatre. It incorporates three tape decks and a six-channel microphone mixer selectable to four output groups. Note the quadrant faders and the loudspeaker selection along the top. Another innovation was that the central control booth was actually in the auditorium. After much negotiation the theatre manager grudgingly sacrificed three seats at the back of the stalls! That is why the conditions are so cramped.

The later part of the sixties and the start of the seventies was an evolutionary period during which people became more aware of the possibilities of sound. Input channels were provided with linear faders and tone controls, and instead of operating at line level only they became switchable to microphone or line levels. This meant that the separate little microphone mixer could either be discarded altogether or kept as an extra sub-mixer for the occasional big show. Extra output channels were added to cater for stereo and the growing requirement for multiple and movable sound sources.

At this point theatre sound technicians realized that they had, by a painful process of trial and error and by striving for better standards, produced the kind of mixing desk that recording studios had evolved many years before. With this realization the technical standards of recording and broadcasting studios began to be applied to the theatre. The quality of the equipment immediately improved. This revolution occurred around 1970. A significant improvement in theatre loudspeaker design, however, lagged a few years behind. Although technicians are now aware of the importance of this final link in the

Photograph 48 Tape/disc console at Chichester Festival Theatre in 1961

Photograph 49 The author at the Old Vic theatre in 1963 operating the newly installed sound system for the first production of the National Theatre Company of Great Britain, *Hamlet*.

Photograph 50 Theatre Y Werin: sound mixing desk 1972. Equipment Electrosonic Ltd. *Photo Theatre Projects Consultants Ltd*

audio chain a surprising number of managers, and even some theatre consultants, do not appreciate that the type of loudspeakers and their positioning is probably the most crucial factor in the success or otherwise of any sound system.

Alongside these improvements in the basic sound system there also came a rationalization of the stage manager's facilities. These are, after all, mainly audio orientated, with various paging systems to dressing rooms, technicians, foyers, bars, etc., as well as the necessary cueing and intercommunication services.

The National Theatre of Great Britain

The National Theatre of Great Britain opened its doors in 1976. Standing on the South Bank of the River Thames adjacent to the Royal Festival Hall it actually houses three auditoria plus a central dressing-room block and numerous offices, workshops, rehearsal spaces and public areas. The Olivier Theatre has an open-cum-thrust stage format, while the Lyttelton has a more conventional proscenium style. The Cottesloe is a very versatile studio which can become anything from an arena theatre to something very akin to a Georgian playhouse.

Paging

One of the biggest complications of a multi-theatre building is the possible overlap of paging to general areas both backstage and in the foyers and bars. The problem was solved by giving each stage manager an interior lit surround for each paging button which indicates when the other stage manager is using the system. If the system is occupied and he needs to make an urgent announcement he presses the button and an indicator in the other theatre starts flashing. Should the second stage manager fail to observe this signal he will lose the system after a preset number of seconds, to the other theatre.

In the general dressing room areas paging is via a single distributed loudspeaker system. Each actor can select 'show relay' on an individual loudspeaker in his make-up cubicle. As well as show relay from three theatres there is also the possibility of switching to a fourth channel to listen to a pre-selected radio station.

Paging is provided to selected backstage areas from rehearsal rooms and the stage door. However, the stage managers have priority at all times and can cut across any other call.

Closed circuit television

A CCTV camera provides a full stage picture for latecomers to watch the performance in the

147

foyers until there is a suitable moment to enter the auditorium. The stage manager has a small television monitor built into the desk to serve as a cueing aid. Each theatre is wired for a second CCTV system for specific technical requirements, such as off-stage chorus wishing to see the conductor.

Intercommunication

There is a standard loudspeaking type of intercom in all the key areas where, during the day, calls may be initiated from any position. Under performance conditions, however, the stage manager has overall control and his unit becomes the master.

The free speech ring intercom system has four channels: stage manager, technical A, B and C. At the main control positions it is possible to select one of the technical channels and the stage manager. Gain controls are provided to set a balance between the two and a speak key routes the associated microphone to either channel. There are many additional points

Figure 148 National Theatre of Great Britain: ring intercom technician's portable unit.

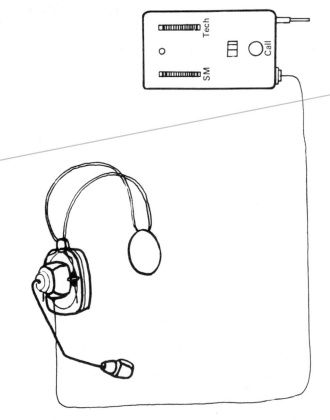

around the theatre where it is possible to connect portable headset units.

The stage manager and the production desk are able to monitor all the channels should they so wish, and the stage manager can in an emergency 'crash-call' over the lot.

Another emergency facility is the provision of telephone handsets sited at a limited number of strategic points which give direct access into the stage manager's communication channel. These can be used in the other direction by the stage manager who is able to flash an associated call light to attract anyone standing in the vicinity.

A final luxury is the possibility of switching a radio transmitter in to any of the channels. Thus roving technicians may listen to instructions via pocket radio receivers with earpieces.

Sound system

As is often the case with large public building contracts the basic specifications had to be approved at an early stage in the construction schedule in order to prepare budgets. We had to anticipate requirements and technical developments some eight to ten years ahead for a theatrical complex the like of which the United Kingdom had never experienced.

There were major battles with the architects over the sizes of control rooms (few theatres in the mid-1960s had control rooms at all) and the large windows which we insisted should be openable; and there were fiercer arguments over our proposals to build effects loudspeakers into the auditorium walls. Many of our chosen locations were rejected and most of our required dimensions for recesses were drastically reduced. However, we did manage to have some small loudspeakers built into the walls of the Lyttelton theatre, and some larger ones in the Olivier where it is more important because the thrust stage places most of the action within the auditorium. Finding space for some large effects speakers in the auditorium ceilings was not such a problem.

For the two main theatres we specified broadcast quality mixing desks including three-band equalization, input sensitivity, two auxiliary sends and PFL on each channel. All of which raised many an eyebrow at the time. Even we wondered secretly whether we might not be overspecifying. Thank goodness we stuck to our guns.

Each desk has sixteen microphone/line input channels selectable to any combination of six

Photograph 51 Sound mixing desk in the Lyttelton Theatre, National Theatre of Great Britain, London 1976. *Photo Theatre Projects Consultants Ltd*

master channels, or 'groups'. Groups E–F are selected at each channel by a single push button with an associated pan control to allow for true stereo.

There are two output presets each with twenty circuits. The upper preset has six colour coded pushes per circuit for selection to the six groups. The lower preset not only has group selection but also incorporates a fader on each circuit. A master switch changes from one preset to the other.

Sixteen of the output circuits are normally tied to sets of amplifiers driving installed loud-speakers. The other four circuits are tied to single amplifiers available for the connection of portable effects speakers. All circuits may be overplugged and rerouted at the patch panel if required.

The installed loudspeakers are as follows: stereo combinations of bass cabinets and horns mounted above the front of the stage in the Upper Theatre and around the proscenium in the Lower, four powerful bass bins and horns mounted in each auditorium ceiling (the Lower

Theatre having two small supplementary units built in below the circle for the rear of the stalls), and nine sets of speakers set into the side and rear auditorium walls.

The control rooms are equipped with a selection of tape machines, a turntable, a simple reverberation unit and space for a specially designed portable sub-mixer shared between the two theatres. A generous quantity of tie lines is distributed throughout each theatre and also to a central sound/communications room. This room houses, apart from all the communications and CCTV control equipment, a studio quality reverberation unit.

The windows of the control rooms are full width and motorized so that they slide silently down into a cavity in the wall. For safety reasons as soon as the window starts to open a warning light appears on the mixing desk and all intercom and monitor loudspeakers are automatically muted.

When I completed the manuscript for the first edition of this book in 1973 the mixers were being manufactured and I wondered with what imagination and dexterity the systems would eventually be used. Now, some nine years or so

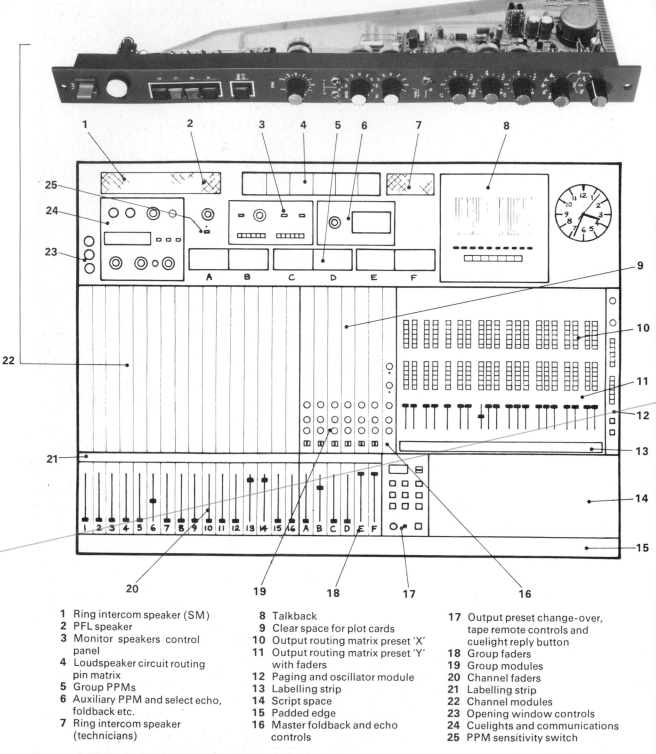

1 Ring intercom speaker (SM)
2 PFL speaker
3 Monitor speakers control panel
4 Loudspeaker circuit routing pin matrix
5 Group PPMs
6 Auxiliary PPM and select echo, foldback etc.
7 Ring intercom speaker (technicians)

8 Talkback
9 Clear space for plot cards
10 Output routing matrix preset 'X'
11 Output routing matrix preset 'Y' with faders
12 Paging and oscillator module
13 Labelling strip
14 Script space
15 Padded edge
16 Master foldback and echo controls

17 Output preset change-over, tape remote controls and cuelight reply button
18 Group faders
19 Group modules
20 Channel faders
21 Labelling strip
22 Channel modules
23 Opening window controls
24 Cuelights and communications
25 PPM sensitivity switch

Photograph 52 The National Theatre, London: Olivier theatre sound control desk. The operator sits side-on to the auditorium and can therefore work extremely close to the open window. The photograph shows one of the sixteen input channel modules incorporating microphone/line sensitivity, tone conrols, bass cut switch, foldback, echo send, pan (associated with groups E–F), group select, channel on/off, and PFL. *Photo courtesy Alice (Stancoil) Ltd*

later, I can say that both mixers have done very sterling work and their various manipulators have produced many exciting sound tracks. But nine years is a long life for such a piece of audio control equipment and so it has been decided that both mixers should be gently put out to grass. Another era passes.

Their replacements are due to incorporate more input channels, more sub-groups and more outputs with the option of adding memory routing and remote control over channel levels via voltage controlled amplifiers (VCAs).

The Barbican Theatre

The Barbican theatre is a part of the Barbican Arts Centre which is at the heart of a very large property development inside that historic square mile, the City of London. The theatre was conceived by the Royal Shakespeare Company as their new London home (they, of course, also have a company at the Memorial Theatre, Stratford-upon-Avon) and the opening production took place in June 1982.

Photograph 53 Barbican Theatre. a) Mixing console during installation, 1981. Inputs and groups in main section with outputs in separate wing on the right. b) Communications section. c) Routing and memory functions. *Photo Steve Stephens Photography*

Photograph 54 Barbican Theatre. The portable production desk with communications unit. *Photo Steve Stephens Photography*

The sound systems for both the National and the Barbican theatres were, in fact, conceived at about the same time. Although the Barbican opened some six years after the National it was originally scheduled to be completed first. This delay meant that we had the opportunity to appraise the first year of operation at the National and make some revisions to the specification. The main requirement seemed to be for more sub-groups and more outputs to increase the flexibility of control over sound effects. The number of channels on the input side was not thought to be too inhibiting as it was always possible to add a separate sub-mixer for shows requiring additional channels for microphones.

There was enough money in the budget and enough time to change the specification for the output end of the desk, but we then became concerned that the projected 24 input channels routing to 10 sub-masters to 26 outputs, plus the duplicate 26 output preset panel, constituted more than 850 switching functions. The later addition of another six inputs, for which the mixer main frame is designed, brings the total up to nearly one thousand switches; a daunting if not impossible prospect for manual operation under the often harassing conditions of a live performance.

So the decision was taken to add some form of memory control to the final specification and on the mixing console especially designed for the Barbican theatre the switching functions are controlled by a microcomputer which can memorize and store 199 cues (or combinations of switching). Sequences of cues are set up via a small key pad which is similar to that of a calculating machine. In the unlikely event of the memory failing, the console can be operated manually by means of banks of push buttons associated with the input and output sections of the mixer. The routing state of the mixer can be seen at any time by means of LED illumination of these push buttons. Alternatively either the preset state or the next cue can be viewed by pressing an appropriate button.

We were keen to dispense altogether with the traditional routing push-buttons relying entirely upon the key pad and a video display. But theatre technicians, probably quite rightly, move forward with caution. The Royal Shakespeare Company sound department have been very enthusiastic at the prospect of memory routing but always insistent upon also having the old familiar controls laid out in the old familiar way – just in case.

While the Barbican sound console is a theatrical 'first' in Great Britain it is also just a first step, for although memory sound consoles are currently in use in some recording studios the basic concept of tying the memory information to a tape of fixed duration does not apply to the theatre. The memory function in a studio is specifically for rebalancing a finite recording, whereas a live show will, by its very nature, contain substantial differences in timing and energy at every performance. We are still a long way in the theatre (or are we?) from memorizing *proportional* routing of inputs to outputs and from the ultimate goal of proportional routing with timed fades.

And then what about all those boring tone controls and auxiliary functions which take up so much space on the panel and are mostly used as preset functions? Similarly, is it really necessary to have so many operational faders when, for example, in an orchestral balance one seldom wishes, or indeed is capable of dealing with other than groups of preset channels?

Examples of typical theatres

But large theatres like the National and the Barbican with specialist requirements for repertoire drama are not the norm. Most modern theatres have a more variable diet and, perhaps, a less extensive budget. Typical are the next examples which are based upon the two auditoria designed by the British firm of architects, Renton, Howard, Wood, Levin, for the National Theatre of Syria in Damascus. One is a traditional European-style tiered proscenium theatre with side boxes, and the other has a thrust stage similar to those at the Festival Theatres in Stratford, Ontario, and Chichester, England; the main difference being that this one has a wrap-around balcony with a pronounced overhang which, of course, makes it a little more difficult for sound.

In both examples suitable positions for loudspeakers were not evident on the preliminary drawings and provision had to be made in close collaboration with the architects.

The proscenium theatre: This 1500-seat theatre was designed to accommodate everything from visiting international opera and ballet companies to local dance and drama, musicals, pop and classical concerts, and conferences. The sound system had to be simple to operate, yet flexible enough to cope with these diverse activities. Maintenance also had to be straightforward so as many standard components as possible were specified throughout both theatres with simple rigging and access a priority.

Above the proscenium opening is a basic mono loudspeaker array providing general coverage of the auditorium. Although there is severe masking beneath some of the boxes and the balconies this overhead position was deemed useful for centre-fill and as a space large enough to install some worthwhile bass cabinets.

In each of the side proscenium zones a space was created for five full range monitors mounted one above the other on a vertical length of pipe. Every seat in the house can see at least four of these loudspeakers which would be used in conjunction with the central system for stereo music and general reinforcement.

As these monitors are not designed for long-throw application eight similar units are sited further out into the auditorium and fed via digital time delay to provide the necessary coverage; and because there is a potential sound-trap below the first and second balconies a number of small ceiling loudspeakers have been incorporated to provide a discreet boost in the speech frequency range.

There is another reason for having a second string of loudspeakers out in the auditorium and that is because of the flexible nature of the orchestra pit/forestage arrangement. The elevators in front of the main stage can be lowered in sections to produce an operatic or a lyric-sized orchestra pit. Alternatively they can be raised to create a small or large forestage; and any activity requiring amplification on the forestage would find the microphones the wrong side of the proscenium loudspeakers thus rendering them ineffectual. So in the forestage condition (perhaps for a folk concert or a conference) the central array would be employed as the source sound with the distributed delay loudspeakers providing a general amplification.

From the control room at the rear of the auditorium it would be possible to balance sound for simple reinforcement situations, to play in the odd sound effect and to record performances. For balancing live concerts, musicals and more ambitious sequences of sound effects a temporary control position has been allocated in the centre of the main floor just in front of the balcony overhangs. Access to all necessary audio wiring is available in a special chamber below the control position. Routes from this room to the stage have also been incorporated for temporary cabling associated with visiting sound – or, indeed, video – systems.

Not shown on the drawing in Figure 149 are the

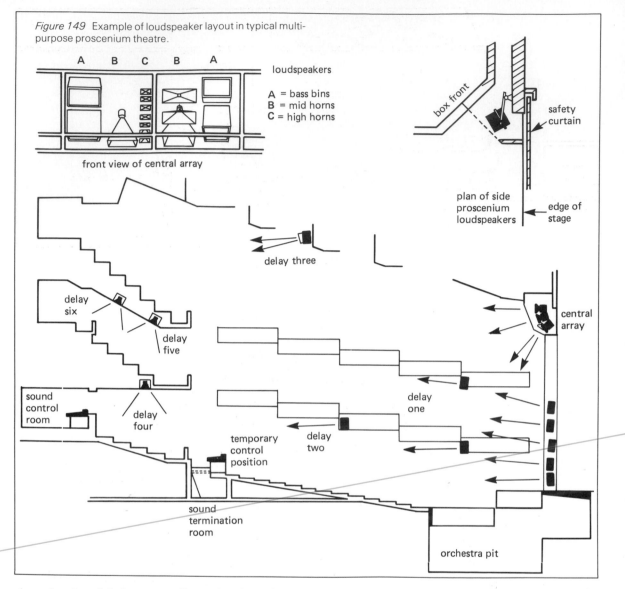

Figure 149 Example of loudspeaker layout in typical multi-purpose proscenium theatre.

front view of central array

loudspeakers

A = bass bins
B = mid horns
C = high horns

box front

safety curtain

plan of side proscenium loudspeakers ← edge of stage

delay three

delay six

delay five

central array

sound control room

delay four

delay one

delay two

temporary control position

sound termination room

orchestra pit

nine circuits of full range effects loudspeakers built into the side and rear walls of the auditorium on each level (27 units in all). On stage, of course, are the usual facilities for portable loudspeakers, microphones, etc.

The thrust stage theatre is mainly designed for drama. The sound system is therefore conceived primarily for the playback of recorded music and sound effects. However, there is an orchestra pit and speech reinforcement could be required for musical productions and also for small group concerts.

Experience with this format of theatre has shown that loudspeakers mounted where the auditorium walls meet the stage are very useful for directional sound effects and, together with a central source, for general reinforcement. So a pair of loudspeakers per level on both sides of the auditorium were included. Central loudspeakers were not considered necessary as a fixture as they would not be required for many productions and could well be in the way of scenic elements or lighting. They therefore ended up as six monitors suspended from a barrel above the stage which can be winched up above the acoustic ceiling (which also houses lighting equipment).

For general sound effects within the auditorium there are a number of full range loudspeakers mounted above the main ceiling. These

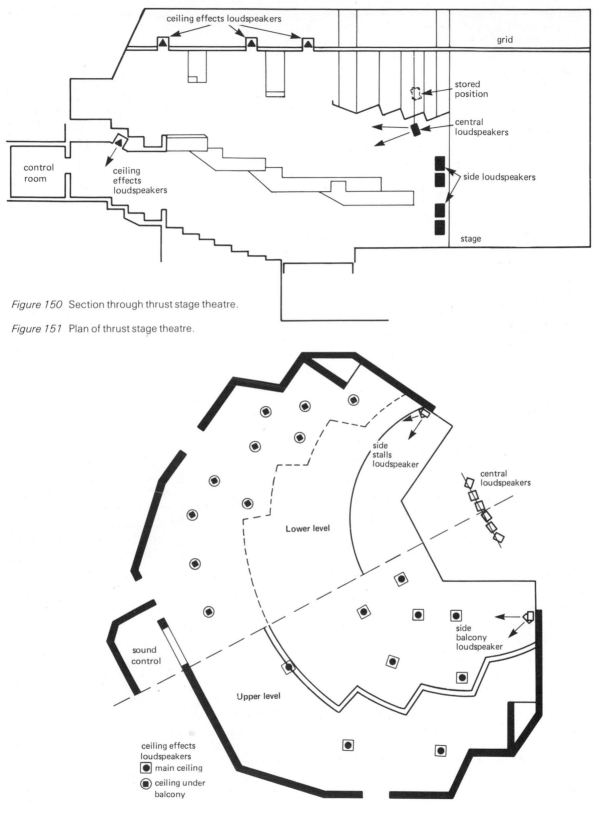

Figure 150 Section through thrust stage theatre.

Figure 151 Plan of thrust stage theatre.

155

Photograph 55 The cuelight control board in the prompt corner at Sadlers Wells Theatre, c. 1930.

Photograph 56 Theatr Y Werin: stage manager's control 1972. Electrosonic Ltd. *Photo Theatre Projects Consultants Ltd*

are supplemented by smaller fill-in units recessed in the ceiling below the balcony. The auditorium effects loudspeakers are in eighteen circuits which can be used together for one overall non-directional effect or can be grouped as required to create the movement of sound in any direction. The ceiling was chosen for these loud-speakers partly because only here was there adequate room for a useful enclosure and partly because with such a wide auditorium it is difficult to throw sufficient sound from a wall on the one side to the audience on the other without the balance being wrong for those people sitting near the source of sound. The only answer is to mount the speakers well above the heads of the audience, which was not possible in this instance.

Photograph 57 Lyric Theatre Hammersmith (1979), Stage manager's control desk.

Photograph 58 Studio Theatre, Lyric Hammersmith. Stage manager's unit next to lighting board in control room. Equipment: Cambridge Electronic Workshops Ltd. *Photo Theatre Projects Consultants Ltd*

1 SM Ring Volume
2 SM Ring Telephone Call Lights
3 SM Ring Loudspeaker
4 Working Lights and
  Rehearsal/Performance Control
5 Technical Ring Loudspeaker
6 Low Voltage Effects Circuits
7 Stop Clock
8 Foyer Paging, Bar Bells and Foyer
  CCTV 3 minute Performance Warn
  Sequence
9 Panel Lights and CCTV Source
  Select
10 CCTV Monitor
11 Ring Intercom Controls

12 House Tabs
13 SM Ring Cueing Control
14 Master Cuelights
15 Microphone
16 Removable Blue/White Light Unit
17 PA to Stage
18 Paging Artists, Technicians
19 Headset 'Hand Mic' Switches
20 Talkback Loudspeaker
21 Talkback Volume
22 Talkback Circuits
23 Pabx External Telephone
24 Cuelights
25 SM Ring Telephone
26 Extension Cuelight 'GO' Circuits

Photograph 59 National Theatre of Great Britain, stage manager's control.
Photo courtesy Pye Business Communications Ltd

Photograph 60 National Theatre of Great Britain: general facilities panel. A
triple compartment metal box with section one for mains, section two for low
level signals and section three for high levels signals. An extendable cuelight
unit may be plugged in at the top of the central panel. A telephone handset
with direct access to the stage manager is on the right hand side of the unit.
Note the dual purpose cable/guard rail. Photo Theatre Projects Consultants Ltd

Photograph 61 Barbican Theatre. Deputy stage manager's cueing desk. *Photo Steve Stephens Photography*

Photograph 62 Barbican Theatre. Stage manager's desk for paging communications, and work lights. *Photo Steve Stephens Photography*

Photograph 63 Centre in the square , Kitchener, Ontario; central loudspeaker array and *Midas* mixing desk in permanent central auditorium (see also inset). Sound consultant Paul Procunier. System installed by Gerr Electro Acoustics Ltd

Photograph 64 Where to place loudspeakers in a beautiful period theatre? In the Lyric Theatre, Hammersmith, completely rebuilt and restored on a new site in 1980, small removable loudspeakers were installed suitable for limited reinforcement and tape playback. *Photo courtesy Steve Stephens Photography. Theatre Consultants, Theatre Projects Consultants Ltd*

Photograph 65 The Theatre Royal, Nottingham, renovated in 1980, also has a limited reinforcement system, this time with bass loudspeakers built into the rear walls of the three lower boxes; mid/high frequency horns are built into specially created recesses below these boxes and full-range loudspeakers are built into the top boxes. Theatre Consultants, Theatre Projects Consultants Ltd. *Photo courtesy Steve Stephens Photography*

Safety Curtain

The O'Keefe Centre, Toronto

Finally, I should like to take a look at the O'Keefe Centre for the Performing Arts in Toronto because despite the enormous size of this theatre the multi-faceted audio installation highlights many of the principles discussed in earlier chapters; and basic principles of sound system design are as valid for a 200-seater school hall as for a 3,000-seater theatre.

The O'Keefe Centre is undoubtedly one of the major theatres in Canada. Not only is it the home of the Canadian Opera Company and the National Ballet of Canada who both perform seasons there every year, but it is an important venue for tours of musicals and plays and for international entertainers of the calibre of Harry Belafonte, Liza Minnelli, Liberace, Tom Jones etc.

Ever since the theatre opened in 1960 it has been dogged by an audibility problem which is due to the sheer size of the auditorium coupled with some inherent acoustic deficiencies. The original sound system appears to have been

totally inadequate and an update of the loud-speaker installation in 1970 obviously did not provide the answer. I was approached in 1976 to make an appraisal and add my findings to the already thick file of reports which the management of the O'Keefe had commissioned during the previous eight to ten years from various eminent acousticians and sound designers from Canada and the States. So it was with this background of rejected reports, stories of singers cancelling performances, and rumours that touring sound engineers regarded the O'Keefe as a place where you had to work hard to achieve second-best, that I began my investigation. When I first walked into the 3,212-seater auditorium I wondered why I had left behind the cosy little

Figure 152 O'Keefe Centre: central array of bass bins, mid frequency horns and tweeters, side array with two pairs of bin/horn systems in the middle plus the reinforcement columns at the top and bottom. Loudspeakers are masked from the auditorium by acoustically transparent panels.

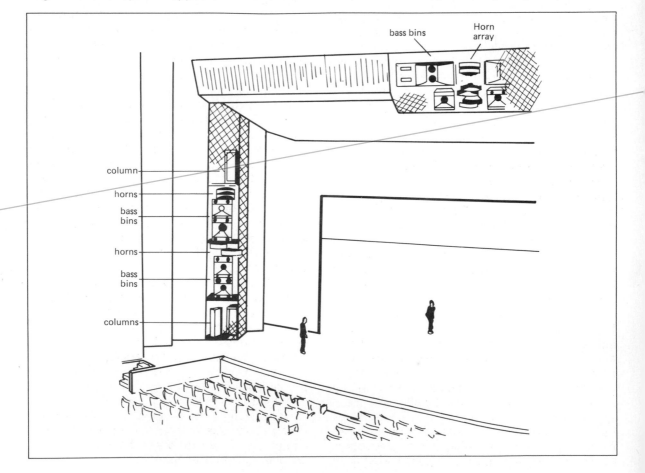

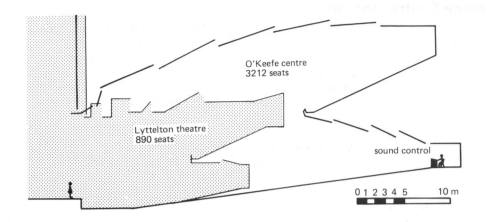

Figure 153 Comparative sizes of the O'Keefe Centre auditorium and that of the Lyttelton in the National Theatre of Great Britain.

1,500 or so seater West End theatres like the Palace and the Theatre Royal, Drury Lane.

To give some idea of the size, if you take a line from the centre of the front edge of the stage on the diagonal to the farthest seat at the rear corner of the balcony the distance is approximately 155 feet (47 metres). Whereas if you take the same measurement in the National Theatre's Lyttelton auditorium the distance is somewhere around 62 feet (19 metres). Furthermore, being a fan-shaped auditorium and with a balcony holding roughly one-third of the audience, well over two-thirds of the seats are in the rear half of the house – sixty feet from the stage and beyond.

The proscenium opening is 60 feet wide by 30 feet high and the stage area is 125 feet wide (including scene dock) by 56 feet. Stage floor to grid is 85 feet. Taking all these factors into account it was obvious that most performers, finding themselves facing such a large auditorium on one of Canada's largest stages, would be thankful for a very efficient Sound Reinforcement system.

I decided from the outset that the requirements for Sound Reinforcement and for the singer/entertainer (or 'Vegas Act' as it is sometimes called) were entirely different. For the reinforcement of a play, musical, or even opera (would you believe?) an extremely even coverage of 'uncoloured' sound is vital together with loudspeakers providing a very good feedback rejection. Whereas for the close microphone technique employed by recording artistes feedback is not such a problem, but it is necessary to provide a big full frequency range sound with plenty of bass to cope with the amplification of musical instruments.

The existing loudspeaker system consisted of a central array of bass bins and multicellular mid/high frequency horns suspended above the orchestra pit. As we have mentioned before this arrangement is favoured by many American and Canadian sound designers because a complete coverage of the auditorium is possible from a point source, thereby minimizing conflicting sound paths which can create unwanted reflections, standing waves and phase cancellations.

Although it is certainly possible to obtain a very even distribution of sound from a central array (and we did) it has always been my contention that *theatrically* it does not work. Moreover there was no way I could envisage any useful sound reaching the seats near to the stage – particularly at the outer extremities – from a central position some 40 feet (12 metres) or more up in the air. But an overhead array is essential with such a wide proscenium opening for general centre fill and for focusing the apparent source of sound into the stage.

The O'Keefe Centre project afforded a superb opportunity to test out some long held theories; one of these being that for successful reinforcement part of the secret is to have the loudspeakers positioned as low as possible (and therefore necessarily to the sides) so as to be in the same height relationship to the audience as the original sound source – the performer – thereby not only assisting the illusion of the sound coming from the stage but automatically taking advantage of natural acoustic gain from reflections off ceilings which have been specifically designed for that purpose.

163

Four loudspeaker systems

After a great deal of calculating and a certain amount of soul-searching the final scheme as presented and accepted by the O'Keefe Centre management called for four separate loudspeaker systems which, in various combinations, would cope with the different requirements as laid out in the brief. These loudspeaker configurations were as follows:

1. *Central Array.* The original overhead central position above the proscenium was retained, but a large section of the ceiling panel and superstructure was cut away in order to make possible a direct shot to every seat in the house. The only loudspeakers utilized from the old system were two ALTEC bass bins each with two 15 inch bass drivers which date back to the original 1960 system. These are supplemented with two JBL bass bins with single 15 inch drivers, and six JBL radial horns for the mid frequencies associated with six JBL pressure units for the highs. The horns, mounted above each other in an arc for minimum phase cancellation, are utilized as follows: one pair cover the balcony (the required vertical distribution of only about 20 degrees is obtained by bolting the two horns together which effectively increases the energy by 6 dB within the 20 degrees), a similarly arranged pair covers the rear orchestra (stalls) under the balcony, and two single horns cater for the mid and front orchestra (stalls) where progressively less sound pressure level is required. The front horn may be muted from the control console if the front block of seats is removed for an extended forestage or for an orchestra pit.

2. *Stereo Music System.* The second loudspeaker system comprises JBL bass bins and horns mounted in specially built towers on the sides of the forestage just in front of the stage proper. With four bass bins and four horns on either side this constitutes a high power system with essentially the same performance characteristics as the central array.

3. *Stereo Reinforcement System.* For a totally natural sound and a very controlled coverage of the auditorium *Bozak* 3-way *'concert'* columns (each having six bass, nine mid range and eight high frequency drivers) are used. Three per side are mounted in the towers along with the bass bin and horn system already mentioned. Two columns are sited for optimum coverage of the balcony and two for the main area of the orchestra (stalls). A triangle of seats in the front near the stage is covered by two more columns which may be muted from the control position if the extended forestage is in use.

4. *Rear Enhancement System.* Because the auditorium is so large it is very difficult to obtain a natural level of sound at the rear without its being very obviously amplified towards the front. We therefore decided to set an overall sound level which would be comfortable throughout the main part of the auditorium and then add an

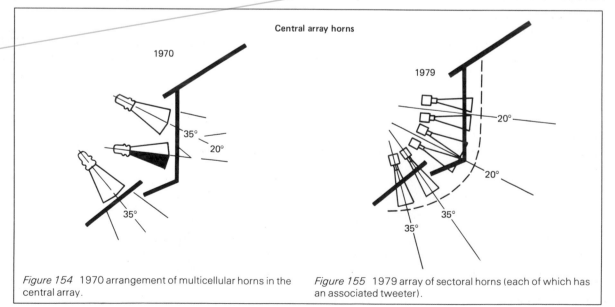

Figure 154 1970 arrangement of multicellular horns in the central array.

Figure 155 1979 array of sectoral horns (each of which has an associated tweeter).

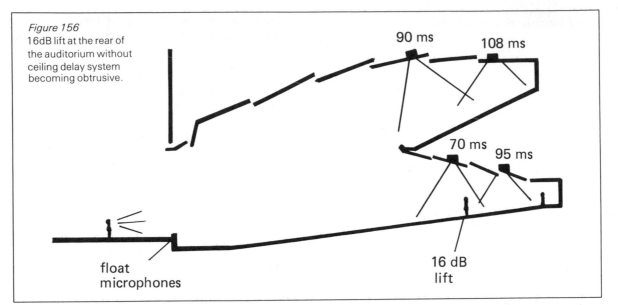

Figure 156
16dB lift at the rear of the auditorium without ceiling delay system becoming obtrusive.

90 ms
108 ms
70 ms
95 ms

float microphones

16 dB lift

'enhancement' system to provide an extra boost at the rear. This consists of twin rows of loudspeakers set flush into the ceilings above the rear balcony and orchestra (stalls) seating areas. Each of these four rows of 8 in. cone loudspeakers (some 55 in all) is fed via a digital delay line set so that the sound from the main system arrives momentarily in advance of the sound from the ceiling speakers. This unobtrusive amplification is in fact an enhancement of the natural ceiling reflection.

Amplification

All the main loudspeakers, including outlets for portable stage monitors and effects speakers, are driven by H/HS.500-D power amplifiers; some eighteen in all. The Enhancement system is driven by four H/H TPA 50-D power amplifiers operating into a 70 volt line.

Each amplifier is fed via a lockable preset gain control on a separate panel, and run with its front panel gain control fully up. Thus, in the event of failure, amplifiers may be interchanged without upsetting the overall balance which took several days to achieve.

Third octave equalizers were provided for each group of loudspeakers, but listening tests (confirmed with pink noise and an IVIE spectrum analyser) showed that equalization of the Enhancement system was not necessary and the natural sound of the Bozak columns could not be improved. The stereo equalizer was re-employed to help iron out a bass absorption problem

at around 80 Hertz in the lower side bins, and the mono equalizer was re-allotted to the foldback system.

The mixing console

The mixer should have been in the centre of the auditorium where the operator could properly balance a stereo mix, but the economics of the permanent loss of ten prime seats proved a powerful argument for an alternative position at the rear of the orchestra (stalls). However, all the wiring is run via a junction box in a room below the centre of the seating slab for a possible future move.

The mixer, designed by Theatre Projects for Rank Strand Sound, has twenty-four mic/line input channels (with full equalization and three auxiliary sends) selectable in mono or stereo as appropriate to eight group output channels. The mono outputs are normalled via a patch field to amplifiers associated with the Central Array and the Enhancement, and the stereo outputs are normalled to the side bins/horns and the side columns. The two remaining outputs are each fitted with four rotary gain controls for selection to any combination of four power amplifiers which connect to socket outlets on stage for portable loudspeakers.

An unusual feature on the mixer is the flexible sub-grouping arrangement. By depressing an internally-lit push button on the groups, any of Groups A–F may be connected to become a Sub Group Master contributing to Groups G and H. A

Photograph 66 O'Keefe Centre: 63 input, 8 group mixing desk at the rear of the stalls, 1979.

pan control associated with each push button assigns the sub group to left or right. The mixer can thus become 24 into 6 into 2. Or, perhaps more typically, 24 into 4 into 2 with the Central Array and Enhancement remaining as separate output groups, perhaps for vocals.

In addition to the twenty-four main input channels there is a 40-channel submixer comprising 10 triple input microphone modules with level controls only and 8 single mic/line input modules with treble/mid/bass tone adjustment. The submixer has available space for another 2 single input plug-in modules. Routing of any combination of submix channels to any combinations of the submix outputs 1–6 is via a pin matrix. The console therefore has a total input capacity of 63 channels (assuming the submixer is all patched to only one channel of the main mixer). Submix outputs 1–6 are normalled on the patchfield to main mixer line inputs 1–6.

The 530 way mini-jack patch panel has been designed with as much 'normalling' as possible so that it is possible to plug up 40 microphones on stage in such a way that they will appear on

the mixer without the necessity for any patch cords in the jackfield. Similarly all the mixer outputs are 'normalled' through the patch to various power amplifiers assigned to groups of loud-speakers. The normalling is via break jacks, so this allows for any facility to be rerouted by over-patching. Insertion points for the main inputs and group outputs also appear on the patchfield which can be used for external signal processing equipment or for any of the SCAMP devices built in to the console (the SCAMP rack contains 8 S01 compressor/limiters with space for another 8 modules).

Another feature of the patching is that the entire jackfield is connected in sections by multi-way plugs and sockets to the installed wiring and the console. Therefore any future change in console location can be easily accommodated by re-routing the multipin extension cables coming from the junction box beneath the centre orchestra floor. This extensive use of multiway connectors is also a flexible arrangement for interface with touring sound systems. Visiting engineers are provided with an outlet box next to the Rear Stalls operating position which provides access to the sound system mic lines, amplifier inputs and main jackfield.

Patching or foldback monitoring to the stage from two auxiliary sends is via the patchfield as separate signals or mixed groups of signals either directly into the monitor amplifier/loudspeaker system or as line level feeds into a portable monitor mixer. Separate mic level feeds are provided via Hybrid Transformers, providing total isolation between main and monitor mixers.

The monitor foldback mixer

The monitor mixer may be connected via multi-connectors down stage left or right. It has 16 inputs with variable cross-point routing to four group outputs. Each of the standard input modules has simple three-band boost and cut equalization plus input sensitivity and mic/line selector switch. These modules are identical to the single input modules on the submixer.

Access to the monitor mixer is by *MIC REPEATS* and balanced line inputs available at the main jackfield. The *MIC REPEATS* are derived from selected microphones on stage which are split by high quality hybrid transformers. Thus, there is total isolation between the 2 mixers. Line inputs are provided to allow the submixer outputs or any other line level signal originating at the main console to be sent to the monitor mixer.

The system is planned so that selection of all microphones used by the monitor mixer is set up at the main jackfield under the control of the main sound operator. This was done to prevent some of the 'surprises' which can occur when such patching is done on stage. However, the balancing of all monitor signals is not affected by the main console.

Echo units

A *Master Room* Dual Echo Unit housed with the amplifier racks provides two separate mono signals or may be combined for stereo operation. Normally one would be reserved for the main sound system and the other used with the stage monitoring system. Reverberation times can be remotely varied at the Mixing Console from 1 to 3 seconds on one half of the unit and 2 to 5 seconds on the other half.

Stage outlets

There are three four-compartment Technical Facilities Panels, one either side of the stage and one in the orchestra pit, for microphones, loudspeakers, communications and power:

1. *Mains*: The mains section of each panel incorporates power outlets reserved for audio.

2. *Microphone level*: Each microphone level compartment has six separate microphone sockets which appear back at the control patchfield, and a multiway socket for a twenty-channel microphone plug box on the end of a 50 ft. multicore cable. The twenty sockets on the stage left plug box multicore (or snake) are labelled 1–20 and are normalled through the patch to mixer inputs 1–20. The stage right snake is also labelled 1–20 but is normalled to the corresponding inputs of the submixer; the idea being that the stage left snake is used for important microphones in an orchestra which require separate equalization and instant access, and the stage right snake is used for microphones which can be grouped; e.g. a string or brass section. The

Photograph 67 Sound engineer Wayne Karlsted beside the foldback monitor mixer looking worried before the first performance with his new sound system.

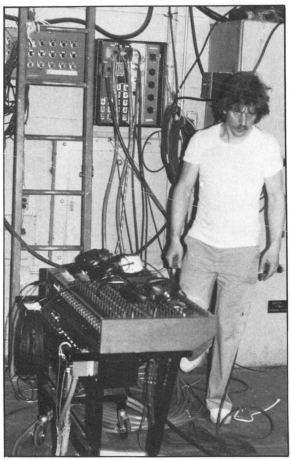

twelve separate sockets are for lead vocalists and off-stage microphones. The provision of 26 similarly arranged circuits in the orchestra pit rear wall and elevator floor allows for the balancing of an orchestra for a musical. There is also a multi-way socket for the microphone level inputs to the foldback mixer on the two stage panels.

3. *Loudspeaker level*: Identical loudspeaker outlets on each Technical Facilities Panel provide for portable foldback monitor and effects loudspeakers. The signals at the four Foldback outlets are derived from the Sound Console via the four outputs of two HH 500-D amplifiers. The four Effects outlets are bi-amped via 2 JBL 5234 Dual crossover units and HH 500-D amplifiers. The wiring and extension cables for 'Foldback' and 'Effects' outlets and loudspeakers are arranged so that the connectors are identical, but erroneous plugging up results in lack of operation rather than erroneous operation. All loudspeaker interconnection is via Cannon EP series connectors. Inputs to all Foldback and Effects circuits are available via the main jackfield.

4. *Line level*: The line level section contains a quantity of 8 tie lines (which can each be picked up at the three Technical Facilities Panels, the Console patch, Rack Room, Balcony Sound Room and Visitors Outlet Panel), plus two communications outlets and a technical earth (ground) on thumb screw terminals. At the two stage positions there are also multiway sockets for the inputs and outputs to the Foldback mixer and for the Communications Master Station.

Communications

The performance communications system was specially designed to be compatible with *Clearcom* which is extensively used by touring companies. The O'Keefe was provided with a single channel headset system with beltpacks which may be plugged in at a number of key technical positions. Each beltpack has adjustment of the listen level, a microphone on/off switch, and an internally lit push for flashing a light signal to all other users of the system; this is primarily to alert any technicians who may have removed their headsets. In practice we have found that the side tone cancellation produces such a good measure of feedback rejection that one can hear (and talk back at) the headset even when it is not being worn.

The control for the communications is a portable unit which may be connected at either side of the stage for use by the stage manager. It also incorporates a second channel which appears with the first at selected locations where are fitted loudspeaking outstations (*squawk boxes* or *biscuits*, as they are sometimes called). At these outstations the technician can, if he so wishes, listen to a mix of Channel A (all the headsets) and Channel B. He may talk to either channel by means of a two-position-and-off key switch. Each of these outstations has a socket for alternative use with headsets. The dual channel system was conceived to allow for communication between the director, lighting designer, and key technicians without interrupting the stage manager's vital communication link. As a safeguard, in case users of the dual channel system have turned down their Channel A listen levels (they cannot mute it completely) the control unit has a 'crash call' facility by means of which the stage manager can override all other signals and be heard at full listening level at each outstation.

Testing the loudspeaker system

It is seldom that one has the opportunity to experiment with different types of loudspeaker configuration properly installed in one large auditorium and it was extremely gratifying to discover that all my theories (at least to the satisfaction of myself and my colleagues) were justified.

The central array provided a very good coverage, with a broad band sound pressure level variation of plus/minus 2.5 dB in the balcony and main orchestra (stalls), with the rear orchestra dropping by some 5dB at the worst point. The higher frequencies not unexpectedly tended to roll off at the rear and sides of the auditorium and particularly down at the front.

The Music System: The bass bins and horns in the side arrays measured on their own provided an SPL tolerance in the balcony of an incredible plus/minus 0.5 dB with the entire lower level of the auditorium varying by only plus/minus 2 dB. The introduction of the Enhancement system greatly improved the overall effect by compensating for high frequency losses at the rear of the house, and the Central Array filled in the centre image and helped to provide a much flatter overall response on the spectrum analyser. Adjusting the balance between the side and central loudspeakers was an interesting and critical operation. As part of our tests we played back a very good stereo recording of a large orchestra and singer; simply by adjusting the output faders associated with the side and overhead loudspeakers we were able to move the voice from side to side and up and down to any position within the proscenium opening. But when the balance was set correctly the singer appeared to be standing centre stage, not at the front but about fifteen feet back; and that seemed to work to a remarkable degree even from the sides of the auditorium. With a performance situation we found that it was an improvement for the seats immediately in front of the side loudspeakers to add some electronic time delay. Experiments showed that about 10 milliseconds was enough to focus the source of sound back to the stage.

The Reinforcement System: The column loudspeakers measured together with the Enhancement system produced an impressive tolerance of plus/minus 2.5 dB with the spectrum analyser showing little variation in the curve throughout the entire auditorium; generally a much smoother response than the bins and horns. The subtle addition of the central cluster provided a fulness to the sound with better imaging for the side seats.

Conformity of sound pressure levels: Although it is an interesting exercise striving for a conformity of sound pressure levels this is not necessarily the ideal. Both the sound pressure levels and the frequency spectrum need to be tailored for different parts of the auditorium to achieve the best acoustic and theatrical effect. For example, in a Reinforcement situation less level is required at the front of the auditorium because one is near enough to receive a good deal of direct energy from the performers. The losses, if any, are liable to be in the higher frequencies, which is where a boost could be provided for maximum intelligibility – perhaps over an orchestra.

Further back in the auditorium the natural voice sound becomes thinner, so more of the bass end is required plus an overall increase in level. Towards the rear of the house one certainly needs the higher frequencies for articulation, but too much level with a full bass content will sound false. For a natural sound a compromise must be reached bearing in mind the psychological effect of the distance between audience and performers.

Photograph 68 Side proscenium loudspeakers viewed from the stage.

But for a singer/entertainer in concert we are less concerned with the natural voice because the amplified sound will be proportionately far louder. Realism therefore gives way to conformity in quality and power. At the back we require the signal to have the same full-frequency response and be as loud as at the front. A fairly usual complication to be borne in mind when

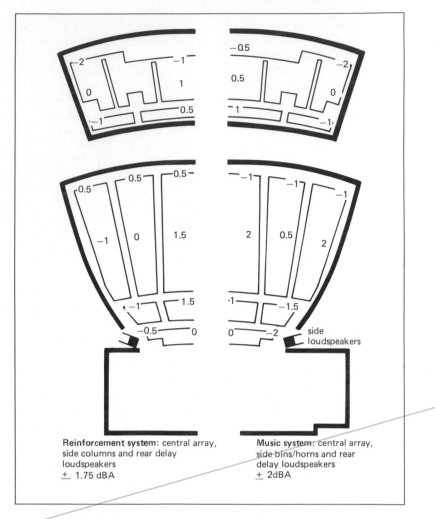

Reinforcement system: central array,
side columns and rear delay
loudspeakers
± 1.75 dBA

Music system: central array,
side bins/horns and rear
delay loudspeakers
± 2dBA

side
loudspeakers

Figure 157 Sound pressure level measurements with pink noise. Note the more
even dispersion achieved with the columns at the sides and front of the main floor.

tailoring the system is that the unfortunate people seated near the stage often experience a great deal of energy from the artistes' foldback monitors. This is mainly the lower frequency spectrum as monitor loudspeakers tend to be pointed away from the audience.

Adjusting the delay: The setting up of the Enhancement system was very interesting. We had measured the distances on the plans and calculated the correct amount of travel time for natural sound to which we added a few milliseconds; but this did not take into account the fact that some people would be sitting nearer the speakers than others and some would be within the range of two sets of speakers on different delay times. So

the final critical settings were arrived at with the aid of one man on stage in front of a microphone alternately talking and knocking two pieces of wood together, another man in the amplifier rack room adjusting delay timings, plus a consensus of two pairs of ears in the auditorium. We were extremely gratified to find that a lift of some 2–3 dB could be attained without being aware that the system was in operation at all. When the setting-up procedure was completed we switched the system off. The effect was dramatic. It was as though the ceiling had been lowered and the sound source moved back twenty feet. For apart from the general increase in level produced by the Enhancement System there is also a restoration of some of the higher frequencies which just simply do not travel that distance. In other words the articulation factor is greatly improved. The delay settings downstairs for the two rows of loudspeakers were 70 m/s and 96 m/s whilst in the balcony they were 90 m/s and 108 m/s.

Although designed primarily for Speech Reinforcement we found that even with singers using a close microphone technique the Enhancement system appeared to improve the acoustics in these relatively low ceiling areas. (Acousticians please note).

The system in use

The system came into use on 20 August 1979 with a concert featuring Cleo Laine and the Johnny Dankworth orchestra. I was told by their manager that on a previous visit to the O'Keefe Centre they only used 10 microphones and spent most of the three-hour orchestral rehearsal trying to obtain a good sound. This time they were using 38 microphones plus four separate mixes of foldback monitoring and, apart from a few comments on the orchestral balance, they were able to concentrate entirely upon their performance.

We were also warned that no matter how excellent a sound installation was provided by the theatre most of the leading singer/entertainers would want to use their own equipment. It was something of a surprise to all concerned that during the first few months performers like Shirley Bassey, Engelbert Humperdinck, Rosemary Clooney and Cleo Laine used the system to the full while Paul Anka, Cher and Johnny Mathis used their own mixing desks tied into the house amplifier/loudspeaker installation.

I was in Toronto whilst Johnny Mathis and Cleo Laine were performing and I was very content to see press reviews for both of these artistes containing phrases like 'excellent diction', 'crystal clear voice' and 'sounding better than ever'; for it is from this kind of reflected glory that a sound man receives his accolade. A sound system which is noticed is usually a bad one.

Later that year the ballet company performed their season and the sound engineer used microphones in the orchestra pit to assist some of the instruments struggling in the nether regions. The critics made no mention, as was customary, of the poor orchestral sound of the O'Keefe.

I was, however, somewhat taken aback when visiting Toronto mid 1981 to have the engineer admit that he had been mixing the opera season 'like a musical'. This was not the intention. I had envisaged that the float microphones would be set at an unobtrusive level for a 'general lift' and then left at that for the performance. Not a bit of it. Nevertheless, the proof of the pudding is that the voices of the opera singers had been electronically amplified for a period of six months before one of the critics made any comment at all; and the comment was, perhaps, more directed at the inadequacies of the particular singer rather than at any shortcomings of the audio installation.

All this proves to me that given the right equipment correctly installed with, most important, a sensitive engineer at the controls, it is perfectly feasible to achieve a level of sound amplification which is at once comfortable for the listener, faithful to the original sound – whether it be vocal or instrumental – and, what is more, appears to be coming from the stage and not emanating from some large conglomeration of ironmongery and coffins suspended above the proscenium.

Interchangeability Cross Reference of Audio Connectors

Description		Cannon	Switchcraft	Amphenol Excellite	Qwick	R.S. Components
Free Cable Connectors Pin Contacts	(3)	XLR–3–12C	A3M	91–453	91–853	X Plug 3–12C
	(4)	XLR–4–12C	A4M	91–457	91–857	X Plug 4–12C
	(5)	XLR–5–12C	A5M	91–461	—	X Plug 5–12C
	(6)	XLR–6–12C		—	—	—
Free Cable Connector Socket Contacts	(3)	XLR–3–11C	A3F	91–454	91–854	X Plug 3–11C
	(4)	XLR–4–11C	A4F	91–458	91–85	X Plug 4–11C
	(5)	XLR–5–11C	A5F	91–462	—	X Plug 5–11C
	(6)	XLR–6–11C		—	—	—
Rectangular Panel Mounts Pin Contacts	(3)	XLR–3–32	D3M	91–455	—	X Socket 3–32
	(4)	XLR–4–32	D4M	91–459	—	X Socket 4–32
	(5)	XLR–5–32	D5M	91–463	—	X Socket 5–32
	(6)	XLR–6–32		—	—	—
Rectangular Panel Mounts Socket Contacts	(3)	XLR–3–31	D3F	91–456	—	X Socket 3–31
	(4)	XLR–4–31	D4F	91–460	—	X Socket 4–31
	(5)	XLR–5–31	D5F	91–464	—	X Socket 5–31
	(6)	XLR–6–31		—	—	—
Round Panel Mount Pin Contacts	(3)	XLR–3–14	C3M	—	91–855	—
	(4)	XLR–4–14	C4M	—	91–859	—
	(5)	XLR–5–14	C5M	—	—	—
	(6)	XLR–6–14		—	—	—
Round Panel Mount Socket Contacts	(3)	XLR–3–13	C3F	—	91–856	—
	(4)	XLR–4–13	C4F	—	91–860	—
	(5)	XLR–5–13	C5F	—	—	—
	(6)	XLR–6–13		—	—	—
Round Panel Mounts (Locknut) Pin Contacts		XLR( )14N*	B( )M*	—	—	—
Round Panel Mounts Socket Contacts		XLR( )13N*	—	—	—	—
Rt. Angle Cable Connector Pin Contacts	(3)	XLR–3–16	R3M	—	—	—
	(4)	XLR–4–16	R4M	—	—	—
	(5)	XLR–5–16	R5M	—	—	—
	(6)	XLR–6–16		—	—	—
Rt. Angle Cable Connector Socket Contacts	(3)	XLR–3–15	R3F	—	—	—
	(4)	XLR–4–15	R4F	—	—	—
	(5)	XLR–5–15	R5F	—	—	—
	(6)	XLR–6–15		—	—	—

*Cannon XLR( )14N overall diameter 17/16″, Switchcraft B( )M 17/64″, therefore panel hole for Switchcraft smaller, otherwise they are similar.

Bibliography

Agfa-Gevaert
Tape Recording Manual
Agfa-Gevaert, London

AKG
Publications on microphones
AKG Equipment Ltd

Alkin, Glyn
Sound with Vision: Sound Techniques for Television and Film
Butterworth & Co, London 1973

Allison, R. F.
High Fidelity Systems: a User's Guide
Dover, New York

Altec
Loudspeaker Enclosures: Their Design and Use
Altec Sound Products Division

Amos, S. W.
Principles of Transistor Circuits
Iliffe, London 1969 and Hayden Book Co., New York

BASF
Your BASF Tape Manual
BASF

BBC
Better Sound: BBC Radio Study Notes
British Broadcasting Corporation, London 1968

Beranek, Leo L.
Music, Acoustics and Architecture
John Wiley & Sons, New York 1962

Bernstein, Julian L.
Audio Systems
John Wiley & Sons, New York 1966

Borwick, John (ed.)
Techniques of Sound Reproduction
Focal Press, London

Briggs, G. A.
Loudspeakers
Rank Wharfdale, Bradford 1958

Briggs, G. A.
Sound Reproduction
Rank Wharfdale, Bradford

Burris-Meyer, H. and V. Mallory
Sound in the Theatre
Theatre Art Books, New York 1959

Common Core Series
Basic Electronics
Technical Press, Oxford 1968

Crabbe, John
Hi-Fi in the Home
Blandford Press, London 1972 and Transatlantic Arts, New York 1972

Crowhurst, Norman H.
Audio Systems Handbook
TAB Books, Pennsylvania 1969 and Foulsham-Tab, Slough 1973

Davis, Don and Carolyn
Sound System Engineering
Howard W. Sams and Co., Inc. Indianapolis, 1975

Dibdin, F. J. H.
Essentials of Sound
Macmillan Publishing, London 1968

Hadden, Burrell
High-Quality Sound Production and Reproduction
Iliffe

Hughes, Robert J. and Peter Pipe
Introduction to Electronics
English Universities Press, London and Doubleday, New York

Jordan, E. J.
Loudspeakers
Focal Press, London 1964 and Hastings House, New York

Judd, F. C.
Tape Recording for Everyone
Blackie & Son, Glasgow 1962

McWilliams, A. A.
Tape Recording and Reproduction
Focal Press, London 1964

Matthews, C. N. G.
Tape Recording
Museum Press, London 1968

Mee, F. G.
Sound
Heinemann, London 1967

Middleton, Robert G.
Tape Recorder Servicing Guide
Foulsham Sams & Co., Indianapolis 1970 and Foulsham-Tab, Slough

Moore, J. E.
Design for Good Acoustics
Architectural Press, London 1961

Nisbet, A.
Techniques of the Sound Studio
Focal Press, London 1963

Olson, Harry F.
Music, Physics and Engineering
Dover, New York 1966

Oughton, F.
Tape Recording & Hi-Fi
Collins, Glasgow and London 1964

Parkin, P. H. and H. R. Humphreys
Acoustics, Noise and Buildings
Faber, London 1969 and Fernhill House, New York

Rindfleisch, Dr H.
Tape Recording Technique
Agfa-Gevaert

Ritter, H.
Tape Questions and Tape Answers
BASF

Robertson, A. E.
Microphones
Iliffe, London 1973

Say, M. G. (ed.)
Electrical Engineers' Reference Book
Butterworth & Co., London 1973

Scroggie, M. G.
Foundations of Wireless and Electronics
Iliffe, London 1970

Sewell, E. C.
BRE Digest 143 Sound Insulation. Basic Principles
HMSO, London

Sproxton, Colin
Hi Fi Yearbook
IPC Electrical-Electronic Press, London

Warring, Ronald H.
Instructions to Radio Constructors
Museum Press, London 1966

Wood, Alexander
The Physics of Music
Methuen & Co., London and Barns & Noble, New York 1964

Yerges, Lyle F.
Sound, Noise and Vibration Control
Van Nostrand Reinhold, New York and London 1969

Theatrical/sound terms

English	French	Italian	German
Theatre			
theatre	théâtre	teatro	Theater
play	pièce de théâtre	lavoro teatrale	Theaterstück
opera	opéra	opera	Oper
act	acte	atto	Akt (Aufzug)
scene	scène	scena	Bild (Szene)
interval	entr'acte	intervallo	Pause
performance	représentation	rappresentazione	Vorstellung
rehearsal	répétition	prova	Probe
stage rehearsal	répétition de scène	prova di scena	Bühnenprobe
general rehearsal	répétition générale	prova generale	Hauptprobe
scene rehearsal	répétition en décors	prova dello scenario	Dekorationsprobe
Staff			
managing director	intendant	direttore del teatro	Intendant
stage director/ producer	metteur-en-scène	regista	Regisseur
director	directeur	direttore	Direktor
actor	acteur	attore	Schauspieler
opera singer	chanteur	cantante	Sänger
assistant stage manager	inspecteur	ispettore	Inspizient
ballet dancer	danseur, danseuse	ballerino, ballerina	Tänzer, Tänzerin
conductor	chef d'orchestre	direttore dell'orchestra	Kapellmeister (Dirigent)
Technicians			
technical director	directeur technique	direttore tecnico	Technischer Leiter
stage carpenter	chef-machiniste	capomacchinista	Theatermeister
stagehand	machiniste	opera o addetto alla scena	Bühnenarbeiter
chief sound man	opérateur des sons	capo di suono	Ton Meister
chief electrician	chef électricien	capo-elettricista	Beleuchtungsmeister
electrician	électricien	elettricista	Beleuchter
machinist	machiniste	macchinista	Maschinist
property man	accessoiriste	addetto agli accessori	Requisiteur
sound operator	opérateur des sons	operatore di suono	Toningenieur
stage decorator	décorateur	decoratore	Dekorateur
painter	peintre	pittore	Maler
carpenter	charpentier	carpentiere	Zimmermann
Stage			
auditorium	salle	sala	Zuschauerraum
orchestra pit	fosse d'orchestre	orchestra	Orchesterraum
stage	scène	palcoscenico	Bühne
back stage	arrière-scène	retroscena	Hinterbühne
side-stage	scène latérale	quinta	Seitenbühne
stage floor	plateau, plancher	tavolato	Bühnenboden
fly gallery	galerie d'équipes	galleria laterale	Arbeitsgalerie
grid, gridiron	cintre	soffitto del palcoscenico	Schnürboden

English	French	Italian	German
rolling stage	scène glissante	scena scorrevole	Schiebebühne
revolving stage	scène tournante	scena girevole	Drehbühne
under machinery	machinerie du dessous	macchinario del sottopalco	Untermaschinerie
trap	trappe	botola	Versenkung
rake	pente	pendenza	Bühnenfall
castor	roulette	rullo	Laufrolle
rostrum	praticable	praticabile	Stellage, Gerüst
step	marche	gradino	Stufe
stairs	escalier	scala	Treppe
counterweight line	équipe à contrepoids	carrucola a contrappeso	Gegengewichtszug
counterweight	contrepoids	contrappeso	Gegengewicht
rope, cord	fil	corda	Seil
wire rope, wire cable	cable	fune	Drahtseil
pipe	porteuse	trave centrale	Laststange
batten	perche supérieure	pertica superiore	Oberlatte
flying equipment	vol	apparecchio aereo	Flugvorrichtung
winch	treuil	argano	Winde
lift	ascenseur	ascensore	Aufzug
proscenium opening	ouverture	apertura	Bühnenöffnung
curtain	rideau	sipario	Vorhang
proscenium	avant-scène	proscenio	Proszenium
scenery	tableau, décors	scenario	Szenerie

Lighting

English	French	Italian	German
stage lighting	éclairage de scène	illuminazione della scena	Bühnenbeleuchtung
dimmer board	commande du jeu d'orgue	quadro elettrico	Bühnenregler
dimmers, resistances	résistances	resistenze	Widerstände
floats, footlights	rampe	luce della ribalta	Rampenlichte
borderlight	herse	luce della bilance	Oberlicht
stage flood	appareils transportables	sostegni trasportabili	Versatzständer
stand, tripod, telescopic stand	pied	sostegno	Ständer, Stativ
lamp	lampe	lampada	Glühlampe
colour medium	écran de gélatine	schermo di mica	Gelatinescheibe
lens	lentille	lente	Linse
focus	foyer	fuoco	Brennpunkt

Sound

English	French	Italian	German
acoustics	acoustique	acustica	Akustik
aerial	antenne	antenna	Antenne
alternating current	courant alternatif	corrente alternata	Wechselstrom
amp	ampère	ampere	Ampere
amplification	amplification	amplificazione	Verstärkung
amplifier	amplificateur	amplificatore	Verstärker
attenuator	attenuer (to attenuate)	attenuare (to attenuate)	vermindern (to attenuate)
bass (low frequencies)	basse	basso	bass
battery	pile	batteria	Batterie
cable	cable	cavo	Kabel
control station	jeu d'orgue	cabina di manovra	Stellwerk
direct current	courant direct	corrente continua	Gleichstrom
disc (gramophone)	disque	disco	Schallplatte
distortion	déformation	distorsione	Verzerrung
echo	écho	eco	Echo
feedback	rétro action		Rückkoppelung
frequency	fréquence	frequenza	Frequenz
fuse	fusible	fusibile	Sicherung
gain (volume)	augmentation	guadagno	Zunahme
headset (earphone)	écouteur	cuffia	Kopfhörer
hiss	sifflement	sibilo	Gezisch
hum	ronronnement	cantarellare	Gesumme
impedance	impédance		Hindernis

English	French	Italian	German
intercom	intercom	intercomunicante	Sprechanlage
loudspeaker	haut-parleur	altoparlante	Lautsprecher
mains	electricité	conduttura principale	Wetz (Strom)
microphone	microphone	microfono	Mikrophon
mono	monaural	monaural	monaural
ohm	ohm	ohm	ohm
plug	fiche	spina	Stecker
radio	radio	radio	Radio
to record	enregistrer	registrare	aufnehmen
recording	enregistrement	registrazione	Aufnahme
record player	phonographe	giradisco	Plattenspieler
reverberation	répercussion	reverberazione	Widerhall
signal	signal	segnale	Signal
sockets	prises	scatole	Anschlussdosen
sound	son	suono	Ton
sound effect	bruitage		Toneffecte
splice	épisser	intrecciare	spleissen
spool	bobine	bobina	Spule
stereo	stereophonique	sterio	stereophonisch
switch	interrupteur	interruttore	Schalter
tape	ruban magnetique	nastro	Tonband
tape recorder	magnetophone	registratore	Tonbandgerät
tone	ton	tono	Ton
transformer	transformateur	trasformatore	Transformator
treble	soprano	sopran	sopran
voltage	voltage	voltaggio	Spannung
wattage	puissance	watt	Watt

General			
long	long	lungo	lang
short	court	corto, breve	kurz
wide	large	largo	weit
narrow	étroit	stretto	schmal
broad	large	largo	breit
large, big	grand	grande, grosso	gross
small	petit	piccolo	klein
on	sur	su	auf
up	en haut	in su, in alto	hinauf, oben
under	sous	sotto	unter
right	à droite	a destra	rechts
left	à gauche	a sinistra	links
downwards	en bas	in giú	abwärts
slow	lent	lento	langsam
fast, quickly	vite, rapide	rapido	schnell
without	sans	senza	ohne
with	avec	con	mit
low	bas	basso	niedrig
lower	plus bas	piú basso	niedriger
high	haut	alto	hoch
higher	plus haut, supérieur	piú alto, superiore	höher
too much	trop	troppo	zu viel
too little	trop peu	troppo poco	zu wenig
more	plus	piú	mehr
less	moins	meno	wenig
a third	un tiers	un terzo	ein Drittel
a quarter	un quart	un quarto	ein Viertel
good	bon	buono	gut
bad	mauvais	cattivo	schlecht
right	juste	giusto	richtig
wrong	faux	falso	falsch
repeat !	répétez !	ripetere !	wiederholen !
once	une fois	una volta	einmal
only once	une seule fois	una sola volta	nur einmal
several times	plusieurs fois	parecchi volte	mehrere Male
the last time	la dernière fois	l'ultima volta	das letzte Mal
alright, OK	en ordre, ça va	in ordine, va bene	in Ordnung
cue	signal, réplique	segno, segnale suggerimento	Zeichen, Signal, Stichwort

English	French	Italian	German
attention !	attention !	attenzione !	Achtung !
begin, go	en marche, on commence	si inizia	los, anfangen
stop !	halte !	alto !	halt !
take care !	attention ! prenez garde !	attenzione !	Vorsicht !
fade out	diminuer	diminuire	ausblenden
fade in	augmenter	aumentare	einblenden
music	musique	musica	Musik
up (more)	encore	piu	mehr
quiet	tranquille	quiete	ruhig
loud	fort	forte	laut
to hear	entendre	sentire	hören
to listen	écouter	ascoltare	zuhören
to hang, to clamp	suspendre	appendere	aufhangen
to mount	équiper	provvedere	ausstatten
to set up	poser	collocare	aufstellen
to earth	mettre à la terre	mettere a fersa	erden

Some useful addresses

United Kingdom

Association of British Theatre Technicians, 4–7 Great Pulteney Street, London W1R 3DF (Organization for collating and disseminating technical information)

Mechanical Copyright Protection Society Ltd, 380 Streatham High Road, London SW16. (For licensing the mechanical copying of a mechanically recorded work on behalf of recording companies)

Performing Rights Society Ltd, 29 Berners Street, London W1. (For licensing the public performance of a mechanically recorded work on behalf of the authors and performers)

Phonographic Performance Ltd, 62 Oxford Street, London W1. (For licensing the public performance of a mechanically recorded work on behalf of the record company)

Society of Theatre Consultants, 4–7 Great Pulteney Street, London W1R 3DF

United States

United States Institute of Theatre Technology, 330 West 42nd Street, Suite 1702, New York, 10036 NY (Organization for collating and disseminating technical information).

Glossary

Absorption Sound conversion of acoustic energy to another form of energy within the structure of sound-absorbing materials.

Acoustical Treatment The use of acoustical absorbents, or any changes or additions to the structure to correct acoustical faults or improve the acoustical environment.

Acoustic Feedback Unwanted acoustic interaction between output and input of an audio system, usually between loudspeaker and microphone or pick-up. It can lead to continuous oscillation.

Acoustics The science of sound; including its production, transmission and effect. In popular parlance applied particularly to acoustical characteristics of halls and rooms.

Aerial Device for capturing radio signals to feed input of receiver or tuner. Also known as antenna.

Air-Borne Sound Sound transmitted through air as a medium rather than through solids or the structure of a building.

Amp Abbreviation of ampere.

Ampere Unit of electrical current flow.

Amplification, Electronic Increasing the intensity level of a sound signal by means of electrical amplification equipment.

Amplifier An electronic device for magnifying electrical signals to a level at which loudspeakers will respond.

Amplitude Magnitude, size. The maximum displacement to either side of the normal or 'rest' position of the molecules of air transmitting sound. (Also applies to any other medium transmitting sound.)

Arm Commonly, pick-up arm. Often applied to the whole pick-up assembly though strictly excludes the cartridge.

Attenuation Reducing the intensity of a sound signal.

Attenuator Device circuit for reducing signal amplitude.

Audible Capable of producing the sensations of hearing.

Baffle Structure for isolating front and rear of loudspeaker diaphragm. Sometimes applied to a loudspeaker cabinet but usually recognized as the board on which the loudspeaker is mounted.

Balance The balance of loudness between instrumental and/or vocal microphones; also between loudspeakers; also tonal balance between bass, middle and treble.

Balanced (line or circuit) System of connections in which two signal carrying conductors are equally 'live'.

Bass Low frequency end of audio spectrum below approximately 150 Hz.

Bass Reflex Type of loudspeaker cabinet with an outlet (vent or port) permitting enclosed air to be put to work to improve efficiency at low frequencies. This is due to the inversion of phase within the enclosure so that the radiations from the port aid the radiations from the cone.

Capacitor microphone Microphone employing a diaphragm so positioned in relation to a fixed member that movement caused by sound waves produces a change of capacitance; this being translated into an audio voltage. Also known as Condenser microphone.

Capstan Accurate spindle which, in conjunction with pinch-wheel, drives the tape on a tape recorder.

Cardioid Microphone with 'heart-shaped' polar response, making it most sensitive in one direction.

Cartridge Tape container with continuous loop of tape (usually $\frac{1}{4}$ in.) for use in cartridge record/playback machine. Also the detachable transducer-plus-stylus part of a pick-up head.

Cassette Preloaded container with tape and spools for use on tape cassette record/playback machine. Usually with four tracks at a speed of $1\frac{7}{8}$ ips. (5 cm/s).

CCIR (International Radio Consultative Committee) Commonly refers to tape replay characteristics.

Channel Sequence of circuits or components handling one specific signal.

Chassis Metalwork on which circuit components are assembled.

Circuit An arrangement of interconnecting electrical and/or electronic components to perform some specific task. Also refers to the diagram of such an arrangement.

Coaxial Cable Type of screened cable with central conductor surrounded by an outer screen.

Condenser microphone (see Capacitor microphone).

Cone Diaphragm of conventional moving coil loudspeaker.

Cone Surround Strip or roll of compliant material fitted to the periphery of the loudspeaker cone to seal it to the frame while permitting axial movement.

C.P.S. Cycles per second (known as Hertz).

Crossover Network Circuit for dividing the signal from an amplifier into frequency bands to feed appropriate loudspeakers; i.e. high frequencies to the tweeter and low frequencies to the woofer, etc.

Crossover Frequency Frequency at which a crossover network divides the signal from one frequency band to another.

Crosstalk Breakthrough of signal between two supposedly separate channels. The level of wanted signal in relation to the unwanted signal is measured and expressed in decibels (dB).

Crystal Natural piezo-electrical transducer used in some pick-ups and microphones. Solid state diode. Also resonant quartz crystal sometimes used for tuning purposes in radio reception.

Current Electrical flow measured in amperes (amps).

Cycle The repetitive pattern in any vibrating system, mechanical, electrical or acoustic. One complete cycle comprises the change of pressure, velocity, voltage or current from a zero point up to a maximum in one direction, down through zero to a minimum in the other direction, then back to zero.

Damping (of loudspeaker enclosure) Process of reducing unwanted resonant effects by applying absorbent materials to the surfaces.

Damping (of loudspeaker) Expresses the ability of the cone to stop moving as soon as the electrical input signal ceases. Poor damping allows motion to continue briefly like an automobile with poor shock absorbers. This hangover creates a 'booming' sound in the bass frequencies masking clarity.

Damping Factor Ratio of loudspeaker impedance to amplifier source impedance. A large ratio improves the loudspeaker damping.

Decibel (dB) A standard unit representing ratios for measuring amplitude. It is used to compare two different levels: e.g. voltages, current or sound pressure levels.

Diaphragm (see Cone) Sound generating element of a loudspeaker. May be a cone driven at its apex or a metal dome driven at its periphery moving in relation to the varying sources of electrical current applied to the loudspeaker circuit.

Diffusion Dispersion of sound within a space so that there is uniform energy density throughout that space.

DIN (Deutscher Industrie Normen (German industrial standards)) Commonly refers to standard plugs, sockets and tape equalization characteristics.

Dispersion The distribution of sound in a space.

Distortion Strictly, any deviation from the original in reproduction.

Drive Unit (or loudspeaker driver) The transducer unit of the loudspeaker as distinct from the enclosure or cabinet.

Drop-Out Momentary reduction or disappearance of signal on a tape recording due to inconsistent tape coating, dirt or mechanical defect.

Dual Concentric Loudspeaker Bass and treble cones or diaphragms are mounted on a common axis and separately driven via a crossover network.

Dual Cone Loudspeaker Two cones mounted on a common axis driven by a single moving coil. The inner cone, being of smaller diameter, is designed for greater efficiency at high frequencies.

Dubbing Copying of a recording by direct transfer.

Dynamic Coil (see Moving Coil).

Dynamic range Range of signal amplitude from highest to lowest found in acoustic programme material (in phons.), or the range which a device will handle (in dB). In equipment the upper limit is set by the overload point and the lower limit by background noise.

Earth Loop Arrangement of interconnections between pieces of apparatus and mains earths resulting in more than one path for the earth side of a signal carrying cable.

Echo Any reflected sound which is loud enough and received late enough to be heard as distinct from the source.

Editing Process of cutting and rearranging sections of recorded tapes.

Efficiency Used in discussing the percentage of acoustic output of a loudspeaker relative to the electrical input available from the amplifier.

Enclosure (Loudspeaker) The acoustically designed cabinet or housing of a loudspeaker drive unit.

Equalization A deliberately introduced change in frequency response, e.g. tone controls, or the electrical correction for a recording characteristic.

Erase head Tape head designed to apply a strong high frequency magnetic field across a fairly wide gap for erasure of recorded material as tape passes head when recorder switched to record mode.

Feedback (see Acoustic Feedback)

Figure of eight microphone Microphone with polar response shaped like a figure of eight making it most sensitive to front and rear and insensitive to the sides.

Flutter Rapid waver of pitch caused by fluctuations of speed in a recording. Heard as a sort of bubbly roughness.

Flutter Echo A rapid reflection pattern between parallel walls, with sufficient time between each echo to cause a listener to be aware of separate signals.

Frequency The rate of repetition in Hertz of musical pitch, as well as that of electrical signals. The number of complete cycles in one second. Low frequency refers to bass tones and high frequency to treble tones.

Frequency range *Bass*: Low frequency end of audio spectrum below approximately 150 Hz. In musical notation top line of the bass clef is A (220 Hz).
Mid-range: Frequency band extending from about 500 Hz to a few kilohertz.
Treble: High frequency end of audio spectrum above 2–3 kHz. In musical notation the bottom line of the treble clef is E (329.63Hz).

Frequency Response The ability of a component to reproduce a range of frequencies is called frequency response. How evenly the component responds to various frequencies within that range describes how 'flat' that response would be.

Fundamental Basic tone produced by the vibration of a whole sonorous body; i.e. excluding harmonics.

Gap Vertical slit in tape recording head, forming poles across which a magnetizing field occurs during the recording process, and into which a corresponding magnetic signal is induced during replay.

Graphic equalizer A particular type of equalizer which operates simultaneously on a relatively large number of frequency bands. Most commonly 27 bands $\frac{1}{3}$ octave wide or 11 bands almost an octave wide. Each band has its own slider control for boost and cut (occasionally for cut only) and these controls are arranged on the front panel in order of increasing frequency horizontally left to right, and increasing gain vertically, thereby giving a graphic representation of the chosen frequency response.

Harmonic Frequency multiple of a fundamental tone. Twice the fundamental frequency is the second harmonic, three times is the third and so on.

Harmonic Distortion A form of distortion in which unwanted harmonics are added to original signal.

Hertz (Hz) Unit of frequency equalling one cycle per second.

HF High frequency.

Horn Acoustic device with cross-sectional area expanding or flaring according to particular mathematical law.

Horn loading Acoustic load offered to a loudspeaker drive unit by horn type enclosure.

Howlround (see Acoustic Feedback).

Hum Unwanted low frequency tone in reproduction usually due to mains and its harmonics.

Impedance A term describing the degree to which a circuit impedes the flow of an alternating current. Measured in ohms.

Induction Production of current across a space due to electric or magnetic fields.

Infinite Baffle Loudspeaker mounting which allows no air paths between front and rear of the diaphragm.

Input Impedance Effective impedance at the input of a circuit.

Intensity The rate of sound energy transmitted in a specified direction through a given unit area.

KiloHertz (kHz) One thousand cycles per second

LF Low frequency.

Line levels Usually the voltages of line level outputs (i.e. the pre-amp stages of tape recorders, mixers, etc.) are greater than those of microphones, and range from about − 20dB up to 0dB (zero level).
The impedances usually found at line inputs and line outputs vary widely even in professional equipment. The original standard was that a line output was 600 ohms and this could be connected to the 600 ohm line input of the next piece of equipment in the chain. The technique used today is to keep the line output (usually) well below 600 ohms, typically 50 to 100 ohms, and the line input never less than 2,000 ohms and usually about 10,000 ohms. The 'low into high' arrangement is highly recommended for professional and semi-professional installations where flexibility is important.

Line source loudspeaker A column or line of loudspeakers in an enclosure producing a fan-shaped pattern of dispersion which is narrow in the vertical plane and wide in the horizontal. The source of sound is from a line of loudspeakers.

Loudspeaker Transducer system for converting electrical energy into sound energy.

Magnetic tape Plastic strip coated with a special oxide film permitting storage and replay of signals by controlled magnetization.

Matching Efficient coupling between electrical or acoustic components achieved by using similar impedances.

Meters PPM: Peak programme meter which provides an accurate measurement of the electrical nature of an audio signal.
VU: Volume indicating meter. A cheaper device which measures the overall loudness but does not display all the peaks of the electrical signal.

Microphone Transducer for converting sound energy into electrical energy.

Mid-range Frequency band extending from about 500 Hz to a few kilohertz.

Mixer A device facilitating electrical mixing of a number of signals in desired proportions.

Monitoring Checking signals during a recording or the operation of a sound system by listening on a separate loudspeaker and/or by watching a level meter.

Moving Coil Type of pick-up, microphone or loudspeaker transducer in which a coil of wire moves in a magnetic field.

Music power Power rating based upon non-sustained tones.

NAB (National Association of Broadcasters (USA)) Commonly refers to various tape standards. Also known as NARTB.

Noise Any unwanted sound.

OHM Unit of electrical resistance or impedance.

Oscillator A device for producing a continuous electrical oscillation, or pure tone, at any desired frequency.

Oscilloscope A device which provides a visual display of the wave form, frequency and amplitude of a signal.

Overloading When distortion occurs because a piece of electronic equipment is being driven beyond its signal handling capacity.

P.A. Public Address system.

Phase Refers to any part of a sound wave or an electrical signal with respect to its passage in time. Loudspeakers are in-phase when the diaphragms are oscillating in the same direction at the same time.

Phase cancellation Occurs when two similar or identical signals are out of step in time. Waveforms displaced by 180 degrees tend to cancel.

Pick-up Device for translating the mechanical motion of a stylus riding in a record groove into electrical voltage. There are two basic types: electro-magnetic and crystal with the former being subdivided into moving armature and moving coil.

Pinch wheel Presses tape against capstan to obtain drive in a tape recorder.

Pink noise Random noise (hiss) weighted so as to contain equal energy per octave bandwidth. It is usually generated by feeding white noise (relatively easy to generate) through a network having a frequency response of – 10dB/Decade. (Pink and white are by analogy with light whereby randomly generated light containing equally visible frequencies appears white, but weighting the lower frequencies (red) would create pink light.)

Pitch The physical response to frequency.

Port Opening or vent in a bass reflex enclosure.

Potentiometer (Pot) A variable resistor used for volume and tone controls

Power Amplifier (see Amplifier)

Power Handling Capacity The amount of electrical power that an electronic device is capable of handling. Especially used when referring to the maximum power output of an amplifier, or the maximum power that can safely be fed to a particular loudspeaker.

Preamplifier Circuit unit designed to accept signals from pick-up, microphone, tape head, etc., applying any necessary equalization and incorporating volume and tone controls. Output feeds power amplifier(s).

Presence Quality of immediacy normally referring to microphone reproduction. Achieved by boosting the upper-middle frequencies.

Pressure Unit Moving-coil loudspeaker drive unit with a metal dome diaphragm usually used in association with a metal horn.

Pure tone A continous electrical oscillation at a given frequency.

Reflection The return from a surface of sound energy not absorbed upon contact with the surface.

Resistance Amount of non-conductivity, or opposition to current flow, measured in ohms.

Resonance The tendency of any physical body to vibrate most freely at one particular frequency as a result of excitation by a sound of that particular frequency.

Reverberation The persistence of sound within a space after the source of that sound has ceased.

Reverberation Time The time in seconds required for a sound to decay to inaudibility after the sound source ceases.

Ribbon A thin corrugated strip of aluminium suspended in a magnetic field used for some microphone transducers.

R.M.S. Root mean square: effective amplitude of an AC voltage waveform (RMS); equal to the DC voltage or current that would produce the same power dissipation in a given load. Always less than peak amplitude except with a square wave.

Room Acoustic The natural acoustics of the listening room.

R.P.M. Revolutions per minute of a record player turntable.

Screen Metallic shield or braiding around cables to prevent electrostatic interference, especially microphone cables.

Sibilance The hissing sound of consonants.

Signal-To-Noise Ratio The ratio of wanted signal to unwanted noise. Measured in decibels.

Sound level meter An electrical instrument for determining sound pressure levels in terms of decibels.

Sound Wave Sound as a disturbance which is propagated in a medium in a wave motion.

Spectrum analyser An electrical instrument for measuring the acoustic energy present in various frequency bands (usually in third octave steps) of a complex sound.

Speech Coil The metal coil in a moving coil loudspeaker.

Speed of sound 1,130 feet (350 metres) per second approximately in air.

Splice Join together two pieces of tape when editing.

Stylus The sapphire, diamond, etc. used in a gramophone pick-up cartridge.

Timbre The proportion of harmonics added to a fundamental frequency producing the individual sound of a musical instrument.

Track (Tape) Recorded path along the length of a magnetic tape.

Transducer Device for converting from one form of energy to another, e.g. a microphone converts from acoustic to electrical.

Treble High frequency end of the audio spectrum; i.e. above 2–3 kHz. In musical notation the bottom line of the treble clef is E (329.63 Hz).

Tweeter Loudspeaker unit for use at high frequencies only.

Unbalanced (line or circuit) System of connections in which one side of the circuit is earthed. The system employs coaxial cables.

Voice Coil The metal coil or moving coil loudspeaker.

Voice frequencies (in Hertz)

Important range for intelligibility		500–5,000
Upper range for harmonics and sibilance		up to 8,000 plus
Fundamental speech range:	Male	75–175
	Female	200–300
Fundamental singing range:	Bass	75–340
	Baritone	90–380
	Tenor	130–480
	Alto	190–640
	Soprano	240–1,000

Volt Unit of electrical force.

Watt Unit of electrical power; volts multiplied by amps.

Wattage Number of watts.

Index